CW00368986

THE JUDGE

1001 SPORTING ARGUMENTS SETTLED

Other books by Norman Giller

The Marathon Kings
The Golden Milers
Olympics Handbook 1980
Olympics Handbook 1984
Olympic Heroes (with Brendan Foster)
The Book of Cricket Lists (with Tom Graveney)
Top Ten Cricket Book (with Tom Graveney)
Cricket Heroes (with Eric Morecambe)
Banks of England (with Gordon Banks)
The Big Fight Quiz Book
TVIQ Puzzle Book
Lucky the Fox (with Barbara Wright)
Watt's My Name (with Jim Watt)
My Most Memorable Fights (with Henry Cooper)
How to Box (with Henry Cooper)
Henry Cooper's 100 Greatest Boxers
The ABC of Soccer Sense (with Tommy Docherty)
The Rat Race (with Tommy Docherty)
The Book of Rugby Lists (with Gareth Edwards)
The Book of Tennis Lists (with John Newcombe)
The Book of Golf Lists
Fighting for Peace (Barry McGuigan biography, with Peter Batt)
TV Quiz Trivia
Sports Quiz Trivia
Know What I Mean? (with Frank Bruno)
Eye of the Tiger (with Frank Bruno)
From Zero to Hero (with Frank Bruno)
Mike Tyson, For Whom the Bell Tolls (with Reg Gutteridge)
Mike Tyson, The Release of Power (with Reg Gutteridge)
Gloria Hunniford's TV Challenge
The World's Greatest Cricket Matches
The World's Greatest Football Matches
A Stolen Life (novel)
Crown of Thorns, The World Heavyweight Championship (with Neil
Duncanson)
The Seventies Revisited (with Kevin Keegan)
The Glory and the Grief (with George Graham)
Carry On Doctor
Carry On England
Carry On Loving
Carry On Up the Khyber
Carry On Abroad
Carry On Henry
Golden Heroes (with Dennis Signy)

Books in collaboration with Jimmy Greaves

This One's On Me
The Final (novel)
The Ball Game (novel)
The Boss (novel)
The Second Half (novel)
World Cup History Book
GOALS!
Stop the Game, I Want to Get On
The Book of Football Lists
Taking Sides
Sports Quiz Challenge
Sports Quiz Challenge 2
It's A Funny Old Life
Saint & Greavsie's World Cup Special
The Sixties Revisited
Don't Shoot the Manager

THE JUDGE

1001 SPORTING ARGUMENTS SETTLED

NORMAN GILLER

MICHAEL GILLER

As featured in

Acknowledgements

The Judge wishes to thank Tim Forrester and his Chameleon editorial team, in particular editor Nicky Paris and production supremo Alastair Gourlay, for their encouragement and expertise; also Michael Giller for his Apple-a-day computer skill, artist David Edwards for his graphic support, and, most of all, Sun Editor Stuart Higgins and Sports Editor Paul Ridley for being shrewd enough judges to have taken the idea on board. The Judge would not be nearly so knowing without a plethora of record books on which to call, and he recommends in particular the six bibles of their sport: *Rothmans Football Yearbook*, *Wisden Cricketers' Almanack*, *The Ring Record Book*, *World of Tennis*, *The Complete Book of the Olympics*, *Golfer's Handbook*, and any number of Guinness sporting record books and particularly those that bear the all-knowing touch of statistical wizard Peter Matthews. For cricket, I have turned to the many works of my old colleague Bill 'The Bearded Wonder' Frindall for the facts and figures, and the football output from Jack Rollin and his offspring has been a constant source of information. My old sparring partners Reg Gutteridge and Ron Olver have kept me informed on the boxing front, and *Boxing News* has, as always, been must reading. Barry Hugman's *Football League Players' Records* is another book that has proved invaluable. Finally, a sincere thank you to VCI chief executive Steve Ayres for lighting the touchpaper. What a good judge!

First published in Great Britain in 1997 by Chameleon Books,
an imprint of André Deutsch Limited
106 Great Russell Street,
London WC1B 3LJ

A subsidiary of VCI plc

Copyright © Norman Giller Enterprises 1997
British Library Cataloguing in Publication Data for this book is available
from the British Library

ISBN 0 233 99134 4

All rights reserved. No part of this publication may be
reproduced, stored in a retrieval system, or transmitted in any form or by any means,
electronic, mechanical,
photocopying, recording or otherwise, without the prior
permission in writing of the publishers.

2   4   6   8   10   9   7   5   3   1

Printed in Great Britain by
WBC Book Manufacturers

CONTENTS

*This book is dedicated to the memory
of Harold John Miller, a master
sports reporter who always
judged all men charitably*

INTRODUCTION

HUNDREDS of sporting arguments have been settled by the Judge in his weekly column in the sports section of the *Sun*. Now 1001 of his answers are featured in this unique book, including many that have not been published before.

The Judge's word has become final for hundreds of sports fans in pubs, clubs, offices and factories across the land as they turn to him for the dispute-settling answers to their sporting questions.

They range from the record book variety to the trivial, and in many instances the stars of sport themselves have come up with the answers. And when even The Judge is struggling for the right answer he consults the huge computer database set up by sports statisticians Michael Giller and Norman Giller, who have had more than fifty sports-linked books published.

Among the widely contrasting subjects covered in the following pages are these questions. See if you can answer them before looking up the Judge's verdict ...

❑　　Did Jimmy Greaves ever score a World Cup finals goal?
❑　　Who was the first world heavyweight champion to retire undefeated?
❑　　What size boots did George Best wear?
❑　　Who has scored most Test centuries for England?
❑　　Was Lester Piggott once thrown by a horse in the Derby?
❑　　Has Frank Bruno ever taken the full ten-second count?
❑　　Who made the first maximum 147 snooker break on TV?
❑　　How many British Open titles has Jack Nicklaus won?
❑　　Who was the first black footballer capped by England?
❑　　What was the name of the dog that found the World Cup?

If you can answer just half of these then you are something of a sports mastermind – just like the Judge! Here's a challenge for you. Try to beat the Judge by coming up with the answer to each question before you read his verdict. Keep a count as you go along, and see if you can correctly answer more than 500 of the questions before reading the Judge's findings. If you can, then you are, without any argument, a great sports judge. We have tested a cross-section of sports fans with the questions and the average score was 290 correct answers.

The Judge thanks all those *Sun* readers who have sent in their questions, many of which are featured in the following pages.

Now it's on with the judging. Let the sporting arguments begin.

Here comes the Judge ...

FOOTBALL

Q **Who was the first England footballer to win 100 international caps?**
Billy Wright was the first player to win a century of England caps (105 in total, 1946-59). Three other centurions who have followed him: Bobby Charlton (106, 1958-70), Bobby Moore (108, 1962-73), Peter Shilton (125, 1970-90).

Q **Did Jimmy Greaves ever score a goal in the finals of a World Cup tournament?**
Jimmy Greaves scored one World Cup finals goal – against Argentina in Chile in 1962. He played in a total of seven World Cup finals matches, four in 1962 and three in 1966. He was injured against France in 1966 and his place was taken in the quarter-final by Geoff Hurst, who retained his position in the team and went on to score his historic hat-trick against West Germany in the final.

Q **Which clubs were founder members of the Football League and in which year did the League start?**
There were 12 founder members in 1888: Accrington, Aston Villa, Blackburn Rovers, Bolton Wanderers, Burnley, Derby County, Everton, Notts County, Preston, Stoke, West Bromwich Albion and Wolves. Three other clubs, Sheffield Wednesday, Nottingham Forest and Halliwell, applied for membership, but were turned down because of fixture-list problems.

Q **Who captained England most times, Billy Wright or Bobby Moore?**
Remarkably, they both led out the England team 90 times, with Wright setting a record of 70 consecutive matches. Their records as captains:
Wright (1948 – 59): P90 W49 D21 L20 F234 A135
Moore (1963 – 73): P90 W57 D20 L13 F171 A75

Q **Where was Graham Taylor born, and what was his record as a player?**
Taylor, the son of a sportswriter, was born in Worksop, Nottinghamshire, on 9 September 1944. He played 189 matches as a full-back for Grimsby (1962-8) before switching to Lincoln City in 1968. A knee injury forced his retirement at the age of 28 after 150 League games.

Q **Who has scored the fastest goal in any match played at Wembley?**
Maurice Cox netted in 20 seconds for Cambridge University in the varsity match against Oxford on 5 December 1979. Bryan Robson holds the

record for the fastest goal at Wembley in a professional match: 38 seconds for England against Yugoslavia on 13 December 1989.

Q How many of the USA team that beat England in the 1950 World Cup finals were American born?

Despite reports that England had been beaten by a team from Ellis Island, all but three of the USA team were born in America. The only goal of the match was scored by Haitian-born centre-forward Larry Gaetjens. What could have been a last-minute face-saving free kick from Alf Ramsey was brilliantly saved by goalkeeper Borghi, who was a professional baseball catcher. The United States were superbly organized by their Scottish captain Ed McIllvenny. The English selectors arrogantly left their best player, Stanley Matthews, out of the team because they were convinced they could beat the Americans without calling on the skills of the Wizard of Dribble. Wrong!

Q What was the line-up of the England team beaten by the United States in the 1950 World Cup finals?

The England team beaten 1-0 by the United States in the 1950 World Cup finals in Belo Horizonte: Williams, Ramsey, Aston, Wright, Hughes, Dickinson, Finney, Mannion, Bentley, Mortensen, Mullen.

Q When were floodlights first used on a British football ground?

The first ever floodlit match was between two Sheffield Association teams in an exhibition match at Bramall Lane on 14 October 1878.
The electric power was generated by a portable engine behind each goal. A huge lamp shedding light to the equivalent of 8,000 standard candles was mounted on the top of a 30-foot tower in each of the four corners of the ground. The first competitive match played in Britain under floodlight was a reserve match between Southampton and Tottenham at The Dell on 1 October 1951. Floodlit football became commonplace from the mid-1950s.

Q What size boots did George Best wear when playing for Manchester United?

The Judge went to George Best for this answer: 'I wear a size eight-and-a-half shoe, but my boots were made to measure and they were nearer an eight.' For the record, George played 361 League games for Manchester United and 37 times for Northern Ireland, and was never ever too big for his boots.

George Best

Q On which grounds were the 1966 World Cup matches staged, and were they the same for Euro 96?

The 1966 grounds were Wembley, White City, Villa Park, Goodison, Old Trafford, Ayresome Park, Hillsborough, Roker Park. The venues for Euro 96: Wembley, Villa Park, Old Trafford, Elland Road, City Ground (Nottingham), St James' Park and Anfield.

Q **Which was the first British football club to win a major European competition?**
Tottenham captured the European Cup Winners' Cup in 1963, beating Atletico Madrid 5-1 in the final in Rotterdam.

Q **Which members of England's 1966 World Cup squad did not play in the Final?**
Ron Springett, Peter Bonetti, Jimmy Armfield, Gerry Byrne, Ron Flowers, Norman Hunter, Terry Paine, Ian Callaghan, John Connolly, George Eastham, Jimmy Greaves. (The 11 who did play: Gordon Banks, George Cohen, Ray Wilson, Nobby Stiles, Jack Charlton, Bobby Moore, Alan Ball, Roger Hunt, Bobby Charlton, Geoff Hurst, Martin Peters.)

Q **Did Paul Gascoigne start the match or come on as a substitute in his first match for England?**
Paul Gascoigne substituted for his fellow-Geordie Peter Beardsley five minutes from the end of England's 1-0 win over Denmark at Wembley on 14 September 1988.

Q **Were Newcastle ever watched at home by a crowd of less than 8,000 in the old First Division?**
The Newcastle United-Norwich City First Division match on 26 April 1978 drew just 7,180 spectators, the lowest Newcastle home attendance since the First World War.

Q **Who was the 'Man in the White Suit' who conducted the singing before FA Cup finals?**
Wembley had two famous crowd conductors. The first was T. P. (Tip) Ratcliffe, and he was followed by Arthur Caiger, who had the popular catch phrase: 'Wave your *Daily Express* song sheets.'

Q **How old was Howard Kendall when he played in the 1964 FA Cup Final?**
Kendall was 17 years, 345 days when he played for Preston against West Ham. He was the youngest to play in a Wembley FA Cup Final until Paul Allen (17 years 256 days) played for West Ham against Arsenal in 1980. James Prinsep was 17 years 245 days when he played for Clapham Rovers in the 1879 FA Cup Final.

Q **Have Arsenal been relegated at any time in their long existence?**
Arsenal – then known as Woolwich Arsenal – were relegated in 1912-13 at the end of a season when they picked up only 18 points. They were re-elected to the First Division as plain Arsenal in the first season after the First World War, and have been in the top table ever since.

Q **Did Gordon Banks play any League matches after the car crash in which he lost the sight of an eye?**
The Judge got this answer from England's master goalkeeper: 'My last League match was for Stoke at Liverpool on 21 October 1972. The date

sticks in my mind because it was the next day that I had the car accident that cost me the sight in my right eye. I managed to make a comeback of sorts in the United States with the Fort Lauderdale Strikers, where I was voted the US League goalkeeper of the year.'

Q **Is it correct that Stanley Matthews and Stan Mortensen once played together for Arsenal?**
Correct. Blackpool team-mates Matthews and Mortensen guested for Arsenal in the famous fog-shrouded game against Moscow Dynamo at Tottenham in 1945. The match was played at White Hart Lane because Highbury was being used as an ARP centre. The Russians won 4-3.

Gordon Banks

Q **Was Kevin Keegan ever sent off while wearing an England international shirt?**
Keegan was sent off for retaliating during an Under-23 match in East Germany in Magdeburg on 1 June 1972. Manager Sir Alf Ramsey said that he would not take any disciplinary action against him because he felt he had been subjected to brutal treatment by his East German marker. He was never sent off in 63 appearances for England in full international matches.

Q **Is it true that Stan Bowles failed to turn up for a European Cup final while with Nottingham Forest?**
Stan Bowles played 19 League games for Forest in 1979-80. He missed the flight to Amsterdam for the second leg of the 1980 European Cup semi-final (it was claimed that he was frightened of flying), and was not selected for the final after putting in a transfer request. He joined Forest from QPR in December 1980. But it did not work out and he soon moved on to Orient and then Brentford.

Q **In how many different positions did Johnny Carey play for Manchester United?**
The former Manchester United and Ireland captain played in every position for the Old Trafford club except outside left. He was capped in six different positions by Ireland, including as emergency goalkeeper.

Q **Who was the first black footballer to establish himself in the League in post-war football?**
The first black footballers to play regular League football were Roy Brown (Stoke City and Watford, 1946-52), Lloyd (Lindy) Delapenha (Arsenal as an amateur, then Portsmouth, Middlesbrough and Mansfield Town, 1947-60), Tommy Best (Chester, Cardiff and QPR, 1947-9). Delapenha was born in Jamaica, while Brown and Best were British born. Charlie Williams, born and raised in Barnsley and later better known as a

comedian, played 158 League games as centre-half for Doncaster Rovers between 1949 and 1958.

Q **Who was the first black footballer capped by England, and who followed him?**
The first 12 black players capped by England were: Viv Anderson (1978), Laurie Cunningham (1979), Cyrille Regis (1982), Ricky Hill (1982), Luther Blissett (1982), Mark Chamberlain (1982), John Barnes (1983), Brian Stein (1984), Danny Wallace (1986), David Rocastle (1988), Michael Thomas (1988) and Des Walker (1988).

Q **Did Everton used to play in black shirts, and when did they switch to blue?**
Everton wore black shirts with a light sash and were nicknamed The Black Watch in their early years. They adopted royal blue in 1901 following several colour changes.

Q **When were substitutes first used in League football, and who was first to come on in the No. 12 shirt?**
Substitutes were first allowed in League football in the 1965-6 season. Keith Peacock, father of Gavin, was the first player to come on as substitute in a League match – for Charlton at Bolton on 21 August 1965.

Q **Is it true that a player once headed four goals in a final at Wembley?**
The glory went to the head of Eddie Reynolds in the 1963 FA Amateur Cup Final. He headed all four goals for Wimbledon in a 4-2 win against Sutton United.

Q **Were ties in the FA Cup competition ever played on a two-leg basis?**
The first post-war FA Cup tournament in the 1945-6 season was decided on a two-legged system up to the semi-finals. Derby County were the eventual winners, beating Charlton Athletic 4-1 after extra-time in the final.

Q **Who was the last player to score in every round of the FA Cup?**
Peter Osgood for Chelsea in 1969-70, including the Final in which he scored against Leeds in the replay at Old Trafford. Six years later Ossie collected an FA Cup winners' medal with Southampton when they beat Manchester United with a Bobby Stokes goal.

Q **How many trophies did Liverpool win under the management of Bob Paisley?**
Liverpool won 13 major trophies in nine seasons under Paisley: six League titles, three League Cups, the UEFA Cup, and, of course, three European Cups. His team also collected the Charity Shield six times (once shared), and won the Super Cup in 1977.

Q **What was the name of the white horse that cleared the pitch before the first FA Cup Final?**
The horse was called Billy and it was ridden by PC George Scorey, who slowly and patiently pushed thousands of spectators off the pitch to make room for Bolton to play West Ham. This opening match at Wembley in

1923 was watched by an estimated crowd of more than 180,000, with 126,047 paying to get in.

Q **What has Jimmy Hill ever achieved in the game apart from being chairman of Fulham?**

Jimmy Hill has been there, done that. He was a good-class player with Reading, Brentford and Fulham, and was also the eloquent PFA chairman who led the fight to abolish the maximum wage of £20 a week. As a manager, he steered Coventry City from the Third Division through to the First before starting a career in television with ITV. He once scored five goals for Fulham in a League match at Doncaster when he was marked by Charlie Williams, who later became a comedian. Hill was a pioneer as a manager, introducing PR ideas that were years ahead of their time.

Q **Who took the corner from which Tommy Smith scored in the 1977 European Cup Final?**

Steve Heighway took the corner from the left in the 65th minute from which Tommy Smith headed Liverpool's second goal in the 3-1 victory over Borussia Moenchengladbach in Rome's Olympic Stadium on 25 May 1977.

Q **Was Diego Maradona sent off during the 1986 World Cup finals in Mexico?**

No, but Maradona did get his marching orders while playing for Argentina against Brazil in the 1982 finals in Spain.

Q **How did Gary Lineker's England goalscoring record compare with that of Jimmy Greaves?**

Gary Lineker scored 48 goals in 80 England appearances between 1984 and 1992. Jimmy Greaves netted 44 goals in 57 matches for England (1959-67). Jimmy made his debut at the age of 19, and played his last match at 27. Gary won his first cap at 23 and his last at 31. Sir Bobby Charlton holds the England goal-scoring record with 49 goals in 106 games (1958-70).

Q **Did Brian Clough score more League goals than Jimmy Greaves, and did they ever play together?**

Cloughie had an incredible strike rate, scoring 197 goals in 213 League games with Middlesbrough, and 54 goals in 61 League games for Sunderland before a knee injury forced him to retire at the age of 28. Greavsie netted a record 357 First Division goals. The majority of Cloughie's goals were scored in the Second Division. They played together in the same England attack in two international matches in October 1959, a 1-1 draw with Wales in Cardiff followed by a 3-2 defeat by Sweden at Wembley. Cloughie carried the can and never played for England again.

Q **Was the 1966 World Cup Final between England and West Germany shown in colour on television?**

Both BBC and ITV covered the match live, but in black and white. The only colour version was in the film *Goal* that was shown later in the year.

Q **Did Ernie Taylor, the former Manchester United inside-forward, ever play for Manchester City?**
No. He played for four clubs: Newcastle United, Blackpool, Manchester United and Sunderland. He played for three clubs in three FA Cup Finals, winning with Newcastle in 1951 and as inside-forward partner to Stanley Matthews for Blackpool in 1953. In 1958 he was given special dispensation to join Manchester United after the Munich disaster, and got a runners-up medal in the Final against Bolton. The ex-submariner had played in an early round for Blackpool.

Q **Who captained Celtic when they won the European Cup in 1967, and who scored the winning goal?**
Billy McNeill was the Celtic skipper of the first British side to win the European Cup. The winning goal in a 2-1 victory over Inter Milan in Lisbon was scored by Steve Chalmers, who deflected a shot from Bobby Murdoch past the Milan goalkeeper in the eighty-fourth minute.

Q **Did George Graham or Herbert Chapman have the better record as Arsenal manager?**
George Graham won six major trophies in eight seasons: two League titles, the FA Cup, the Littlewoods Cup, the Coca-Cola Cup and the European Cup Winners' Cup. Chapman, who took over at Highbury in 1925, won the League title in successive seasons and Arsenal were on the way to a hat-trick when he died in January 1934. His team also lifted the FA Cup in 1930. He had earlier guided Huddersfield to two consecutive championships and the FA Cup. The Judge's verdict: 'Graham is the more successful on paper, but remember that Chapman did not have the League Cup or Europe to aim at.'

Q **Did Kenny Dalglish ever play a competitive game for Blackburn Rovers?**
Kenny Dalglish played his last 'proper' game of football with Liverpool at Coventry on 5 May 1990 in his role as player-manager, and had retired before taking over as manager of Blackburn. He scored 118 goals in 355 League matches for Liverpool, adding to his 112 Scottish League goals with Celtic.

Q **For which clubs has Steve Bruce played, and was he capped by England?**
Bruce, one of the best uncapped defenders in modern football, served his apprenticeship with Gillingham and then played 203 League games for the Kent club. Norwich City signed him in 1984 and he made 141 League appearances for the Canaries before moving on to Manchester United in 1987 for his greatest days as Old Trafford captain. He joined Birmingham in the summer of 1996 after skippering the United 'double double' team.

Q **Did Joe Mercer play more matches for Everton or Arsenal?**
Joe Mercer played 184 League and FA Cup games for Everton and 273 League and Cup games for Arsenal.

Q **Is it correct that Tottenham and Arsenal both played their wartime home matches at White Hart Lane?**
Correct, and to prove it there is a plaque in the Spurs boardroom from the Arsenal directors thanking Tottenham for letting them use White Hart Lane while Highbury was converted into an Air Raid Precautions centre during the Second World War.

Q **Which footballer was said to be 'ten years ahead of his time'?**
This was the label hung on Martin Peters by England manager Alf Ramsey.

Q **Did Terry Venables ever play in the European championship finals fo England?**
Terry Venables won just two caps for England in 1964, and neither game was in the European championships. His first cap completed a unique record. He is the only person to have played for England at schoolboy, amateur, youth, Under-23 and full level.

Q **Was Bryan Robson the first million-pound player when he joined Manchester United from West Brom?**
The fee was £1,500,000 when Bryan Robson signed for United in 1981. Trevor Francis was the first British player to move for £1,000,000 when he joined Nottingham Forest from Birmingham City in 1979.

Q **Did Jamie Redknapp ever play for West Ham under the management of his father, Harry?**
No. Harry introduced Jamie to football when he was in charge at Bournemouth, and he moved to Liverpool after making 13 League appearances.

Q **With which League club did Stuart Pearce start his career, and has he ever played for QPR?**
Stuart first played for Coventry City before joining Forest in 1985, and he has never played for QPR. He started his career with non-League Wealdstone.

Q **Did Andy Cole play for Fulham before joining Newcastle United?**
Andy Cole played for Fulham while on loan from Arsenal in 1991. He was later loaned to Bristol City, who then signed him for £500,000 before selling him on to Newcastle United for £1,750,000 in March 1993 (Arsenal collected ten per cent of the fee). Manchester United bought Cole for £7,000,000 in 1995.

Q **Was Kevin Keegan playing in a local Doncaster league before starting his professional career?**
The Judge checked it out with Kevin, who said: 'Before joining Scunthorpe I played for the Peglers' Brass Works team in the Doncaster league, and also for their reserves in the Bentley League. Those were the days when I would also squeeze in Saturday morning matches for the Enfield House youth club and Sunday morning games for the Lonsdale Hotel team. I was football daft and was finally given my big chance by

Scunthorpe after Coventry had turned me down because they reckoned I was too small.'

Q How many goals did Pele score during his career both at club and international level?

Pele (Edson Arantes do Nascimento) scored 1,283 first-class goals, including 97 in 111 international matches for Brazil. His most productive season was 1958 when, aged 17, he scored six goals in the World Cup finals for Brazil and finished the year with a haul of 139 goals – 130 of them for his club, Santos, for whom he played from 1955 to 1974. He netted nine goals in World Cup finals in all, collecting winners' medals in 1958, 1962, and 1970. Pele also played in the 1966 finals in England but was hacked out of the tournament by some brutal tackles. He missed the 1962 final because of injury.

Q Who was the first footballer sent off in any match at Wembley?

We have to go back to the 1948 Olympics when the captain of Yugoslavia, Boris Stankovic, was sent off while playing against Sweden. The first professional footballer ordered off at Wembley was Argentinian captain Antonio Rattin, who got his marching orders for disputing the referee's decisions during the 1966 World Cup quarter-final against England. The first player sent off in an FA Cup Final at Wembley was Manchester United's Kevin Moran for a reckless tackle on Everton's Peter Reid in the 1985 Final.

Pele

Q True or false: Goalkeeper Bruce Grobbelaar once scored a goal for Crewe Alexandra?

True. Goalkeeper Grobbelaar scored from the penalty spot against York City in his 24th and final match for Crewe in the last match of the 1979-80 season. He then played in Vancouver before dropping everything and signing for Liverpool.

Q How many players have captained England since the war who have played for Southampton?

Nine: Alf Ramsey, Mick Mills, Dave Watson, Peter Shilton, Mark Wright, Kevin Keegan, Mike Channon, Alan Ball and Alan Shearer.

Q Did Bobby Charlton or Denis Law score more League goals for Manchester United?

Bobby scored 198 League goals between 1956 and 1972. Denis netted 171 League goals for United between 1962 and 1972.

Q When was the last transfer transaction between Liverpool and Manchester United?

It is almost an unwritten rule that these intense rivals do not do transfer business. The last deal between the clubs saw Phil Chisnall move from Old Trafford to Anfield for £30,000 on 15 April 1964.

Q **On which ground did Chelsea win the FA Cup in 1970, and who scored the winning goal?**
The replay was staged at Old Trafford because the Wembley pitch was unfit after being trampled on by showjumping horses. Chelsea's winning goal was a far-post header by David Webb that clinched victory for Dave Sexton's team over a Leeds United side managed by Don Revie. Chelsea went on to capture the European Cup Winners' Cup the following season by beating Real Madrid in a replay in Athens.

Q **Who is Aston Villa's all-time top goal scorer in League matches?**
Harry Hampton, who netted 215 League goals between 1904 and 1915. 'Pongo' Waring was top scorer for a single season with 49 goals in 1930-31.

Q **What is the record for most League goals in a season by an individual?**
The great William Ralph (Dixie) Dean's record of 60 goals for Everton in the 1927-8 season is never likely to be beaten. In the final match of the season he scored a hat-trick against Arsenal at Goodison Park to beat the 59-goal record set in the previous season by Middlesbrough goal ace George Camsell, whose goals were netted in the Second Division.

Q **Did the late Laurie Cunningham ever play for Manchester United?**
Laurie Cunningham played five matches for Manchester United (two as a substitute) in the 1982-3 season during a loan transfer from Real Madrid. He scored one goal. Laurie was killed in a road smash while back in Spain.

Q **What is the attendance record for any match at Hampden Park?**
A crowd of 149,547 saw Scotland beat England 3-1 on 17 April 1937.

Q **What was Mike Channon's football record before he switched to training horses?**
Mike Channon, born in Wiltshire on 28 November 1948, played for Southampton (twice), Manchester City, Newcastle United, Bristol Rovers, Norwich and Portsmouth. He will best be remembered for his scoring feats with Southampton (a club record 185 goals in 511 League games). He won 46 England caps, scored 21 goals and captained the team three times. Mike collected an FA Cup winners' medal with Southampton in 1976.

Q **Who scored England's second goal in the 1966 World Cup final?**
It was Martin Peters who shot England into a 2-1 lead against West Germany in the seventy-eighth minute of the match in which his West Ham clubmate Geoff Hurst scored an historic hat-trick.

Q **Was Bryan Robson the first England captain for his namesake Bobby Robson?**
Ray Wilkins was captain for Bobby Robson's first match, a 2-2 draw in

Denmark in 1982. Bryan Robson became captain two games later against Greece.

Q **For which clubs has England goalkeeper David Seaman played?**
Rotherham-born Seaman was an amateur with Leeds before starting his League career with Peterborough (1982-4). He then played for Birmingham City (1984-6) and QPR (1986-90) before joining Arsenal in 1990.

Q **Is Leeds United and former Manchester United player Lee Sharpe a Devonian or a Mancunian?**
Neither. Sharpe was born in Halesowen, West Midlands. He moved to Old Trafford from Torquay United in 1988 and on to Leeds United in August 1996.

Q **Did the Compton brothers, Denis and Leslie, play football for England?**
Denis Compton did not win an England cap at football. He played only in unofficial wartime internationals. Big brother Leslie won two caps at the age of 38 and was the oldest player to make his England debut. Both played cricket for Middlesex, but only Denis played in Tests for England. Both were in Arsenal's FA Cup winning team in 1950.

Q **From which club did Manchester United sign Lou Macari and how many goals did he score for them?**
Tommy Docherty returned to the Celtic club where he had started his playing career to make Lou Macari one of his first signings for Manchester United in January 1974. Macari's transfer fee was a then Scottish record £200,000, and it broke up his prolific partnership at Celtic with a young striker called Kenny Dalglish. In his ten years with United Macari scored 78 League goals in 311 matches.

Q **What was Kenny Dalglish's goal scoring record with Celtic, Liverpool and Scotland?**
Dalglish scored 112 goals in 202 League matches for Celtic while helping them win nine major domestic titles in ten years. He was equally productive when moving to Liverpool in 1977 for the then British record transfer fee of £440,000. He netted 118 goals in 355 League games and was a member of the all-conquering Liverpool team that won three European Cup finals, the FA Cup in 1986, the League Cup four years in a row and six First Division championships. He is the only player to have scored a century of goals in both the Scottish and English Leagues. In a Scottish record 102 international appearances he equalled Denis Law's record of 30 goals for Scotland.

Kenny Dalgl

Q **Who was the first ever substitute to play in a full England international match?**
Wolves winger Jimmy Mullen came on for injured Jackie Milburn in the tenth minute of the international match against Belgium at the Heysel Stadium in Brussels on 18 May 1950. It was England's final warm-up game before the unhappy 1950 World Cup adventure. England were trailing 1-0 at half-time, and it was Mullen who equalized in the first attacking move of the second-half to put England on the way to a 4-1 victory.

Q **What squad of players did Sir Alf Ramsey select to defend the World Cup in Mexico in 1970?**
Gordon Banks, Keith Newton, Terry Cooper, Alan Mullery, Brian Labone, Bobby Moore (captain), Francis Lee, Alan Ball, Bobby Charlton, Geoff Hurst, Martin Peters, Peter Bonetti, Tommy Wright, Jack Charlton, Norman Hunter, Emlyn Hughes, Colin Bell, Peter Osgood, Jeff Astle, Allan Clarke, Nobby Stiles, Alex Stepney. Only full-backs George Cohen and Ray Wilson and striker Roger Hunt were missing from the team that won the Cup in 1966.

Q **Which England manager had the best record: Walter Winterbottom, Alf Ramsey or Bobby Robson?**
Judge for yourself:
> Winterbottom (1946-62): P139 W78 D33 L28 F383 A196
> Ramsey (1962-73): P113 W69 D27 L17 F224 A99
> Robson (1982-90): P95 W47 D30 L18 F154 A60
Winterbottom's teams were picked in most instances by a selection committee based on recommendations from Walter. It was not until Alf Ramsey took over in 1962 that the amateur selectors stopped interfering.

Q **Who were the ten most capped players during the reign of Walter Winterbottom as England manager?**
Billy Wright (105), Tom Finney (76), Johnny Haynes (56), Jimmy Dickinson (48), Bobby Charlton (39), Ron Flowers (39), Stanley Matthews (36), Ronnie Clayton (35) and, equal ninth, Roger Byrne (33), Bryan Douglas (33), Nat Lofthouse (33).

Q **Who were the ten most capped players during the reign of Alf Ramsey as England manager?**
Bobby Moore (100), Gordon Banks (73), Bobby Charlton (67), Alan Ball (66), Martin Peters (66), Geoff Hurst (49), Ray Wilson (46), George Cohen (37), Alan Mullery (35), Jack Charlton (35).

Q **Who were the ten most capped players during the reign of Bobby Robson as England manager?**
Peter Shilton (83), Terry Butcher (69), Bryan Robson (65), Kenny Sansom (59), Chris Waddle (59), John Barnes (58), Gary Lineker (58), Peter Beardsley (45), Gary Stevens (41), Glenn Hoddle (40).

Q **From which club did Jim Baxter join Rangers the first time around?**
Jim Baxter joined Rangers from Raith Rovers. He later played in England with Sunderland and Nottingham Forest before winding down his career at Ibrox. 'Slim Jim' retired at the age of 30.

Q **True or false: More than 70 goals were scored on the same day in just two matches in Scotland?**
True. Seventy-one goals were scored in one day in two first round Scottish Cup ties on 5 September 1885. Arbroath beat Bon Accord 36-0 and Dundee Harp beat Aberdeen Rovers 35-0.

Q **How many clubs has former England captain Gerry Francis managed?**
Francis served his managerial apprenticeship with Exeter City and Bristol Rovers before taking over as manager of his old club Queen's Park Rangers. He moved to White Hart Lane as manager of Tottenham in 1994.

Q **Did George Best ever play World Cup football for Northern Ireland?**
George Best, sadly, never played in the World Cup finals. His talent deserved to be seen on the greatest of all stages. He did, however, play for Northern Ireland in 12 World Cup qualifying matches for the finals of 1966 (6), 1970 (2), 1974 (2) and 1978 (4). Northern Ireland manager Billy Bingham resisted demands by the media to recall him for the 1982 finals in Spain.

Q **When were numbered shirts first worn in an FA Cup Final?**
This was in the 1932-3 FA Cup Final between Everton and Manchester City. Everton shirts were numbered from 1 to 11, and City wore shirts numbered from 12 to 22. Everton, with their attack led by the legendary 'Dixie' Dean, won 3-0. It was another seven years before numbered shirts became compulsory.

Q **With what clubs did Liam Brady play before going into management?**
Brady passed with honours for Arsenal, Juventus, Sampdoria, Ascoli, West Ham United and Celtic.

Q **How many League matches did Ian Callaghan play for Liverpool, and to what club did he move?**
Ian Callaghan played a club record 640 League matches for Liverpool before winding down his career with Swansea City, where his old Anfield clubmate John Toshack was the manager.

Q **Why is the Sheffield Wednesday club nicknamed 'The Owls'?**
Their ground was known as Owlerton before becoming Hillsborough in 1914. Owlerton was the district, which was renamed as Hillsborough.

Q **Has the same player ever played for two different teams on the same day?**
It was fairly common during the wartime programme. For instance, on Christmas Day 1940 Tommy Lawton played for his own club Everton against Liverpool in the morning and guested for Tranmere Rovers against

Crewe Alexandra in the afternoon. Len Shackleton, the Clown Prince, appeared for the two Bradford clubs: his own Park Avenue and as a guest for City.

Q How and when did Crystal Palace Football Club get its name?

The original Crystal Palace team was founded back in 1861 by staff working at the Great Exhibition in Joseph Paxton's Crystal Palace and was one of the sides to contest the very first FA Cup in 1871, getting as far as the semi-final. The present Crystal Palace club dates back to 1905 and used the Crystal Palace ground as its first home until 1915, when the army claimed the site during the First World War. The club was later based at Herne Hill, the Den, and the Nest, before the Eagles eventually landed at Selhurst Park in 1924, four years after joining the Football League.

Q Why is Derby manager Jim Smith known as a member of 'The 92 Club'?

In 1986 Jim Smith completed the unique record of travelling to every one of the 92 League grounds for first-team fixtures in the role of manager. He was enrolled as a member of 'The 92 Club' which is exclusive to people who can prove they have visited every one of the Football League grounds to witness a first-team game. Jim Smith started managing at Colchester United in 1972 and has since been in charge at Blackburn Rovers, Birmingham City, Oxford United, Queen's Park Rangers, Newcastle United, Portsmouth and Derby County.

Q Where was Ron Atkinson born, and did he ever play for Aston Villa?

Ron is a Scouser, born in Liverpool on 18 March 1939. He and his brother Graham, four years younger, joined Aston Villa while apprentices with BSA Tools, but he never played in the first-team. It was at Oxford United that he established himself as a driving midfield player who earned the nickname 'The Tank'. He played 383 League games for Oxford, with his brother, the orchestrator of the team. Ron started in management with Kettering Town. He has since travelled the managerial roundabout with Cambridge United, West Bromwich Albion, Manchester United, Atletico Madrid, Sheffield Wednesday, Aston Villa and Coventry City.

Q Why is it called a hat-trick when a player scores three goals?

The term 'hat-trick' was borrowed from cricket. It dates back to the days late last century when bowlers were presented with a new hat by a hatter's shop whenever they succeeded in taking three wickets with three balls. Going by the original meaning, it is not correct to credit a player with a 'hat-trick' in football if his sequence of three goals is broken by a goal from another player for the same side. But three goals by any player is now accepted as a hat-trick.

Q Have two players ever been credited with the same own goal?

Jim Milburn and Jack Froggatt were credited with the same own goal in the First Division match between Leicester City and Chelsea on 18 December 1954. Both connected with the ball simultaneously to shoot the ball into the Leicester net.

Q **Which club was first to reach the FA Cup semi final from the old Third Division?**
It was Millwall in 1936-7, and they were finally beaten by eventual Cup winners Sunderland. Millwall provided their greatest shock when they eliminated the reigning League champions, Manchester City, in the quarter-finals.

Q **With which club did Peter Beardsley start his career, and did he ever play for Manchester United?**
Peter Beardsley started his career with Carlisle United for whom he played 102 League matches. He was briefly with Manchester United but did not play any League games for them. Peter joined Newcastle United after two spells with Vancouver Whitecaps. He moved on to Liverpool and then Everton before manager Kevin Keegan, his old Tyneside team-mate, brought him back to Newcastle in 1993.

Q **Did Welsh international striker Ron Davies ever play for Manchester United?**
Ron Davies joined Manchester United from Portsmouth in a straight swap for George Graham in November 1974. He played just eight League games for United.

Q **How old was Stanley Matthews when he played his final match?**
Stanley Matthews was five days past his 50th birthday when he made his final League appearance for Stoke City against Fulham on 6 February 1965. He remains the oldest footballer to have played in the First Division. Five weeks earlier he had become the first footballer to be knighted. Sir Stanley continued to play well into his 60s in exhibition matches around the world, flourishing the 'Wizard of Dribble' skills that made him a legendary player with Stoke City, Blackpool and, ofcourse, England.

Stanley Matthews

Q **Who is the oldest footballer to have appeared in a Football League match?**
New Brighton manager Neil McBain was 52 years and 4 months old when he picked himself as emergency goalkeeper in a

Third Division North match at Hartlepool on 15 March 1947. His team was beaten 3-0.

Q **Who is the oldest footballer to have played in the FA Cup?**
Billy Meredith, the Welsh Wizard, was 49 years 8 months old when he played for Manchester City against Newcastle United in the 1924 FA Cup semi-final.

Q **Which two teams featured in the first live televised League match?**
Blackpool v Bolton Wanderers on Friday 9 September 1960. The idea was to make it a regular Friday night series on ITV, but the game – won 1-0 by Blackpool – was so dull that the option was not taken up for further live coverage, mainly because several of the top clubs refused to allow cameras at their grounds. In August 1964 BBC2 started screening a regular 55-minute edited version of the *Match of the Day*. This was cut back by ten minutes following protests to the League by the Football Association, who warned that the game was in danger of becoming over exposed. The first FA Cup Final televised in part was the 1937 match between Sunderland and Preston. The 1947 Final between Charlton and Burnley was shown in its entirety.

Q **When was the first League match shown in colour on British television?**
The First Division game at Anfield between Liverpool and West Ham United on 15 November 1969 was the first colour transmission. The first FA Cup final screened in colour was the 1968 match between West Brom and Everton.

Q **True or false: Stan Mortensen played his first international match for Wales?**
True. Blackpool goal hunter Stan Mortensen made his international debut in a wartime match at Wembley on 25 September 1943 for Wales. He was at Wembley as an England reserve, and was called into the match in the second-half as a substitute for injured Welsh half-back Ivor Powell.

Q **Were substitutes used during the 1966 World Cup finals?**
No. It was 1970 before substitutes were allowed in the World Cup finals. Tommy Wright and Peter Osgood were the first England substitutes in the World Cup, replacing Keith Newton and Francis Lee in the 1970 group match against Romania in Guadalajara.

Q **Which England players were substituted in the 1970 World Cup match against West Germany?**
Manager Sir Alf Ramsey sent on Colin Bell for Bobby Charlton and Norman Hunter in place of Martin Peters. England were leading 2-0 and lost the quarter-final 3-2 after extra-time.

Q **Against which team did Brian Kidd score four goals for Manchester City?**
Leicester City. The date: 22 January 1977. Mike Doyle scored the other goal in a 5-0 victory. Kidd netted a total of 152 League goals while playing for Manchester United, Arsenal, Manchester City, Everton and Bolton.

Q **Was Bobby Moore the captain when he played for Fulham against West Ham in the 1975 FA Cup Final?**
No. Alan Mullery was the Fulham skipper. Bobby skippered West Ham when they beat Preston in the Final in 1964.

Q **How many Welsh players were in the Cardiff team that beat Arsenal in the 1927 FA Cup Final?**
The Cardiff City team comprised three Welshmen, one Englishman, three Scots and four Irishmen. Cardiff won 1-0 with a seventy-third minute goal by Scot Hugh Ferguson that was fumbled into the net by Arsenal's Welsh goalkeeper Dai Lewis. He claimed that he lost control of the greasy ball because it skidded off his shiny new jersey. Arsenal goalkeepers have since always had their new jerseys washed before wearing them for the first time. The Cardiff team: Farquharson, Nelson, Watson, Keenor, Sloan, Hardy, Curtis, Irving, Ferguson, Davies, McLachan.

Q **From which club did Arsene Wenger join Arsenal as manager?**
Wenger joined Arsenal from leading Japanese club Grampus Eight.

Q **Did Billy Wright ever score for England in an international match at White Hart Lane?**
Yes, with a 40-yard lob against Italy on 30 November 1949. It was one of only three goals that Billy scored in his 105 appearances for England. He skippered this team at White Hart Lane that beat Italy 2-0: Williams, Ramsey, Aston, Watson, Franklin, Wright, Finney, Mortensen, Rowley, Pearson, Froggatt.

Q **Did goalkeeper Frank Swift have a brother who also played in goal as a professional?**
Frank Swift played with distinction for Manchester City and England, while his older brother, Fred, was a good-class pre-war goalkeeper with Bolton Wanderers and Oldham Athletic.

Q **Was Peter Shilton the first goalkeeper to captain England?**
That honour went to Frank Swift, who captained England for the first of two matches against Italy in Turin in 1948. England won 4-0.

Q **What was the score when Tottenham beat Everton in Bill Nicholson's first match as manager?**
Tottenham won 10-4 at White Hart Lane in October 1958. As Bill Nicholson came into the dressing-room after the final whistle, man of the match Tommy Harmer said: 'Don't expect this sort of score every week, Boss!'

Q **For which clubs has Mark Hateley played, and has he had more clubs than his father, Tony?**
Mark Hateley has played for Coventry, Portsmouth, AC Milan, AS Monaco, Glasgow Rangers, QPR and Leeds. His father, Tony, was a have-boots-will-travel centre-forward in the 1960s and played for Notts County (twice), Aston Villa, Chelsea, Liverpool, Coventry, Birmingham and Oldham.

Q **When Moscow Dynamo played in England in 1945, what was the name of their goalkeeper?**
It was Alexei 'Tiger' Khomich, who was rated second only to the legendary Lev Yashin as the greatest of all Russian goalkeepers.

Q **Did Paul Gascoigne play more games for Newcastle United or Tottenham?**
Gazza played exactly 92 League games for both Newcastle and Tottenham. He was already lined up for a move to Lazio from Spurs when he received a crippling knee injury in the 1991 FA Cup Final against Nottingham Forest.

Q **How old was Bobby Moore when he first captained England?**
Bobby was at 22 the youngest player ever to captain England when he deputized for injured Jimmy Armfield against Czechoslovakia in Bratislava on 20 May 1963. He led England to the first victory under Alf Ramsey in the new manager's fourth match in charge. Armfield returned to skipper England for the next six matches, and then Moore took over as full-time captain against Uruguay at Wembley on 6 May 1964. England won the match 2-1. He was captain in 90 matches in all, skippering the team for the last time in his 108th and final appearance against Italy at Wembley on 14 November 1973.

Bobby Moore

Q **Did Bobby Moore ever play in the same team as Johnny Haynes?**
Johnny Haynes was England captain when Bobby Moore made his debut against Peru in Lima in the match before the 1962 World Cup finals. England won 4-0, Jimmy Greaves scoring a hat-trick. Moore, replacing Bobby Robson, played in all four World Cup games with Haynes.

Q **Who was the top scorer in the 1966 World Cup finals?**
Eusebio, the 'Black Panther' of Portugal. He scored nine goals, including four in a remarkable match against North Korea at Goodison Park when Portugal struck back to win 5-3 after trailing by three goals.

Q **Why is it that West Ham United are known by older supporters as 'The Irons'?**
West Ham began life as Thames Ironworks, a side formed in 1895 by workers at a shipyard in East London. They became West Ham United in 1900.

Q **Which player was nicknamed the 'Galloping Major', and why?**
Ferenc Puskas was nicknamed the 'Galloping Major' when playing for crack Hungarian club Honved, a formidable force in the 1950s. Honved was the Army team of Hungary, and Puskas had the rank of major although doing little soldiering. One of the greatest left-footed players of all time, he left Hungary following the 1956 revolution and joined Real Madrid where he formed a prolific partnership with Alfredo di Stefano.

Q **True or false: A player has made more than 400 consecutive League appearances?**
True. Harold Bell made 401 consecutive appearances for Tranmere Rovers between 1946 and 1955. The record reached 459 games including cup ties.

Q **What is the record attendance for any match involving British clubs?**
Celtic and Leeds United were watched by a crowd of 135,826 when they met in the second leg of the European Cup semi-final at Hampden Park on 15 April 1970. The aggregate attendance for the two legs was 181,331.

Q **What is the longest a British goalkeeper has gone without having to pick the ball out of the net?**
Former England goalkeeper Chris Woods went a total of 1196 minutes with Glasgow Rangers without conceding a goal (13 games from 26 November 1986 to 31 January 1987). The Football League record was set in 1979 by Reading goalkeeper Steve Death, who kept a clean sheet for 1103 minutes (24 March to 18 August). The world record is 1275 minutes, set by Atletico Madrid goalkeeper Abel Resino in 1991.

Q **Who has been the youngest player to appear in League football?**
The record is shared by two players. Both Albert Gerard (Bradford Park Avenue v Millwall, 1929) and Ken Roberts (Wrexham v Bradford Park Avenue, 1951) were exactly 15 years 158 days old when making their debuts. Goalkeeper Derek Forster (Sunderland v Leicester City, 1984) holds the old First Division record at 15 years 185 days.

Q **What is the highest number of penalties converted by any one player in a single season?**
Francis Lee netted 13 spot-kicks for Manchester City in the old First Division in 1971-2. His nickname was Lee Won Pen because he convinced so many referees that he had been fouled. He took two penalties for England, and missed them both (against Portugal and Wales in 1969). Francis, who became a wealthy businessman and racehorse trainer, liked Manchester City so much that he bought the club and became chairman of the board.

Q **Have there been any Chinese players in the Football League?**
Hong Kong-born Cheung Chi-Doy played two matches for Blackpool in 1960-1, and Sammy Chung – half Chinese – played for Reading, Norwich and Watford between 1953 and 1964 before becoming an outstanding coach. Buxton-born Frank Soo played for Stoke, Leicester City and Luton.

Q **Who was the first European Footballer of the Year, and how many British players have won the award?**
Stanley Matthews, then with Blackpool, was the first winner in 1956 when the French football weekly France Football launched the award after conducting a poll among European football writers. British winners since have been Denis Law (1964), Bobby Charlton (1966), George Best (1968) and Kevin Keegan (1978, 1979).

Q **True or false: Denis Law once scored seven goals and finished on the losing side?**
True. Denis Law scored six goals for Manchester City in an FA Cup tie at Luton in 1961. The match was abandoned because of a waterlogged pitch. When it was replayed at Luton four days later, Law scored again but City lost 3-1. Seven goals, and he was on the losing side! Denis told The Judge: 'As we trooped off through the mud the referee apologized to me for having to call the game off. I told him that I was used to it. Exactly the same thing happened after I had scored six goals in a schoolboys match.' There was consolation for Denis two years later when he was the man of the match as Manchester United beat Leicester City in the FA Cup Final. In between, he had a short spell with Torino.

Q **Why is Derby County's ground known as the Baseball Ground?**
It was originally built as a baseball stadium by a local foundry owner, who had fallen in love with the game while visiting the United States. Derby County's first home was the Racecourse Ground, which they shared with the county cricket team. They moved to the nearby Baseball Ground in 1895 as the interest in baseball dwindled. Some gypsies camping at the ground were forced to move, and a curse was laid on the ground. In 1946 the Derby players visited a gypsy encampment and asked for the curse to be lifted. The following week they beat Charlton 4-1 in the FA Cup Final at Wembley. A new, all-seater Derby stadium has been erected.

Q **How many times did Liverpool win the old Football League First Division championship?**
Liverpool had a record 18 League championship triumphs: 1901, 1906, 1922, 1923, 1947, 1964, 1966, 1973, 1976, 1977, 1979, 1980, 1982, 1983, 1984, 1986, 1988 and 1990.

Q **What was Jamie Redknapp's contribution to England's Euro 96 campaign?**
Redknapp came on as a substitute for Stuart Pearce in

Jamie Redknapp

29

the forty-sixth minute of the crucial group match against Scotland. The score was 0-0. Within seven minutes of coming on to the pitch he started the move that led to Alan Shearer giving England the lead. He was then influential in bossing the midfield and had played an important part in helping England move into a 2-0 lead through Paul Gascoigne when he was injured and had to go off in the eighty-fourth minute. His contribution to Euro 96 lasted just 38 minutes, but it was considered vital.

Q What and when was the Battle of Highbury?
This was the label hung by the media on a vicious encounter between England and Italy, then world champions, at Highbury in 1934. England, including seven Arsenal players, beat the previously all-conquering Italians 3-2. England were the 'Old Masters' and the game was billed as being for the unofficial championship of the world. The Italians had been offered huge bonuses as an incentive to win the prestige game, and tempers boiled over when their star player, Luisito Monti, limped off with a broken toe after a clash with Ted Drake in the tenth minute. Eddie Hapgood, the England left-back and captain, had his nose broken by an Italian elbow and there were so many injured players limping around that the pitch resembled a battlefield. Eric Brook (2) and Ted Drake put England 3-0 clear inside the first 15 minutes.

Q Has an England player ever scored from the penalty spot on his international debut?
Allan Clarke, playing in his first game for England, slotted home a penalty in their World Cup finals match against Czechoslovakia in Mexico in 1970. It was the only goal and came on what was his wife's birthday, their wedding anniversary and the anniversary of his transfer from Fulham to Leicester City. Sir Alf Ramsey had asked before the kick-off who would volunteer to act as penalty taker. He was amazed to find Clarke the only player putting up his hand before what should have been a nerves-jangling debut.

Q Which three teams were in England's group in the 1970 World Cup finals in Mexico?
Romania (won 1-0), Brazil (lost 1-0) and Czechoslovakia (won 1-0) in Guadalajara. Engand went through to the quarter-finals in Leon where they were beaten 3-2 by West Germany in extra-time after leading 2-0.

Q Were the two John Astons who both played for Manchester United related?
John Aston was a Manchester United inside-forward who was converted into a full-back by Matt Busby. He won 17 England caps in the immediate post-war years, and later became chief scout at Old Trafford. His son, Johnny, was a winger who played a prominent role in United's 1968 European Cup winning team.

Q Have a father and son ever played together in the same League team?
Alec Herd and his son David played inside-right and inside-left respectively for Stockport County against Hartlepool United in what was the final Third Division (North) match of the 1950-51 season at Edgeley Park.

David, later a top-flight player with Arsenal, Manchester United and Scotland, scored in a 2-0 win. The Easthams, George and George Jnr, often played together for Ards in the Irish League.

Q Was Liverpool midfield player Craig Johnston ever capped by England?
Only at England Under-21 level. Craig Johnston was born in South Africa, brought up in Australia, had a Scottish grandfather and Irish grandmother, and is a British citizen. He was turned down when he wanted to play for Scotland because he had England honours, and in 1987 he was selected for the full England squad for the game against Yugoslavia, but did not play.

Q Did Oleg Blokhin count himself as a Russian when he won the European Footballer of the Year award?
Oleg Blokhin was a Ukranian rather than a Russian when he was voted European Footballer of the Year in 1975 in the days of the Soviet Union. A gifted left-winger with Dynamo Kiev, he became the Soviet Union's top goal scorer of all time with 302 goals, as well as scoring a record 44 goals in 108 internationals. He was past his peak when allowed to transfer to Austria's Vowarts Steyr in 1988 and he wound down his career in Cyprus.

Q Was Pele the leading goal scorer in the 1958 World Cup finals?
No. Pele scored six goals, but even he was overshadowed by the prolific goal scoring of Just Fontaine. The French-Moroccan netted a record 13 goals in helping France into third place behind Brazil and Sweden.

Q Has David Beckham played for any club other than Manchester United?
Beckham, an East Londoner from the Orient territory of Leytonstone, joined Manchester United as a trainee in January 1993. He was briefly loaned to Preston in March 1995 to get some League experience, and he scored two goals in five appearances for the Deepdale club. He made his Premiership debut for United in a goalless draw with Leeds on 2 April 1995, one week after returning to Old Trafford from Preston. He was courted by Spurs and Arsenal when a schoolboy player.

Q Which of the Football League clubs has had most grounds?
Queen's Park Rangers have had 13 grounds since being founded in 1885, finally arriving at Loftus Road, Shepherds Bush, London, in 1931, and settling there in 1963 after several flirtations with nearby White City stadium.

Q For how many English League clubs did Danny Blanchflower play?
Belfast-born Blanchflower joined Barnsley from Irish club Glentoran in 1949. He moved to Aston Villa two years later, and then to Tottenham for his greatest years in 1954. Danny was an inspirational midfield motivator and skipper of Spurs until a knee injury forced his retirement in 1964. His triumphs with Tottenham included the League and FA Cup double in 1961, a second FA Cup in 1962 and the European Cup Winners' Cup in 1963. He was voted Footballer of the Year in 1958 and 1961 and collected a then record 56 Northern Ireland caps. Danny, whose brother, Jackie, was an Irish international centre-half who survived the Munich air crash, later

became a perceptive journalist and was briefly manager of Chelsea. He died in 1993.

Q **With which club did Dave Beasant play before joining Wimbledon?**
Beasant joined Wimbledon from Edgware Town for £1,000 in 1979. He has since played for Newcastle United, Chelsea and Southampton and had short spells on loan to Wolves and Grimsby Town.

Q **Has any player won English, Scottish and Irish Cup medals?**
Jimmy Delaney had a unique collection of English, Scottish, Northern Ireland and Republic of Ireland cup medals which were won during skilled wing duty with Celtic (1937), Manchester United (1948) and Derry City (1954). At the grand age of 44, he won a runners-up medal with Cork (1956). He also played for Abderdeen and Falkirk, and was known as 'Old Bones'.

Q **How old was Ian Wright when he started his League career with Crystal Palace?**
Wright was 21 when he joined Crystal Palace from Sunday club side Greenwich Borough in August 1985.

Q **Did Everton centre-forward Duncan Ferguson start his career with Rangers?**
Ferguson joined Rangers from Dundee United, who signed him from Carse Thistle. He moved to Everton from Rangers for £4,400,000 in July 1993.

Q **Did Alan Shearer win any England caps while with Southampton?**
Shearer made his debut for England while with Southampton, scoring a minute before half-time with a shot on the turn against France at Wembley on 19 February 1992.
He had won two more caps (against CIS and France in the Euro 92 finals) before joining Blackburn for £3,600,000 in July 1992.

Q **Whom did David Platt succeed as England captain, and for which club was he playing?**
Platt's first game as England captain was in the World Cup qualifier against San Marino on 17 February 1993 when he scored four goals in a 6-0 win at Wembley. He was a Juventus player at the time, and took over the captain's armband from the injured Stuart Pearce. Platt was later named as skipper by Terry Venables for his first game as manager against Denmark on 9 March 1994, and he scored the only goal of the match.

Alan Shea

Q **How many League matches did John Lyall play for West Ham United?**
Just 31 before a broken leg ended his playing career at the age of 21.

32

Q **Were Rangers or Celtic featured in the first Scottish League match shown live on television?**

Neither were involved. The first game screened live in Scotland was the First Division match between Clyde and Aberdeen at the Shawfield Stadium on 3 September 1955.

Q **Has any player scored in the final of two World Cups and finished on the winning side each time?**

Brazilian striker Vava was first to achieve this feat (1958 and 1962) and was followed by Pele (1958 and 1970). They were team-mates when Pele made his World Cup debut in the 1958 finals in Sweden at the age of 17. Both scored in the final against Sweden. Vava found the net again in the 1962 final against Czechoslovakia, and Pele scored in the 1970 final against Italy. Paul Breitner scored for West Germany in the 1974 and 1982 finals, but was on the beaten side (by Italy) the second time around.

Q **What is the biggest defeat suffered by any of the home countries in a live televised football match?**

The unfortunate distinction falls to Scotland. They were hammered 7-0 by Uruguay in the 1954 World Cup finals in Switzerland. It was the first time that Scotland had been shown in a live match.

Q **Has a British referee ever taken charge of a World Cup Final?**

Southampton referee George Reader was the man in charge of the match in which Uruguay clinched the 1950 World Cup with a 2-1 win over host country Brazil in front of a near-200,000 attendance at the Maracana Stadium in Rio. This was when the tournament was decided on a league basis, but it is generally accepted as the final. Reader later became chairman of Southampton. Englishman Bill Ling was in charge of the 1954 final, and Wolverhampton master butcher Jack Taylor refereed the 1974 final between West Germany and Holland when he gave a penalty after just 90 seconds.

Q **Why are Peterborough United known to their fans as 'Posh'?**

The nickname was given to them by their supporters when they wore a posh new strip at the start of the 1934-5 season. They were elected to the League in 1960-61, and won the Fourth Division championship at the first attempt with a record haul of 134 goals. Terry Bly scored 52 of them.

Q **What is the highest number of goals scored by a player in any one League match?**

Joe Payne netted ten goals for Luton Town in their 12-0 defeat of Bristol Rovers in a Third Division (South) match on Easter Monday 13 April 1936. It was only his fourth League match, and he was making his first appearance at centre-forward after joining the club as a half-back from Biggleswade Town. A coal miner, he later played for Chelsea, West Ham and Millwall.

Q **Where was Gary McAllister born, and with which club did he start his career?**

McAllister was born in Motherwell on Christmas Day 1964. He first came to the attention of scouts while playing for Fir Park Boys Club and he joined Motherwell in 1981. He has since played for Leicester City, Leeds United and Coventry City, and he has captained Scotland.

Q **Have any clubs gone through an entire League season without a single defeat?**
It has happened just three times, twice in the English League and once in the Scottish. 'Proud Preston' won the first League championship in 1888-9 without a single defeat. They had to play just 22 matches that season. Liverpool repeated the feat in 1893-4 when going through their 28 Second Division matches undefeated. Rangers achieved it in 1898-9 when going 18 matches without defeat in the old Scottish First Division. The nearest in modern times was Arsenal's one defeat in 38 matches on the way to the First Division title in 1990-91.

Q **From which club did Arsenal sign Swedish winger Anders Limpar?**
Limpar joined Arsenal from Cremonese for £1,000,000 in the summer of 1990. He moved on to Everton for £1,600,000 in March 1994.

Q **Who was the first player to appear in more than 1,000 matches with English clubs?**
Pat Jennings, exceptional Northern Ireland goalkeeper, was first to reach the 1,000-match milestone on 26 February 1983 when playing for Arsenal at West Bromwich Albion. His previous clubs were Watford and Tottenham. He also played 119 matches for Northern Ireland.

Q **How many all-London FA Cup finals have featured at Wembley?**
Four, or five if you include a replay – Tottenham 2, Chelsea 1 in 1967, West Ham 2, Fulham 0 in 1975, West Ham 1, Arsenal 0 in 1980, Tottenham 1, QPR 0 (replay after a 1-1 draw) in 1982.

Q **Which English footballer is credited with the most hat-tricks during his career?**
Dixie Dean, who completed 37 hat-tricks while playing for Tranmere Rovers and Everton. He scored 379 League goals in all. Dixie also netted 18 goals in 16 England appearances, plus 47 in 18 other representative matches. His FA Cup haul was 18 goals in 33 ties, including one in the 1933 final.

Q **Did Dixie Dean play for any clubs other than Everton and Tranmere?**
Dixie started his League career with Tranmere in 1923 and scored 27 goals in 29 League matches before joining Everton in 1925. He netted 349 goals in 399 games for Everton, and added three more during nine appearances with Notts County in his final season of 1938-9.

Q **How many players have won the European Footballer of the Year award more than once?**
Seven – Alfredo di Stefano (Real Madrid, 1957, 1959), Johan Cruyff (Ajax, 1971, 1973, 1974), Franz Beckenbauer (Bayern Munich, 1972, 1976), Kevin Keegan (Hamburg, 1978, 1979), Karl-Heinz Rummenigge (Bayern Munich, 1980, 1981), Michel Platini (Juventus, 1983, 1984, 1985), Marco Van Basten (AC Milan, 1988, 1989, 1992).

Q **Against which team did Ryan Giggs score his first League goal for Manchester United?**
Giggs scored his first League goal in the Manchester derby against Manchester City at Old Trafford on 4 May 1991. It was the first match in which 17-year-old Giggs had started after one brief appearance as a substitute. Manager Alex Ferguson pulled him off late in the game and replaced him with Mal Donaghy. He became a regular in the United attack the following season.

Q **For which League clubs did QPR manager Stewart Houston play?**
Defender Houston joined Chelsea from Port Glasgow in 1967. His career record: Chelsea (6 games), Brentford (77), Manchester United (204), Sheffield United (93) and Colchester United (106).

Ryan Giggs

Q **What is the biggest winning margin in a Football League match?**
Newcastle United 13, Newport County 0. Len Shackleton, the Clown Prince of football, was making his Newcastle debut in this Second Division match on 5 October 1946 and scored six of the goals. This equalled the record set by Stockport County, who beat Halifax Town 13-0 in a Third Division (North) match on 6 January 1934.

Q **Where and when was Joe Royle born, and for which clubs did he play?**
Royle was born in Liverpool on 8 April 1949, and scored 152 goals in 467 League games with Everton (229), Manchester City (98), Bristol City (100) and Norwich City (40). He scored two goals in six England appearances at centre-forward.

Q **How much did Liverpool pay for Ian Rush the first time around and how many League goals did he score for them?**
Rush cost Liverpool £300,000 when he joined them from Chester at the age of 18 in 1980. He scored 139 goals in 224 First Division games before a short spell with Juventus. On his return to Anfield he added another 90 in 245 League matches before joining Leeds in the summer of 1996. His 229 League goals was short of the Liverpool club record of 245 set by Roger Hunt (1959-69).

Q **Which club holds the record for fielding most players in a single season?**
Birmingham City set a new record in 1995-6 when their then manager Barry Fry selected 46 players. Not one of their players was an ever-present, and Birmingham finished in the middle of the First Division. By the start of the following season Fry was in charge at Peterborough.

Q What is the individual goal scoring record for any Scottish League match?
It is held by Celtic goal master Jimmy McGrory, who found the net eight times in a First Division match against Dunfermline Athletic at Celtic Park on 14 September 1928. He was noted for his heading power, but netted all eight goals with his feet. McGrory scored a club record 397 goals for Celtic between 1922 and 1939, and – including a brief loan spell with Clydebank – notched 550 goals, 410 of them in 408 Scottish League matches.

Q Why are Norwich City known to their supporters as 'The Canaries'.
Their former ground was The Nest, which was carved out of an old chalk pit. This coupled with their yellow and green shirts brought them their Canaries nickname. They moved to Carrow Road in 1935.

Q How many times did Jimmy Greaves score five goals in a match?
Three, all for Chelsea and in consecutive seasons: v Wolves (1958-9), v Preston (1959-60) and v West Bromwich Albion (1960-61). He completed a record six hat-tricks in the 1960-61 season on his way to another record of 357 First Division goals.

Q Which footballer holds the world record for most goals in a career?
Brazilian centre-forward Artur Friedenreich was credited with 1,329 goals during a career that spanned 26 years from 1909. The son of a German father and Brazilian mother, he played for Germania, Ipiranga, Americano, Paulistano, São Paulo and Flamengo. His haul included nine goals in 17 matches for Brazil.

Q How many football clubs have won the League championship in three successive seasons?
Three – Huddersfield Town (1923-4 to 1925-6), Arsenal (1932-3 to 1934-5) and Liverpool (1981-2 to 1983-4).

Q What is the highest number of goals scored in a single season in the Scottish Premier Division?
The record was set by Rangers in 1991-2 when they scored 101 goals in their 44 matches. Fifty goals came at Ibrox, and 51 in away matches. Ally McCoist (34) and Mark Hateley (21) led the goal rush.

Q Has a club ever conceded more than 100 goals in the FA Premiership?
Swindon Town hold the record for goals against, conceding exactly 100 on their way to relegation in the 1993-4 season. The most goals conceded in the old First Division was 125 by Blackpool in 1930-31.

Q On which ground did Ted Drake score his record seven First Division goals?
Drake's seven-goal haul came for Arsenal at Villa Park on 14 December 1935. It was very nearly eight goals because he struck the crossbar with another shot. His seven goals equalled the record set by James Ross for Preston against Stoke City on 6 October 1888.

Q **What is the highest attendance for a European Cup final?**
The 127,621 crowd that gathered to see the 'match of the century' in which Real Madrid beat Eintracht Frankfurt 7-3 at Hampden Park, Glasgow, on 18 May 1960.

Q **Has Teddy Sheringham played for any club other than Millwall, Nottingham Forest and Tottenham?**
Sheringham had a five-match loan spell with Aldershot in 1985 while with Millwall.

Q **Has any English player scored a hat-trick of penalties in a European tie?**
No, but Scot John Wark achieved the feat in a UEFA Cup tie for Ipswich against Aris Salonika of Greece in 1980-81. He scored a total of four goals in the match, including three from the spot. He finished with an individual record 14 goals in the tournament, with Ipswich winning the UEFA Cup by beating AZ 67 of Holland 5-4 on aggregate in the final. Wark signed three times for Ipswich in between playing for Middlesbrough and Liverpool.

Q **Where was Coventry City and former Crystal Palace winger John Salako born?**
Salako was born in Nigeria on 11 February 1969. He was brought up in London and joined Crystal Palace as a trainee straight from school.

Q **Did George Graham play football for any Scottish League clubs?**
Graham, born in Bargeddie, Lanarkshire, joined Aston Villa straight from school in 1959-60, and was an apprentice at Villa Park until making his League debut against Liverpool at 18. He later played for Chelsea, Arsenal, Manchester United, Portsmouth and Crystal Palace.

Q **Has Great Britain ever won the Olympic football gold medal?**
Yes, twice – in the 1908 Games in London, and in Stockholm in 1912 (with an England team entered). In each final they defeated Denmark (2-0 and 4-2). Vivian Woodward, the finest amateur player of the first decade of the twentieth Century and a star with Chelsea and then Tottenham, played in both matches. Great Britain, represented by Upton Park Football Club, also won the unofficial tournament in Paris in 1900.

Les Ferdinand

Q **Did Les Ferdinand win any club honours while playing club football in Turkey?**
Ferdinand collected a Turkish Cup Final winners' medal while on a loan spell to Besiktas from QPR in 1988-9. He had been bought from Hayes for £15,000 in 1987, and Rangers made a huge profit when selling

him to Newcastle for £6 million in 1995. He also had a three-match loan period with Brentford while with QPR before establishing himself in the first-team. He scored 80 League goals for Rangers.

Q Who was the first Fourth Division player to represent his country in a full international?
Crystal Palace goalkeeper Vic Rouse, who made his debut for Wales in their 4-1 defeat by Northern Ireland in the 1959 Home Championship.

Q Did Tommy Docherty, as he has often said, really have more clubs than Jack Nicklaus?
The Doc played for Celtic, Preston, Arsenal and, briefly, for Chelsea. As a manager, he was in charge at Chelsea (1962), Rotherham United (1967), QPR (for 28 days in 1968), Aston Villa (1968), Porto (1970), Hull City (assistant manager, 1971), Manchester United (1972), Derby County (1977), QPR again (1979), Sydney Olympic (1980), Preston North End (1981), South Melbourne (1982), Wolves (1984), Altrincham (1987). Well, he certainly had as many clubs as Jack Nicklaus carries in his bag. The Doc also had a spell in charge of the Scottish international team between the Hull and Manchester United jobs. In addition he captained Scotland as a player.

Q Which Football League manager has won the Manager of the Year award most times?
Liverpool master Bob Paisley, with six awards – 1976, 1977, 1979, 1980, 1982 and 1983.

Q Has there been an England manager who has not played First Division football?
Graham Taylor spent his playing career with Grimsby Town and Lincoln City. Walter Winterbottom was reduced to playing only a handful of games at centre-half for Manchester United because of a spinal problem.

Q Why are Mansfield Town known to their supporters as 'The Stags'?
It is a reference to the deer that roam the nearby Sherwood Forest.

Q Who was the European footballer known as 'Little Napoleon'?
Raymond Kopa, the legendary French field marshal who had Polish parents and the original name of Kopazewski. He played for Angers, Reims and Real Madrid. It was in two spells at Reims that he had his greatest moments in harness with crack marksman Just Fontaine. A pass master who could almost make the ball sit up and talk, Kopa was voted European Footballer of the Year in 1959. He played in European Cup finals with both Reims and Real Madrid.

Q Has there ever been a match with two referees officiating at the same time?
There have been several experimental games using this dual method of control, the first an England v 'the Rest' team at West Bromwich on 27 March 1935. It was the idea of Sir Stanley Rous, a former top referee who became President of FIFA.

Q **Which club defence gained the nickname of the 'Iron Curtain?'**
This was the name given to the famous Rangers rearguard of the immediate post-war years: Brown, Young, Shaw, McColl, Woodburn and Cox. The famous defence, noted for its strength and composure under pressure, broke up when centre-half Willie Woodburn was banned for life in 1954 after punching an opponent.

Q **When were Football League matches first played on a Sunday?**
The power blackout crisis of 1974 meant the Football League authorities had to allow Sunday football, and the first match was Millwall v Fulham on 20 January 1974. It was 1981 before League football on a Sunday was introduced on a regular basis. The 1974 tie between Cambridge United and Oldham Athletic was the first FA Cup tie played on a Sunday.

Q **Which international team was known as the Wembley Wizards?**
The Scotland team of 1928 that beat England 5-1 at Wembley. It included 'Wee Blue Devils' Alex James, Alan Morton and Hughie Gallacher. The tallest player in the Scottish attack stood 5 foot 6 inches.

Q **Why are Scottish club Ayr United known as the Honest Men?**
It is inspired by a couplet in praise of the town of Ayr by Robbie Burns in his poem 'Tam o'Shanter':
> *Auld Ayr, wham ne'er a town surpasses,*
> *For honest men and bonnie lassies.*

Q **Which was the first Football League club to install undersoil heating?**
Everton were first to have an undersoil heating system in 1958 following experiments at their training ground. Hibernian were the first Scottish club to install undersoil heating in 1980.

Q **How many goals did the great Gerd Müller score in international matches?**
Müller, nicknamed Der Bomber, scored 62 goals in 68 games for West Germany. He was top scorer in the 1970 World Cup with ten goals, and in the same year became the first German elected European Footballer of the Year. He helped Bayern win three European Cups, and scored the winning goal for West Germany against Holland in the 1974 World Cup final.

Q **Did Bobby Moore ever play *against* England?**
Yes. He captained Team America against England in 1976. The American team also inluded Tommy Smith, Mike England and Pele.

Q **Which was the first Third Division side to win a Final at Wembley?**
Queen's Park Rangers in 1967. Inspired by a magical goal from Rodney Marsh, they came from behind to beat First Division West Bromwich Albion 3-2 in the League Cup final.

Q **What was Alf Ramsey's record as a Football League club manager?**
Sir Alf took over as manager of Ipswich in 1955 after a distinguished playing career as a right-back with Southampton, Tottenham and England.

In seven years at Portman Road he steered Ipswich from the Third Division (South), including winning the Second and First Division titles in successive seasons (1960-61 and 1961-2). He then became the most successful of all England managers, briefly returning to club management for an unhappy spell with Birmingham City in 1978. As a player Sir Alf was such a calculating right-back that he was known as 'The General', and he won Second and First Division championship medals in successive seasons with the push-and-run Tottenham team of the 1950s. He was capped 32 times by England.

Q Has a goalkeeper ever been voted European Footballer of the Year?

Yes. Lev Yashin, Russia's famous Man in Black, was elected European Footballer of the Year in 1963. He had started out as an

Sir Alf Ramsey

ice hockey goaltender and switched full time to football in 1951 when he became Moscow Dynamo's first-team goalkeeper. Yashin played in the World Cup finals of 1958, 1962 and 1966, and was a reserve in 1970. He won 78 caps with the Soviet Union team, and collected six Soviet championship medals with Moscow Dynamo. It was claimed that during his career he saved more than 150 penalties. He had a spell in charge at Moscow Dynamo at the end of his playing career.

Q Where was Eusebio born and did he play club football in any country other than Portugal?

Euesbio Da Silva Ferreira was born on 25 January 1942 in Lourenço Marques (now Maputo), Mozambique, which was then under Portuguese rule. He was a youth player with Sporting Lourenço Marques, the nursery club of Sporting Lisbon. Benfica snapped him up under the noses of their great rivals in 1961 and a year later he scored two magnificent goals to help Benfica beat Real Madrid 5-3 in the European Cup Final. He won seven Portuguese championship medals with Benfica, was voted European Footballer of the Year in 1965 and was top World Cup scorer in the 1966 finals with nine goals. The Black Panther of football very nearly won the 1968 European Cup Final for Benfica when he forced a magnificent save from Manchester United goalkeeper Alex Stepney with the score at 1-1. Eusebio wound down his career with clubs in Mexico and Canada before returning to Portugal where they have built a statue of him at Benfica's Stadium of Light.

Q How many matches did it take Ian Wright to find the net while wearing an England shirt?

Ian Wright, a prolific goal scorer at club level, went nine international matches before he broke his duck with England. He scored his first goal against Poland in Katowice in a World Cup qualifier on 29 May 1993 after coming on as a substitute for Carlton Palmer.

Q **When did the first European Championship take place, and who were the winners?**
The qualifying tournament for the first Championship (then called the European Nations Cup) began in 1958, with the final four matches taking place in France in 1960. The Soviet Union beat Yugoslavia 2-1 in the Final.

Q **Was George Best capped more times than his Manchester United team-mate Denis Law?**
Best was capped 37 times by Northern Ireland, Law 55 times by Scotland.

Q **Who was the first player sent off while wearing an England shirt in a full international?**
Alan Mullery, then with Tottenham, had that unfortunate distinction. He was ordered off for retaliating in the 1968 European Championship semi-final against Yugoslavia in Italy.

Q **Did Terry Paine play all his League matches for Southampton?**
Paine played a then record 713 League games for Southampton, and later added another 111 to the total at Hereford. A winger turned midfield schemer, he played 19 games for England including one in the 1966 World Cup finals. He later emigrated to South Africa.

Q **Was Franz Beckenbauer captain of the West German team in the 1966 World Cup?**
No. That honour went to Hamburg centre-forward Uwe Seeler, who was also captain for the 1970 finals. Beckenbauer, just 20 when the 1966 finals were played, was West Germany skipper when they won the 1972 European Championship and the 1974 World Cup.

Q **How many teams entered the first European Cup, and was Britain represented?**
Sixteen teams entered the first European Cup tournament in 1955-6: Sporting Lisbon, Partizan Belgrade, Voros Lobogo, Anderlecht, Real Madrid, Servetee Geneva, Rot Weiss Essen, Hibernian, Aarhus, Stade de Reims, Rapid Vienna, PSV Eindhoven, Djurgaarden, Guardia Warsaw, AC Milan, Saarbrücken. Hibernian represented Scotland even though they had finished only fifth in the Scottish First Division. Chelsea were the English champions, but they were prevented from entering by the short-sighted bosses of the Football League. Real Madrid won the first final (beating Reims 4-3 in Paris) for the first of five successive triumphs. Hibernian were beaten 3-0 on aggregate by Reims in the two-leg semi-final.

Q **Exactly how far out was David Beckham when he scored from long range in the opening match of the 1996-7 season against Wimbledon?**
The Sky TV computer showed that he was 57·4 yards from goal when the

Manchester United midfielder launched his perfectly flighted shot from just inside his own half.

Q **What is the full name of Brazilian star striker Romario?**
Romario de Souza Faria. He was born in Rio de Janeiro, Brazil, on 29 January 1966.

Q **Did Ryan Giggs play for England schoolboys, and was he on Manchester City's books?**
Giggs played for Manchester Schools and was the English Schools captain nine times. His partner in attack was Nick Barmby. He joined Manchester City on associate schoolboy forms, but it was United who signed him on 1 December 1990, two days after his seventeenth birthday. Ryan was born in Cardiff, and moved to Manchester in 1975 when his father signed for Swinton Rugby League club. He changed his name from Ryan Wilson.

Q **Has striker Mark Hughes played for more than one overseas club?**
Hughes played for two – Barcelona and Bayern Munich (on loan) before his return to Manchester United, who sold him to Barcelona for £2,300,000 in 1986.

Q **With which club was Dean Saunders playing when he made his international debut for Wales?**
Saunders was playing for Third Division Brighton when he made his first appearance for Wales as a substitute against the Republic of Ireland in 1986.

Q **How many times did the Charles and Allchurch brothers appear together for Wales?**
John and Mel Charles and Ivor and Len Allchurch appeared together in the same Welsh international team on three occasions, the first against Northern Ireland at Windsor Park, Belfast, on 20 April 1955. The Allchurch brothers played together for Wales in eight matches, and the Charles brothers were in the same Welsh team on 15 occasions. John, 'The Gentle Giant', was equally at home in the middle of defence or at centre-forward.

Q **Is it right that Tony Adams could have joined West Ham when he left school?**
The Judge went to Tony Adams for this answer: 'West Ham were my local club and I supported them when I was a boy, particularly as my Dad had been on their books. I had the chance to sign for the Hammers, but I looked at their set-up and the one at Arsenal and preferred what I saw at Highbury. It seemed very relaxed at West Ham, while Arsenal stressed there would be a lot of hard work involved and that appealed to me.'

Q **Did Robbie Fowler score in his first-team debut for Liverpool?**
Yes, against Fulham in a Coca-Cola first leg tie against Fulham at Anfield on 22 September 1993. In the second leg he scored five goals. He netted 15 goals in his first 24 games until a hairline shin fracture put him on the sidelines for two months. He scored on his return against Aston Villa in the final match of the 1993-4 season.

Q **For which clubs did Eric Cantona play before joining Manchester United?**
Auxerre, Bordeaux, Montpellier, Marseille, Nîmes and Leeds. He was offered a trial by Sheffield Wednesday before joining Leeds from Nimes for £900,000 on 6 Februrary 1992, and switched to Manchester United for £1,200,000 on 27 November 1992.

Q **With which League club did David Platt start his footballing career?**
Platt was an apprentice with Manchester United, but he was released before making it into the first-team and signed on a free transfer with Crewe in January 1985. He has since travelled the football roundabout with Aston Villa, Bari, Juventus, Sampdoria and Arsenal for total transfer fees of around £22,000,000.

Q **Did Franz Beckenbauer play for any club side other than Bayern Munich?**
'Kaiser Franz' was with Bayern from his youth days in 1959 until his retirement from international football in 1976 after winning 103 caps. He then played for New York Cosmos for four years before retiring in 1980.

Q **How many times did the Charlton brothers play together for England?**
Alf Ramsey picked them together in 28 international matches between 1965 and 1970, and they were on the losing side during this sequence just twice – against Austria in 1965 and against Scotland in 1967. Jack scored six goals for England in his 35 games, the fifth and sixth of them coming with headers from 'kid' brother Bobby's corners (v Romania and Portugal in 1969).

Q **What was Alfredo di Stefano's nationality, and for which clubs did he play?**
Di Stefano was Argentinian by birth, born in Barracas, a deprived suburb of Buenos Aires on 4 July 1920. His father played for River Plate, and his grandfather was a fine footballer who emigrated to Argentina from Italy. Alfredo played international football for Argentina, Colombia and Spain, and his clubs were Los Cardales, River Plate, Hurcan (on loan), Millonairos of Bogota, Real Madrid and Espanol of Barcelona. It was at Real that he enjoyed his greatest triumphs, inspiring them to five successive European Cup triumphs.

Q **Did Ferenc Puskas win an Olympic gold medal with Hungary?**
Yes. Puskas captained the team that beat Yugoslavia in the 1952 Olympic final in Helsinki. The following year he skippered the 'Magical Magyars' side that hammered England 6-3 in their first ever defeat at Wembley.

Q **Is it true that Brazilian winger Garrincha had two left feet?**
Garrincha, a nickname meaning Little Bird, was crippled by polio when he was a child and his right leg was so badly twisted that surgeons feared he would never walk properly. An operation left him needing to wear two left boots. Garrincha (real name Manoel Francisco dos Santos) was deadly

with both of them. He won the first of his 51 Brazilian caps in 1955, and was a key player in the World Cup triumphs of 1958 and 1962. Sadly, he led a reckless life off the pitch and died of alcohol poisoning at the age of 49.

Q Why was Tom Finney known as the 'Preston Plumber'?

Finney was called the Preston Plumber because throughout his career with Preston (187 goals in 433 League games) he ran a family plumbing and electricians' business. He played the first of his 76 internationals for England against Northern Ireland in Belfast on 28 September 1946, and scored in a 7-2 victory. It was the first of what was then a record 30 goals. The first time the selectors dared play Finney and his great wing rival Stanley Matthews in the same attack Portugal capitulated to a 10-0 defeat in Lisbon on 27 May 1947. Tommy Lawton and debutant Stan Mortensen each scored four goals as they fed on the wing wizardry of Matthews on the right and Finney on the

Tom Finney

left. His final appearance for England was against the Soviet Union at Wembley on 22 October 1958. England won 5-0, with a hat-trick from Johnny Haynes.

Q Did Billy Bremner and Don Revie ever play together in the same Leeds United team?

Bremner made his Leeds debut as a winger at the age of 17 in 1959 alongside player-manager Don Revie, who was twice his age. Over the next 15 years Bremner was to become Revie's right hand man and captain.

Q Who has been the youngest player capped by each of the home countries this century?

Duncan Edwards, Manchester United (England, 18 years 183 days v Scotland, 2 April 1955); Norman Whiteside, Manchester United (Northern Ireland, 17 years 42 days v Yugoslavia, 17 June 1982); Denis Law, Huddersfield Town (Scotland, 18 years 235 days v Wales, 18 October 1958); Ryan Giggs, Manchester United (Wales, 17 years 332 days v Germany, 16 October 1991).

Q Who was the first goalkeeper to be voted Footballer of the Year?

Manchester City goalkeeper Bert Trautmann was elected Footballer of the Year by the Football Writers' Association in 1956, the year the Maine Road club beat Birmingham City 3-1 in the FA Cup Final at Wembley. Trautmann, who had been a German prisoner of war, played through the last 15 minutes of the final suffering from what was later diagnosed as a broken neck. He was a magnificent last line of defence for City through a run of 508 League games. His real Christian name is Bernhard.

Q **How old was Dennis Bergkamp when he made his first-team debut for Ajax?**

Bergkamp was 17 and still at school. He sat school examinations in the morning and then in the afternoon flew to join the Ajax team for a European Cup tie against Malmö the next day. His parents were Manchester United fans and named their son after their hero, Denis Law. He arrived at Arsenal from Inter-Milan for £7,500,000 in June 1995.

Q **Which non-League side once put six goals into the Derby County net in an FA Cup tie?**

Boston United, fielding six former Derby players, beat Third Division Derby 6-1 in an FA Cup second round tie at the Baseball Ground in December 1955. Ex-Derby striker Geoff Hazeldine scored a hat-trick, and Boston right-winger Reg Harrison had helped Derby win the Cup nine years earlier.

Q **How many European Cup goals did Tommy Gemmell score for Celtic?**

Eight, which was a remarkable haul for a full-back. The most memorable was the equalizer that he blasted against Inter-Milan in the 1967 European Cup Final which set Celtic up for a 2-1 victory and the honour of becoming the first British club to win the European Cup. He also scored against Feyenoord in the final three years later when Celtic were beaten 2-1.

Q **Has any player won more than five European Cup winners' medals?**

The record is six, set by Real Madrid's flying left-winger Francisco Gento. He won them all with Real, along with 12 Spanish championship medals during an 800-game career in which he scored 256 goals. Jet-paced Gento had a long-running partnership on the left of the Real attack with the skilled Jose Hector Rial, and they rivalled the impact of Puskas and di Stefano with their contribution to the team.

Q **With which club did Ray Houghton make his League debut, and was he born in Ireland?**

Houghton, born in Glasgow in 1962, moved to London with his Irish father when he was ten. He made his League debut as a substitute for West Ham, who gave him a free transfer after his one appearance in 1982. Malcolm Macdonald then signed him for Fulham, and he has since played with distinction for Oxford United, Liverpool, Aston Villa, Crystal Palace and the Republic of Ireland.

Q **What was John Greig's record as a player with Rangers?**

Greig played a club record 496 League matches for Rangers between 1962 and 1978. Much of his career coincided with when Jock Stein's Celtic were invincible, but he still managed to establish himself as one of the Glasgow greats as a commander in midfield and defence. He was a driving captain for much of his 16 years at Ibrox, and helped steer Rangers to the European Cup Winners' Cup finals of 1967 (beaten 1-0 by Bayern

Munich) and 1972 (beat Moscow Dynamo 3-2). Greig played 44 times for Scotland and was an inspirational skipper. Scottish Footballer of the Year in 1966 and again in 1976, he later had a brief but relatively unsuccessful spell as manager at Ibrox where his off-the-pitch input is still valued.

Q **Was Ruud Gullit ever the captain of the Dutch international team?**
Gullit skippered the Dutch team that won the European Championship in 1988. In the same season he was a key man for European Cup winners AC Milan, a year after being elected European Footballer of the Year.

Q **Did Brian Clough sign Francis Lee when he joined Derby County?**
No. Dave Mackay had taken over from Clough as manager and bought Lee from Manchester City. He linked up with another Mackay signing, Bruce Rioch, and between them they scored 27 goals in the 1974-5 season as Derby recaptured the League title won two years earlier by Clough's team.

Q **Who made the pass to Geoff Hurst when he scored his third goal in the 1966 World Cup Final?**
England skipper Bobby Moore played the ball through to his West Ham team-mate Geoff Hurst, who went on to complete his historic hat-trick in the final minute against West Germany at Wembley on 30 July 1966. They then knew it was all over!

Q **Is it right that striker John Aldridge started his League career in Wales?**
Aldridge was a full-time toolmaker and a part-time player with South Liverpool when Newport County launched his professional career in 1979. He scored 69 goals for Newport and then 73 League goals for Oxford before returning home to Liverpool in 1987. Aldridge filled in for Ian Rush with 56 goals, and then added 23 to his collection during a spell with Real Sociedad. He has since topped a century of goals at Tranmere to join the exclusive club of players who have broken the 300 goal barrier.

Q **How old was Stan Collymore when he made his League debut?**
Collymore, born in Stone in 1971, had been released by Wolves and was playing non-League football with his local Stafford club when discovered by Crystal Palace, who gave him his first League game at the age of 20 in a goalless draw with QPR. Palace sold him to Southend United for £100,000 after one goal in 20 League games. Then 15 goals in 30 games attracted

Stan Collymore

46

Nottingham Forest, who bought him for £200,000 in 1993 before selling him to Liverpool for an £8,300,000 profit in 1995.

Q **Why was Arsenal and England winger Cliff Bastin known as 'Boy'?**
It was a nickname that stuck from when he won every honour in the game while still in his teens. 'Boy' Bastin, who joined Arsenal from his local club Exeter City, had won five League championship medals, two FA Cup winners' medals and 21 England caps when his career was halted by the Second World War. He was still only 27. A fast, direct outside-left who was equally adept at inside-forward, Bastin scored 157 goals in 367 League games, which is a prodigious scoring rate for a winger.

Q **How many goals did Wolves striker Steve Bull score for England?**
Four in 13 matches, including a goal in his debut when coming on as a substitute for John Fashanu against Scotland at Hampden Park on 27 May 1989. He was the first Third Division player capped since Peter Taylor in 1976. Bull notched two goals against Czechoslovakia at Wembley on 25 April 1990 and another against Tunisia when coming on for Gary Lineker.

Q **What was the longest that Gary Lineker went without scoring a goal for England?**
Lineker had a run of seven barren matches from June 1988 until April 1989. He ended his drought with a headed goal against Albania in a World Cup qualifying match at Wembley. He also laid on two goals for Peter Beardsley in the 5-0 victory.

Q **Did Gary Lineker ever miss from the penalty spot while playing for England?**
Yes, in his seventy-sixth appearance for England. He needed one goal to equal Bobby Charlton's all-time record of 49 goals for England when he missed his spot-kick against Brazil at Wembley on 17 May 1992. His international career ended four matches later when pulled off by manager Graham Taylor in the Euro 92 match against Sweden. Lineker was left stranded on 48 goals.

Q **How old was Trevor Francis when he made his League debut, and for how many clubs did he play?**
Francis made his debut for Birmingham City at the age of 16, and two months before his seventeenth birthday he scored four goals in a League game against Bolton. His clubs: Birmingham City (1970-79), Nottingham Forest (1979-81), Manchester City (1981-2), Sampdoria (1982-6), Atalanta (1986-7), Glasgow Rangers (1987-8), Queen's Park Rangers (1988-90). He also had a spell with Detroit Express and played 76 League games as player-manager of Sheffield Wednesday.

Q **How many League matches did Clive Allen play for Arsenal?**
None. Allen joined Arsenal from QPR for £1,250,000 in June 1980 as the first teenage million-pound footballer. He moved on to Crystal Palace in a £1,350,000-rated swap deal for Kenny Sansom just two months later.

Q **With which club was striker Cyrille Regis playing before starting his League career?**
Regis was discovered playing for Hayes in the Isthmian League. West Bromwich Albion bought him for £5,000 in 1977.

Q **Has Rangers striker Ally McCoist played for any English clubs?**
McCoist joined Sunderland from his first club St Johnstone in 1981 for £400,000 when he was 20, but after only eight goals in 56 League games he moved back to Scotland with Rangers for £185,000.

Q **Who has scored most Football League goals in total?**
Arthur Rowley, who notched 434 goals while playing for West Brom, Fulham, Leicester City, and Shrewsbury Town from 1946 to 1965. He played in a total of 619 League games. His brother, Jack, was an exceptional centre-forward with Manchester United and England. Arthur was a more prolific goal scorer but was never capped. Most of his goals were scored outside the First Division. He started out as an amateur with his local club Wolves.

Q **Has any non-League side won the FA Cup this century?**
Just one – Tottenham Hotspur in 1901 when they were in the Southern League. They beat Sheffield United 3-1 in a replay at Burnden Park after a 2-2 draw at Crystal Palace.

Q **Did Diego Maradona help Napoli win any honours during his spell with Napoli?**
Maradona joined Napoli from Barcelona in 1984, and helped them win their first ever Italian League title in 1987. They also won the Italian Cup. In 1988 he collected his only European medal when he steered Napoli to victory over Stuttgart in the UEFA Cup final. Before getting involved in a drugs scandal he also captained Argentina's 1986 winning World Cup team and led them to the runner's up position against West Germany in the 1990 final.

Q **Which manager was first to select Les Ferdinand as an England international?**
Graham Taylor gave Ferdinand, then with Queen's Park Rangers, his first cap in the World Cup qualifier against San Marino at Wembley on 17 February 1993. He scored the final goal in a 6-0 victory.

Q **Has any player been leading scorer in successive seasons in the top two divisions?**
Centre-forward Kerry Dixon went one better, top scoring in three successive seasons – with Reading in the Third Division in 1982-3 and then with Chelsea in the following two seasons in the Second and old First Division.

Q **Did Johnny Haynes ever hold the Fulham goal scoring record?**
Haynes was famous for making rather than taking goals, but he managed 157 goals in 657 League games between 1952 and 1970 – a Fulham record that survived until Gordon Davies beat it in 1989.

Q **Which is the oldest of the Glasgow giants, Rangers or Celtic?**
Rangers were founded in 1873, Celtic in 1887. In their first official match in May 1888, Celtic beat Rangers 5-0.

Q **Did Graeme Souness play any League matches for Tottenham?**
No. Souness served his apprenticeship with Tottenham, but never really settled. He once ran off home to Scotland because he was homesick. Graeme was impatient for first-team football, and manager Bill Nicholson reluctantly let him go when Jack Charlton took him to Middlesbrough for £30,000 in 1973. Within a year he had won a place in Scotland's team.

Q **Is it right that Brian McClair started his career with Aston Villa?**
Correct. He joined Villa straight from school, but returned to Scotland after a year to study for a maths degree at Glasgow University. He made his Scottish League debut with Motherwell before going on to greater things with Celtic and Manchester United.

Q **Has the redoubtable Vinnie Jones ever played for an overseas club?**
Jones had a season on loan with Swedish club IFK Holmsund before joining Wimbledon from Wealdstone for £10,000 at the start of his League career in 1986. He has since travelled the soccer roundabout with Leeds, Sheffield United and Chelsea before returning to Wimbledon in 1993. Born in Watford on 5 January 1965, football's most infamous hard man of the modern era is a Welsh international.

Q **Who has been the oldest man to captain a World Cup winning team?**
Goalkeeper Dino Zoff was 40 years and three months old when he captained the Italian team that beat West Germany 3-1 to win the 1982 World Cup Final in Madrid.

Q **For which overseas clubs did Ray Wilkins play, and was he capped while playing abroad?**
Wilkins joined AC Milan from Manchester United in 1984 and had a spell with Paris St Germain before moving to Rangers in 1987-8. Ray (or 'Butch', as he was then known) made his debut for Chelsea at the age of 17, following his father, George, into the game. His other League clubs have been QPR and Crystal Palace. Following an unsuccessful run as player-manager at QPR, he returned to Scotland in September 1996 to join Hibs on a short-term contract as a player. Ray won 22 of his 84 caps while playing for AC Milan.

Q **Where was the first ever FA Cup Final played and what was the attendance?**
A crowd of 2,000 gathered at the Kennington Oval to see Wanderers beat Royal Engineers 1-0 in the first FA Cup Final in 1872.

Q **What is the biggest attendance for an FA Cup Final away from Wembley?**
The crowd record was set in 1913 when 120,081 jammed Crystal Palace to see Aston Villa beat Sunderland 1-0.

Q **Has goalkeeper Neville Southall played for any team other than Everton?**
Southall started his League career with Bury in 1980 at the age of 21 after playing for his local team, Winsford United. He had a nine match loan-transfer period with Port Vale in 1982 while waiting to establish himself at Everton.

Q **For which clubs did Howard Wilkinson play before going into football management?**
Wilkinson started with Sheffield United as an amateur before playing as a winger with Sheffield Wednesday and Brighton. He returned to Hillsborough as manager before a reign as Leeds manager that ended in September 1996.

Q **Was Dino Zoff the first goalkeeper to captain a World Cup winning team?**
No. That honour went to his countryman Giampiero Combi, who skippered the Italian team that won the World Cup in 1934.

Q **Did Neil Webb start his League playing career with Nottingham Forest?**
No. Webb followed his father as a professional at Reading, and then moved to Portsmouth before joining Forest for £250,000 in May 1985.

Q **How many goalkeepers have been voted Footballer of the Year?**
Four goalkeepers have won the coveted Football Writers' Association award since its inception in 1948: Bert Trautmann (1956), Gordon Banks (1972), Pat Jennings (1973 and 1976) and Neville Southall (1985).

Q **Against which team did Bryan Robson score within a minute of a World Cup Finals match?**
England captain Robson scored in 27 seconds against France in the 1982 World Cup finals in Spain, which was then the quickest ever World Cup finals goal.

Q **How many times was Frank McLintock on the losing side in Wembley finals?**
The Judge went to Frank McLintock for this answer: 'I lost twice at Wembley with Leicester City in FA Cup finals and then in two League Cup finals with Arsenal. I was beginning to think I would never win there when I was privileged to captain the Arsenal team that clinched the double in the 1971 final against Liverpool. A year later we lost in the FA Cup centenary final against Leeds. I have to confess that Wembley was not my favourite ground!'

Q **Has any player won the World Cup both as a captain and as a manager?**
Franz Beckenbauer completed this unique double when he managed the West Germany team that beat Argentina in the 1990 World Cup Final in Italy. Sixteen years earlier he had skippered the West German side that beat Holland 2-1 in the 1974 final in Munich.

Q **How many goals did England concede on the way to winning the World Cup in 1966?**
Three. The first came from a Eusebio penalty in the semi-final against Portugal, and Helmut Haller and Wolfgang Weber scored for West Germany in the final. It remains the best defensive record for a World Cup winning team. England's defence: Banks, Cohen, Wilson, Stiles, Jack Charlton, Moore.

Q **Which FA Cup match has taken the longest to decide?**
Alvechurch and Oxford City took six matches (11 hours) before Alvechurch went through after their 1972 final qualifying round marathon. In the competition proper, Stoke City went through at the fifth time of asking after 9 hours 22 minutes of third-round play against Bury in 1955.

Q **What is the quickest hat-trick by an England player in a full international?**
The record was set by Tottenham goal hunter Willie Hall, who completed a hat-trick in just three and a half minutes when playing for England against Ireland at Old Trafford on 16 November 1938.

Q **What was the longest undefeated run by Brian Clough's Nottingham Forest?**
Forest went a record 42 consecutive First Division matches without defeat between 20 November 1977 and 9 December 1978.

Q **Who scored the goals when England hammered Scotland 9-3 and what were the teams?**
The match was played at Wembley on 15 April 1961. England scorers: Jimmy Greaves (3), Johnny Haynes (2), Bobby Smith (2), Bobby Robson and Bryan Douglas. Dave Mackay and Davie Wilson scored for the Scots to make it 3-2 just after half-time before Scotland's defence fell apart. The teams: England – Springett, Armfield, McNeil, Robson, Swan, Flowers, Douglas, Greaves, Bobby Smith, Haynes, Bobby Charlton. Scotland – Haffey, Shearer, Caldow, Mackay, McNeill, McCann, McLeod, Law, St John, Quinn, Wilson.

Q **Against which team did Ted MacDougall score nine goals in the FA Cup?**
MacDougall's record nine-goal haul was for Bournemouth against Margate in the first round of the FA Cup on 20 November 1971. The individual record for a preliminary round of the FA Cup is 10 goals by Chris Marron for South Shields against Radcliffe on 20 September 1947.

Q **Which player has made most appearances for any one League club?**
Full-back John Trollope, 770 League games for Swindon Town,1960-80.

Q **How many League titles did Celtic win when Jock Stein was their manager?**
Under Stein's dynamic leadership (1965-74) Celtic won the Scottish League ten times, the Scottish Cup seven times and the League Cup six

times. There was also, of course, the European Cup in 1967. He had a brief period in charge at Leeds United before taking over as Scotland's team manager. A miner after leaving school, the 'Big Man' played for Albion Rovers, Llanelli and Celtic before starting his managerial career with Dunfermline Athletic.

Q **From which club did Middlesbrough buy Fabrizio Ravanelli, and against which team did he score a hat-trick in his debut?**
Ravanelli joined Middlesbrough from Juventus in the summer of 1996, and he started his career in England with a hat-trick against Liverpool in the first match of the 1996-7 season. The match finished in a 3-3 draw.

Q **Which footballer was first to win the PFA Player of the Year award?**
This honour went to Leeds United defender Norman 'Bites Yer Legs' Hunter when the award was first introduced in 1973.

Jock Stein

Q **How many English players were in Liverpool's 1986 FA Cup winning team at Wembley?**
Not one. The team that beat Everton 3-1 to complete the League and Cup double consisted of four Scots, three Irish, one Welsh, one Dane, one Australian and one Zimbabwean. The team, managed by Scot Kenny Dalglish: Grobbelaar, Lawrenson, Beglin, Nicol, Whelan, Hansen, Dalglish, Johnston, Rush, Molby, MacDonald.

Q **Against which team did Alan Shearer score his first League goal for Newcastle United?**
Shearer opened his Newcastle account with a free-kick blasted into the Wimbledon net two minutes from the end of his home Premiership debut at St James' Park on 21 August 1996.

Q **What have been the greatest number of spot-kicks needed to decide a penalty shoot-out in Britain?**
This was in a Freight Rover Trophy quarter-final (Southern section) between Aldershot and Fulham on 10 February 1987. It took 28 alternate penalties, with just seven missed, before Aldershot finally won 11-10.

Q **Who is the most capped international footballer in the world?**
The record is claimed by Hector Chumpitaz, who made 150 appearances for Peru from 1963 to 1982. But many of the games were against club sides, and it is generally accepted that goalkeepers Thomas Ravelli (127 caps for Sweden) and Peter Shilton (125 for England) are the most capped

players in games against full international teams. Majed Abdullah made 147 appearances for Saudi Arabia between 1978 and 1994.

Q **Who was manager of Arsenal when they signed Charlie Nicholas?**
Terry Neill was in charge at Highbury when Nicholas joined Arsenal from Celtic for £750,000 in June 1983.

Q **Has there ever been a crowd of less than 5,000 to watch an international football match in Britain?**
The lowest attendance was the 2,315 spectators who paid to watch Wales against Northern Ireland at the Racecourse Ground, Wrexham, on 27 May 1982.

Q **What has been the longest unbeaten sequence by any League club in a single season?**
Burnley set the record in the old First Division in 1920-21. They went 30 matches unbeaten on their way to winning their first League championship by four points from Manchester City.

Q **What has been the longest sequence by a League club without recording a win?**
Cambridge United reluctantly hold this record. They went 31 matches in the old Second Division without a single win in 1983-4 and were relegated with 24 points from 42 games.

Q **Is midfield player Gary Speed an English-born Welsh international?**
Speed, who joined Everton from Leeds in a £3,500,00 transfer in the summer of 1996, was born in Hawarden, North Wales, 8 September 1969.

Q **How many international caps did Peter Osgood win with England?**
Osgood was capped four times between 1970 and 1974 while with Chelsea.

Q **Who scored the goal when the Republic of Ireland beat Italy in the 1994 World Cup finals?**
Ray Houghton scored the only goal of the match in the 12th minute.

Q **What is the quickest goal ever conceded by an England international team?**
San Marino scored after nine seconds in the 1994 World Cup qualifier.

Q **How many times have West Ham United won the FA Cup?**
Three, beating Preston (1964), Fulham (1975) and Arsenal (1980).

Q **Which Scottish footballer was given the nickname of Caesar?**
Billy McNeill, captain of the Celtic team that dominated Scottish football in the 1960s. He was a soldier's son who attended a rugby-playing school, but it was the round-ball game that held his attention. McNeill was the rock at the heart of the Celtic defence, and survived the 9-3 defeat by England in his international debut to win 28 more Scottish caps. He later had two spells as Celtic manager and was also in charge at Aston Villa and Manchester City.

Q **Had Alan Ball joined Everton before the 1966 World Cup Final?**
Blackpool sold Ball to Everton for a then record £110,000 on 15 August 1966, 16 days after he had helped England win the World Cup. It was British football's first six-figure fee.

Q **Have Sheffield Wednesday won the League title and FA Cup more times than Sheffield United?**
Wednesday have won the League title four times (1903, 1904, 1929 and 1930), United once (1898). United have captured the
FA Cup four times (1899, 1902, 1915 and 1925),
Wednesday three times (1896, 1907 and
1935). Wednesday also won the League
Cup in 1991.

Q **Did Ron Greenwood win a League championship medal as a player?**
Greenwood played 21 games for Chelsea's League championship winning team of 1953-4. His career playing record: Bradford Park Avenue (1946-7), Brentford (1948-52), Chelsea (1952-4), Fulham (1954-5). He was a constructive centre-half who made a name for himself as an innovative coach at Arsenal and then as manager of West Ham United before succeeding Don Revie as England manager.

Q **How many post-war FA Cup Finals have gone to replays?**

Ron Greenwood

Six: Chelsea v Leeds (1970), Tottenham v Manchester City (1981), Tottenham v QPR (1982), Manchester United v Brighton (1983), Manchester United v Crystal Palace (1990), Arsenal v Sheffield Wednesday (1993). All the replays were staged at Wembley, except the Chelsea v Leeds match which was played at Old Trafford.

Q **Are Matthew Le Tissier and Graeme Le Saux from the same Channel Island?**
Le Tissier comes from Guernsey, Le Saux from Jersey.

Q **Which country was first to host the World Cup finals?**
Uruguay in 1930. Host countries since: France (1934, 1998), Italy (1938, 1990), Brazil (1950), Switzerland (1954), Sweden (1958), Chile (1962), England (1966), Mexico (1970, 1986), West Germany (1974), Argentina (1978), Spain (1982), United States (1994).

Q **When was the first international match staged at Wembley – before or after the first FA Cup Final?**
England and Scotland drew 1-1 in the first international at Wembley on 12 April 1924. The first Wembley FA Cup final between Bolton and West Ham was on 28 April 1923.

Q **Who scored the first hat-trick for England in a Wembley international?**
Chelsea centre-forward Roy Bentley scored all three goals when England beat Wales 3-2 at Wembley on 10 November 1954.

Q **For which clubs did Bobby Gould play, and was he ever capped?**
Gould did not win any international caps during a career in which he played for Coventry City, Arsenal, Wolves, West Bromwich Albion, Bristol City, West Ham United, Wolves, Bristol Rovers and Hereford. He managed the Wimbledon team that won the FA Cup in 1988, and later had spells in charge at his old clubs West Brom and Coventry. Bobby was creating a new career for himself as a sports talk-show host on Sky Television when he was enticed back into football by the job of manager of the Welsh international team.

Q **In which World Cup finals were penalties introduced to decide a winner of a drawn match?**
The first World Cup match to be decided by penalties was the 1982 semi-final between West Germany and France in Seville. Germany went through to the final 5-4 on penalties following a 3-3 draw after extra-time.

Q **Was the great midfield maestro Michel Platini Italian by birth?**
Platini was born to Italian parents in Joeuf, France, on 21 June 1955. His father, Aldo, had emigrated to France as a maths teacher, but was drawn to his first love of football and he was the coach at Nancy when his son joined him first as an amateur and then professional. Michel became a star with St Etienne and then Juventus, where he was voted European Footballer of the Year for three successive seasons.

Q **For how long was Paolo Rossi out of the game before his return to play in the 1982 World Cup?**
Rossi returned to Italian football in April 1982 after serving two years of a three-year suspension for allegedly being involved in match fixing. Just 11 weeks later Rossi's six goals helped Italy win the World Cup in Spain.

Q **How did Denmark qualify for the 1992 European Championship finals?**
War-torn Yugoslavia were forced to pull out, and Denmark were invited to take their place at the last minute. They had finished a point behind Yugoslavia in their qualifying group. The Danes beat Germany 2-0 in the final.

Q **How many League goals did Alan Shearer score in total for Blackburn Rovers?**
Shearer scored 112 goals in 138 League appearances for Blackburn before his £15,000,000 transfer to Newcastle United in the summer of 1996.

Q **What is the record run of home matches without a defeat by an English club?**
Liverpool went unbeaten for 85 games at Anfield from January 1978 to

January 1981 (63 League games, 7 European Cup, 9 League Cup, 6 FA Cup).

Q **From which club did Manchester City buy Georgiou Kinkladze, and who was manager when he signed?**
Kinkladze moved from Dynamo Tbilisi, his hometown club in Georgia, for £2,000,000. He was Alan Ball's first signing as City manager in July 1996.

Q **How much did Chelsea pay for the Italian striker Gianluca Vialli?**
Vialli joined Chelsea on a free transfer in the summer of 1996, four years after costing Juventus £12,000,000. He was Ruud Gullit's first signing as Chelsea manager, and was lured by a £1,400,000 a year contract.

Q **Has an English manager ever won the Dutch championship with Ajax?**
Yes. Vic Buckingham achieved it in 1960. The ex-Spurs player was in charge at Barcelona, Seville and Ethnikos, and also managed in England at Bradford Park Avenue, West Brom, Sheffield Wednesday and Fulham.

Q **How many British clubs have won the European Cup Winners' Cup?**
Nine since the first final in 1961: Tottenham (v Atletico Madrid,1963), West Ham (v Munich 1860,1965), Manchester City (v Gornik Zabrze,1970), Chelsea (v Real Madrid,1971), Rangers (v Moscow Dynamo,1972), Aberdeen (v Real Madrid,1983), Everton (v Rapid Vienna,1985), Manchester United (v Barcelona, 1991), Arsenal (v Parma,1994).

Q **Who has scored the fastest goal in an FA Cup final?**
Bob Chatt claimed a goal after just 30 seconds for Aston Villa against West Bromwich Albion in the 1895 final at Crystal Palace. The ball was scrambled clear and was then deflected into the net by Villa centre-forward John Devey. It has never been satisfactorily proved which of them scored, but the fact that the time has now been accepted as 40 seconds leans towards Devey as the marksman. Roberto Di Matteo's goal in 43 seconds for Chelsea against Middlesbrough on 17 May 1997 is the fastest in a Wembley FA Cup final, beating the previous record of 45 seconds set by Jackie Milburn when scoring an instant goal for Newcastle United against Manchester City in 1955.

BOXING

Q **Who was the first opponent to force Muhammad Ali to take a count?**
Ali was known as Cassius Clay when Sonny Banks dropped him with a
left hook in the first round of his eleventh professional fight in New York
on 11 February 1962. Ali got up at two and forced a fourth-round stoppage. The only other opponents to drop him were Henry Cooper and Joe
Frazier, each with left hooks. Chuck Wepner claimed to have knocked him
down in the ninth round of their contest, but Ali insisted it was a slip and
later produced photographic evidence to prove it.

Q **Was Floyd Patterson the first Olympic heavyweight champion to
challenge for the professional world heavyweight title?**
Floyd Patterson was Olympic champion at middleweight. The first heavyweight gold medallist to challenge for the world title was 1956 champion
Pete Rademacher, who was knocked out in six rounds by Patterson in his
professional debut in 1957.

Q **True or false: Alan Minter once beat heavyweight hero Henry
Cooper?**
Alan Minter knocked out Henry Cooper in one round in London on 20
January 1975. It was not Our 'Enery, of course, but an American with the
same name. Cooper retired in 1971, a year before Minter turned profes-
sional.

Q **How many boxers has manager Terry Lawless guided to world
championships?**
Four: welterweight John H. Stracey, lightweight Jim Watt, light-middleweight Maurice Hope and flyweight Charlie Magri. Lawless also
steered Frank Bruno to his first two world title challenges.

Q **Did Vince Hawkins ever fight Stan Rowan for the British
middleweight title?**
Vince Hawkins was British middleweight champion from 1946 to 1948;
Stan Rowan was British bantamweight champion in 1949. They never
fought each other.

Q **Were they world title defences when Tommy Burns knocked out two opponents on the same night?**
Tommy Burns ko'd Jim O'Brien and Jim Walker in one round each in San Diego on the evening of 28 March 1906. They were exhibition bouts.

Q **Was Rocky Marciano the only undefeated heavyweight champion of the world?**
Rocky Marciano was the only world heavyweight champion to go through his entire career undefeated (49 fights, 49 wins). Gene Tunney retired as unbeaten champion, but suffered one defeat as a light-heavyweight against Harry Grebb. James J. Jeffries and Joe Louis retired as unbeaten heavyweight champions, but were beaten in comeback title fights.

Q **What was the result when Joe Bugner fought Jack Bodell and what titles were at stake?**
Bodell outpointed Bugner over 15 rounds in a European, Commonwealth and British heavyweight title fight at Wembley Arena on 27 September 1971. Bugner was making his first defence of the titles taken from Henry Cooper six months earlier.

Q **Which British champion was nicknamed the Dartford Destroyer?**
Dave Charnley, who was European, Commonwealth and British lightweight champion from 1957 to 1965. Born in Dartford, Kent, on 10 October 1935, he twice made unsuccessful world title challenges against Joe 'Old Bones' Brown.

Q **Where was Chris Eubank born, and where did he start his professional career?**
Eubank was born in Dulwich on 8 August 1966, but he spent his teenage years in New York. He turned professional while in the United States and had his first five fights in Atlantic City, winning each of them on points over four rounds between October 1985 and March 1987. He made his British debut with a first round stoppage against Darren Parker at Copthorne, West Sussex, on 15 February 1988.

Q **How many professional fights did Henry Cooper have, and did he ever box abroad?**
Cooper's record (1954-71):
Fights 55, W40, L14, D1.
He won 27 inside the distance, and was stopped eight times, with five defeats caused by eye injuries. Henry fought abroad five times (in Stockholm, Dortmund twice, Frankfurt and Rome).

Q **Did Randolph Turpin ever fight Don Cockell and, if so, for which title?**
Turpin stopped Cockell in 11 rounds in a British and Empire light-heavyweight title fight at London's White City on 10 June 1952.

Q **How long did Randolph Turpin hold the world middleweight title?**
Sixty-four days. He took it from Sugar Ray Robinson with a 15-round

points victory at Earls Court, London, on 10 July 1951, and was stopped in ten rounds in the return at the Polo Grounds, New York, on 12 September.

Q Who were the contestants in the first world title fight staged in Las Vegas?
It is often misreported that the Jack Johnson-Jim Flynn contest in 1912 was the first to be staged in the gambling city of Las Vegas, Nevada. But they actually fought in Las Vegas, New Mexico. The first world title fight staged in Las Vegas, Nevada, was the welterweight contest in which Benny (Kid) Paret outpointed Don Jordan on 27 May 1960.

Q Has a British boxer ever won two Olympic gold medals?
Londoner Harry Mallin won gold medals in the middleweight division at the 1924 and 1928 Olympics. He and his brother, Fred, won ten ABA titles between them.

Q Was Frank Bruno ever coached by former world heavyweight champion Floyd Patterson?
The Judge got this answer from Bruno: 'Floyd Patterson spent a couple of days working in the gymnasium with me early in my career, and concentrated on improving my left jab. He gave me some useful tips, but it did not go as far as coaching.'

Q Did Chuck Wepner go the full 15 rounds against Muhammad Ali?
Not quite. Ali stopped Wepner in the fifteenth and final round in a world title defence in 1975.

Q Who was Jack Dempsey's opponent in the first fight to draw a million-dollar gate?
Georges Carpentier, who was knocked out in four rounds by Dempsey on 2 July 1921. A crowd of 80,183 fans paid $1,789,238 to see the contest which was promoted by Tex Rickard at a specially constructed outdoor arena in Jersey City.

Q Is it right that Georges Carpentier fought in every weight division?
Georges Carpentier boxed in every weight division from flyweight to heavyweight. 'The Orchid Man' weighed in at 7 st 2 lbs when he had the first of his 106 official professional fights on 24 February 1907, when he was aged 14. In his last contest on 15 September 1926, he scaled 12 st 4 lbs. During his 19-year career he won European titles at welterweight, middleweight, light-heavyweight and heavyweight as well as every French championship from lightweight to heavyweight. He also crossed the Atlantic to win the world light-heavyweight title.

Q How old was Jersey Joe Walcott when he won the world heavyweight title?
Walcott became, at 37 years 6 months, the then oldest man to win the world heavyweight crown when he knocked out Ezzard Charles with a classic left hook in the seventh round on 18 July 1951. He won the title at the fifth time of asking after two defeats by Joe Louis and two by Ezzard Charles.

Walcott's ring record over a span of 23 years was:
69 fights, 50 wins, 18 losses (6 stoppages),
30 inside-the-distance wins, one draw. He lost the title to Rocky Marciano on 23 September 1952, when knocked out in the 13th round. Rocky knocked him out in the first round in the return. George Foreman, aged 45, took over from Walcott as the oldest world heavyweight champion when he knocked out Michael Moorer in the tenth round in Las Vegas on 5 November 1994.

Jersey Joe Walcott

Q **What was the real name of Jersey Joe Walcott, and where was he born?**
Walcott, born in Merchantville, New Jersey, on 31 January 1914, was called Arnold Raymond Cream. He borrowed his ring name from a famous welterweight boxer who had been world champion at the turn of the century.

Q **Who have been the European-born holders of any version of the world heavyweight title?**
Bob Fitzsimmons (born Cornwall), Max Schmeling (Germany), Primo Carnera (Italy), Ingemar Johansson (Sweden), Francesco Damiani (Italy), Lennox Lewis (London), Michael Bentt (London), Frank Bruno (London), Henry Akinwande (London). Herbie Hide was born in Nigeria, and Sheffield-born Johnny Nelson won the little-recognised WBF title.

Q **In which round did John H. Stracey stop Jose Napoles to win the world title?**
Stracey stopped Napoles in the sixth round to capture the world welterweight title in Mexico City on 6 December 1975. The Bethnal Green fighter climbed off the floor in the first round to win. Cuban Napoles, nicknamed 'Mantequilla' (smooth as butter), announced his retirement after what was only his seventh defeat in 84 fights.

Q **Who was the only man to defeat former world heavyweight champion Gene Tunney?**
Harry Greb gave Tunney a thrashing before outpointing him over 15 rounds in a fight for the American light-heavyweight title in 1922. In four subsequent contests between these two all-time greats, Tunney won three and the fourth was a 'no decision' draw. Tunney's defeat by Greb was the only blot on his 83-fight record and he retired as undefeated world heavyweight champion in 1928. Greb did most of his fighting at middleweight and became world champion of that division after his first fight with Tunney, reigning from 1923 to 1926.

Q **Who was the first opponent to put Naseem Hamed on the canvas?**
Daniel Alicea, of Puerto Rico, knocked Naseem Hamed down in the first
round of his world featherweight title defence at Newcastle on 8 June
1996. Hamed got up quickly, and won on a stoppage in the next round. It
was his twenty-second unbeaten fight.

Q **Which world champion was nicknamed the 'Toy Bulldog'?**
Mickey Walker, who was world welterweight (1922-6) and middleweight
champion (1926-31). The tenacious, all-action fighter from the Irish district of Elizabeth, New Jersey, got his nickname because he was always
taking on and beating opponents bigger than himself in a 163-fight career.

Q **What was the line up of the British amateur team that beat the USA
10-0?**
The Great Britain team that beat the United States 10-0 at Wembley on 2
November 1961: flyweight: Alan Rudkin; bantam: Peter Bennyworth;
feather: Frankie Taylor; light: Dick McTaggart; light-welter: Brian
Brazier; welter: Jim Lloyd; light-middle: Derek Richards; middle: John
Fisher; light-heavy: Dennis Pollard; heavyweight: Billy Walker. The highlight, seen live by millions on BBC television, was a sensational one-
round knock out victory by West Ham 'golden boy' Billy Walker over the
giant Philadelphian Cornelius Perry.

Q **Was former world flyweight champion Charlie Magri born in
London?**
Magri was born in Tunisia, and was brought to London when still a baby.
He was brought up in Stepney, and started boxing as an amateur at the
Arbour Square Boxing Club in London's East End. He won four succes-
sive ABA flyweight championships before turning professional under the
guidance of manager Terry Lawless in 1977.

Q **Has there ever been boxing staged at the London Palladium?**
There have been several promotions at the theatre, including Bombardier
Billy Wells defending his British heavyweight title against Bandsman
Blake with a fourth-round knock out victory on 3 March 1914.

Q **True or false: Howard Winstone had only two fingers on his right
hand?**
Winstone, the Merythr Marvel, lost the tops of three fingers on his right
hand when working a machine in a factory during his amateur days. There
was a reduction in his punching power but not his skill, and he won all but
six of his 67 professional fights between 1959 and 1968.

Q **Was Howard Winstone holding any titles when he retired from the
ring?**
Winstone hung up his gloves after losing his WBC world featherweight
title to Cuban Jose Legra at Porthcawl on 24 July 1968. He retired as
undefeated British and European featherweight champion. He took part in
17 title contests during his career, defending the British championship six
times and winning eight European title fights. Winstone lost three thrilling
world title fights against Mexican featherweight king Vicente Saldivar.

Q **Has any boxer won a world title more than four times in the same weight division?**
The record is held by the great Sugar Ray Robinson, who won the world middleweight title five times. He regained the championship for a fourth time by outpointing Carmen Basilio over 15 rounds in Chicago on 25 March 1958. Robinson had a total of 23 world title contests, six of them in the welterweight division and several that were not universally recognized. The total includes a challenge for the light-heavyweight crown against Joey Maxim in sweltering conditions that forced his retirement at the end of the thirteenth round when he was well ahead on points. It was his only stoppage.

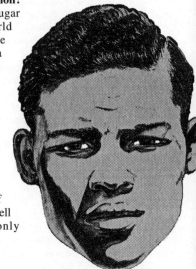

Joe Louis

Q **Did Muhammad Ali ever fight former world light-heavyweight champion Archie Moore?**
Muhammad Ali (then Cassius Clay) stopped Archie Moore in four rounds in a non-title fight in Los Angeles on 15 November 1962. It was Ageless Archie's last but one contest in a 234-fight, 27-year career.

Q **How many times did Joe Louis defend the world heavy-weight championship?**
Louis successfully defended the world title a record 25 times after taking it from James J. Braddock with an eighth round knock out win on 22 June 1937. His last winning defence was an eleventh round knock out victory over Jersey Joe Walcott on 25 June 1948. The only title fight he lost was in a comeback against Ezzard Charles when he was outpointed over 15 rounds on 27 September 1950.
The Louis title defences,

       1937: Tommy Farr (wpts15);
       1938: Nathan Mann (wko3), Harry Thomas (wko5), Max
           Schmeling (wko1);
       1939: John Henry Lewis (wrsf1), Jack Roper (wko1), 'Two Ton'
           Tony Galento (wrsf4), Bob Pastor wko11);
       1940: Arturo Godoy (wpts15), Johnny Paychek (wrsf2), Arturo
           Godoy (wrsf8), Al McCoy (wret6);
       1941: Red Burman (wko3), GusDorazio (wko2), Abe Simon
           (wrsf13), Tony Musto (wrsf9), Buddy Baer (wdisq7), Billy
           Conn(wko13), Lou Nova (wrsf6);
       1942: Buddy Baer (wko1), Abe Simon (wko6);

1946: Billy Conn (wko8), Tami Mauriello (wko1);
1947: Jersey Joe Walcott (wpts15);
1948: Jersey Joe Walcott (wko11).

Q **In which countries were Frank Bruno, Lennox Lewis and Naseem Hamed born?**
All were born in England. Bruno was born in Hammersmith, London, of West Indian parentage. Lewis was born in Stratford, London, of West Indian parentage. Naseem Hamed was born in Sheffield. His parents emigrated from the Yemen.

Q **How many world heavyweight championship belts are there?**
There are four main heavyweight titles: World Boxing Association (WBA), World Boxing Council (WBC), World Boxing Organization (WBO) and the International Boxing Federation (IBF). Four other organizations claim world status, but they do not have universal recognition: International Boxing Organization (IBO), World Boxing Federation (WBF), International Boxing Council (IBC) and World Boxing Union (WBU).

Q **Was Ken Norton the only boxer to break Muhammad Ali's jaw or did Joe Frazier break it as well?**
The Judge went to Ferdie Pacheco, Muhammad Ali's doctor in his peak years, for the answer: 'Ali's jaw was badly swollen the first time he fought Frazier, and we thought it might be broken. But x-rays showed only bruising. The only time his jaw was broken was in his first fight with Ken Norton.'

Q **How did former world heavyweight champion Tommy Burns get his name?**
Tommy's real name was Noah Brusso. He borrowed the name of a jockey friend so that his anti-boxing parents did not know he was fighting for a living. Noah was the twelfth of 13 children born to a French father and German mother, and was brought up in a log cabin in Ontario.

Q **How old was Bob Fitzsimmons when he left England for New Zealand?**
Fitzsimmons was eight years old when he emigrated with his family from Helston in Cornwall to New Zealand in 1870. He learned to box in New Zealand where he worked for his father as a blacksmith.

Q **Did Herol Graham win an ABA championship before turning professional?**
Graham was ABA middleweight champion in 1978, and started boxing for pay six months later.

Q **Were the two Ali-Liston fights televised live in Britain?**
The BBC wanted to show the first Ali-Liston fight live, but in those days (25 February 1964) they had to wait for the 'Telstar Earlybird' satellite to come into range. Film of the fight was screened at 6 a.m. and repeated the same evening. The second 'fight', all over inside a round when Liston

went down and out to a phantom punch, was shown live at around three in the morning of 25 May, 1965. The venue was Lewiston, Maine. Harry Carpenter was the commentator for both fights.

Q Was the Frank Bruno-Tim Witherspoon world title fight shown live on television?
Not in the United Kingdom. The fight was staged at Wembley Stadium in the early hours of Sunday morning, 20 July 1986. ITV screened a break-fast-time recording of the fight, and BBC showed it on the Sunday evening.

Q Was Frank Bruno ever counted out, either as an amateur or professional?
Frank Bruno took the full ten-second count once, against James 'Bonecrusher' Smith in the tenth and last round of his twenty-second fight. The referee stopped his world title fights against Tim Witherspoon, Lennox Lewis and Mike Tyson (twice). He lost one of his 21 amateur contests on points, a defeat he reversed by stopping Irish amateur champion Joe Christle.

Q Did Liverpool idol Nel Tarleton challenge for the world championship?
Tarleton was involved in 12 championship contests during his 19-year, 144-fight career from 1926 to 1945, and all 12 went the full distance of 15 rounds. He won seven, drew one and lost four. Two of his defeats came in world featherweight title fights against American southpaw Freddie Miller, both contests staged in the open air at Anfield football ground. Tarleton continued to box for eight years after having a lung removed in 1937.

Q At which weight was Sugar Ray Leonard an Olympic champion?
Leonard won the gold medal at light-welterweight in the 1976 Montreal Olympics. He held versions of the world championship at welterweight, light-middleweight, middleweight, super-middleweight and light-heavy-weight.

Q Did Tommy Hearns or Sugar Ray Leonard win most world titles?
Leonard won five titles, while Hearns laid claim to six titles: welter, (WBA), light-middle (WBC), middleweight (WBC), super-middle (WBO), light-heavyweight (WBC), light-heavy (WBA).

Q What was the relationship between Walter McGowan and his manager Joe Gans?
Joe Gans was Walter's father. He was a former fighter who took his name from one of the great old-time lightweight champions. Joe taught his son to box and guided him to the world flyweight championship. Walter, from Lanarkshire, was also an outstanding bantamweight and lost only four of 40 fights. His career was cut short by recurring eye injuries.

Q Who was the first man to win titles in more than two weight divisions?
Bob Fitzsimmons, Cornwall-born, New Zealand-raised, won the middle-

weight title in 1891, the heavyweight crown in 1897 and the newly introduced light-heavyweight championship in 1903.

Q **What have been the most number of knock downs recorded in a world title fight?**
Britain's Danny O'Sullivan was dropped 14 times by South African Vic
Toweel on his way to a tenth-round defeat in a world bantamweight title
fight in Johannesburg on 2 December 1950.

Q **True or false: Kirkland Laing once beat the great Roberto Duran?**
True. The Nottingham-based welterweight outpointed Roberto Duran in a
10 rounds non-title fight in Detroit on 4 September 1992.

Q **What was Nigel Benn's winning sequence before his first defeat?**
Benn had won 22 fights, all inside the distance, when he was knocked out
in six rounds by Michael Watson in a Commonwealth middle-weight
championship contest at Finsbury Park, London, on 21 May 1989. The
former Royal Fusilier was an outstanding amateur with the West Ham
Club. He turned professional in 1987, the year after winning the ABA
middleweight title. Only one of his opponents had lasted more than four
rounds before he lost to Watson.

Q **Who has been the youngest boxer to win a world championship?**
Wilfred Benitez was 17 years 173 days old when he took the WBA world
light-welterweight title from Colombian Antonio Cervantes on 6 March
1976. He was born in New York and raised in Puerto Rico, and also won
world titles at welterweight and light-middleweight.

Q **How many British football grounds have been used to stage championship boxing?**
They include Anfield (Liverpool), Ibrox (Rangers), Hampden Park, Loftus
Road (QPR), Highbury (Arsenal), Ninian Park (Cardiff City), Old
Trafford (Manchester United), Shawfield Park (Clyde), St Andrew's Park
(Birmingham), Villa Park (Aston Villa), White Hart Lane (Tottenham),
and, of course, Wembley Stadium.

Q **Is it true that Chris Eubank was the first opponent to beat Barry McGuigan?**
No. It was Eubank's brother, Peter, who inflicted the first defeat on
McGuigan in what was the Irishman's third fight. He was outpointed over
eight rounds in Brighton.

Q **Who was the first man to beat Sugar Ray Robinson, and was it in a title fight?**
Robinson was unbeaten for 39 fights before dropping a 10-rounds points
decision to Jake LaMotta in a non-title fight on 5 February 1943. It was
their second of five meetings and the only one in which Robinson came
off second best. He then went unbeaten for the next eight years and 91
fights. Britain's Randolph Turpin was the second man to beat him, a
points defeat that Robinson quickly reversed. He won 110 of his 202
fights inside the distance, and avenged four of his 19 defeats. He had his

first professional fight in 1940 and his last, a points loss to Joey Archer, in 1965.

Q **What was the first world championship contest shown live on television?**
The Willie Pep-Chalky Wright featherweight title fight in New York on 29 September 1944. Pep won on points over 15 rounds.

Q **Did Barry McGuigan and Azumah Nelson box each other in the 1978 Commonwealth Games?**
They were in different weight divisions. McGuigan won the bantamweight gold medal, and Nelson was the featherweight champion.

Q **Which was the champion who always sang 'When Irish Eyes Are Smiling' in the ring after his fights?**
Rinty Monaghan, the Belfast fighter who was world flyweight champion from 1947 to 1950.

Q **Did former stablemates Jim Watt and John H. Stracey ever fight each other?**
Only as amateurs. They met in the semi-finals of the ABA lightweight division in 1968, and Watt won on a first-round knock out. Both later became world professional champions under the guidance of manager Terry Lawless, Stracey at welterweight and Watt at lightweight.

Q **In which year was the first Lonsdale Belt awarded, and who was first to win it?**
The original belts were donated to the National Sporting Club by Lord Lonsdale in 1909 and were known as the National Sporting Club Challenge Belts. Freddie Welsh, the Pride of Pontypridd, was the first winner of an NSC Belt when he outpointed Johnny Summers over 20 rounds to win the British featherweight title at the NSC on 8 November 1909. His fellow Welshman, 'Peerless' Jim Driscoll, was first to win an NSC Belt outright. The British Boxing Board of Control renamed the award the Lonsdale Belt, and Benny Lynch was the first winner when he knocked out Pat Palmer in eight rounds in defence of his British flyweight title in Glasgow on 16 September 1936. Eric Boon was the first outright winner of the renamed Lonsdale Belt.

Q **What was the result when Ken Buchanan boxed Jim Watt, and which of them had most fights?**
Buchanan outpointed Watt over 15 rounds in a British lightweight title fight in Glasgow on 29 January 1973. Their records:
      Buchanan: 69 fights, 61 victories, 8 defeats.
      Jim Watt: 46 fights, 38 victories, 8 defeats.

Q **Was Floyd Patterson undefeated when he first won the world heavy weight title?**
Patterson had been beaten once, a disputed eight-round points defeat by former world light heavyweight champion Joey Maxim in his fourteenth fight.

Q **Were the Finnegan brothers British champions in the same weight division?**
Chris Finnegan was British, European and Commonwealth champion at light-heavyweight. Kevin held the British and European titles at middleweight.

Q **Who was the first black boxer to win a British championship?**
A colour bar operated in British boxing until 1948. Dick Turpin, older brother of Randolph, became the first black champion when he took the British and Empire middleweight titles with a 15-rounds points victory over Vince Hawkins at Villa Park, Birmingham, on 28 June 1948.

Q **Did Gene Tunney have a ring nickname, and did he ever fight in Europe?**
Tunney was known as the Fighting Marine. He came to Europe with the US Expeditionary Force during the First World War, and won the Forces light-heavyweight title in Paris in 1914.

Q **Who was the first southpaw boxer to win the world heavyweight championship?**
Michael Moorer, who won the WBO version of the title when he twice climbed off the canvas to stop Bert Cooper in five rounds on 15 May 1992.

Q **How old was Jack 'Kid' Berg when he had his first professional fight?**
Berg, the Whitechapel Windmill, had his first fight at the Premierland in London's East End at the age of 13 in 1922. He had 192 officially recorded fights, winning 157 and losing 26. Berg won the world light-welterweight title in 1930 when it was not a universally recognized division. He stopped American Mushy Callahan in 10 rounds at the Royal Albert Hall in 1930.

Q **Who were Henry Cooper's opponents in British heavy-weight title fights?**
Henry took the title from:
Brian London (wpts15, 1959).
His defences were against:
Joe Erskine (wrsf12, 1959),
Joe Erskine (wret5, 1961),
Joe Erskine (wrsf9, 1962),
Dick Richardson (wko5, 1963),
Brian London (wpts15, 1964),
Johnny Prescott (wret10, 1965),
Jack Bodell (wrsf2, 1967),
Billy Walker (wrsf6, 1967).

Henry Cooper

He then relinquished the title and regained it from Jack Bodell (wpts15, 1970), and lost in a controversial points defeat by Joe Bugner (1971) in what was his last fight.

Q How many fights had James 'Buster' Douglas won before taking the world title from Mike Tyson?
Buster Douglas had won 29 of his 35 fights before challenging Tyson for the world heavyweight title in Tokyo on 11 February 1990. He knocked out Tyson in the tenth round after surviving a 'long count' knock down in the eighth. He lost the title in his first defence against Evander Holyfield.

Q Where and when did Dennis Andries start his professional boxing career?
Andries was born in Guyana, but grew up in Hackney, East London, where he boxed as an amateur for the Colvestone club. He made his professional debut in Newport with a second-round knock out win over Ray Pearce on 16 May 1978.

Q How old was Mike Tyson when he won the world heavyweight title?
Tyson became the youngest world heavyweight champion when he knocked out Trevor Berbick in two rounds in his twenty-eighth fight. He was 20 years four months old. Floyd Patterson had been the previous youngest champion at 21 years 11 months.

Q Who was the first boxer to beat Joe Bugner, and how old was he when he made his debut?
Seventeen-year-old Bugner was knocked out in the third round of his professional debut by Paul Brown at Shoreditch Town Hall in 1967. Bugner, born in Hungary, came to Britain with his mother when she fled what was then an Iron Curtain country during the 1956 Uprising against the Russians. He was coached and managed for the first half of his career by Andy Smith, who steered him to two fights with Muhammad Ali. Bugner was outpointed each time by Ali, first over 12 rounds and then over 15 in a championship fight in Kuala Lumpur. He continued his career into his 40s after becoming an Australian citizen, losing in two trips back to Europe against Frank Bruno and Scott Welch.

Q Who beat Evander Holyfield when he competed in the 1984 Olympic Games?
Holyfield was overpowering New Zealander Kevin Barry in the light-heavyweight semi-final when he landed a punch after the bell at the end of the second round and was disqualified. A distraught Holyfield had to settle for a bronze medal, and he then turned professional after winning 160 out of 174 amateur contests.

Q How many fights did Jimmy Wilde win inside the distance?
Wilde, the Ghost with a Hammer in his Hand, stopped 100 of his 145 opponents, and dozens more in unrecorded fairground booth fights. He had to give away weight in nearly every one of his contests, but the Tylorstown Terror was such a fierce puncher that he soon cut his opponents down to size. He was the first world flyweight champion, reigning

from 1916 until coming out of retirement in 1923 to put the title on the line against Pancho Villa, who knocked him out in seven rounds. His only other inside the distance defeats were by Tancy Lee (which he later reversed) and a seventeenth round stoppage by American Pete Herman when he attempted to take the bantamweight crown from him in 1921.

Q **When and where was the first British Commonwealth title fight contested?**

Peerless Jim Driscoll outpointed Australian Charlie Griffin in a 15-rounds-featherweight fight billed as for the British Empire championship at London's National Sporting Club on 24 February 1908.

Q **What is the highest number of rounds ever contested in a boxing match?**

We have to go back to 1825 and the bare-knuckle days. Jack Jones beat Patsy Tunney at Cheshire in a match that lasted 276 rounds and a total of 4 hours 30 minutes. This was under Jack Broughton rules which demanded the end of a round when one fighter was knocked down. There was a 30-seconds break between each round. The longest bare-knuckle battle lasted 6 hours 15 minutes between Jim Kelly and John Smith in New South Wales, on 3 December 1855. The longest gloved fight lasted 6 hours 19 minutes and was contested by Andy Bowen and Jack Burke in New Orleans on 6 April 1893. The referee declared it a 'no contest' when neither man could continue.

Q **Did any opponent knock down Larry Holmes before his knock out defeat by Mike Tyson?**

Holmes got off the floor to win in world heavyweight titles defences against Earnie Shavers (wrsf11 1979) and Renaldo Snipes (wrsf11 1981).

Q **How many weights did Henry Armstrong hold at one and the same time?**

Three: featherweight, lightweight and welterweight. He also made a challenge for the middleweight crown but was held to a draw by Ceferino Garcia. Armstrong, nicknamed Homicide Hank, won 143 and drew 8 of his 175 fights between 1931 and 1945. His real name was Henry Jackson, and he fought in his early days as Melody Jackson after winning 58 out of 62 amateur contests. He became an ordained minister six years after his retirement.

Q **When was the last scheduled 20-rounds world championship contest?**

Joe Louis knocked out Abe Simon in the thirteenth round of a world heavyweight title fight scheduled for 20 rounds on 21 March 1941.

Q **Did Henry Armstrong ever take part in a world championship contest in London?**

Armstrong won on points over 15 rounds when he defended his world welterweight title against British champion Ernie Roderick at Harringay Arena on 25 May 1939.

Q **True or false: Sugar Ray Robinson once beat Henry Armstrong?**
True. Armstrong was coming to the close of his 175-fight career and Robinson was into the fourth year of his 202-fight marathon when Sugar Ray outpointed Homicide Hank in a non-title fight over ten rounds in New York on 27 August 1943.

Q **Did Terry Downes ever fight Sugar Ray Robinson for the world middleweight title?**
There was no championship at stake when Downes outpointed Robinson over ten rounds at Wembley Arena on 25 September 1962.

Q **How many times has Mike Tyson fought outside the United States of America?**
Three times: twice as a professional and once as an amateur. His final contest as an amateur was a victory over Hakan Brock in an international tournament in Tampere, Finland. He made two defences of his world heavyweight title in Tokyo, stopping Tony Tubbs in two rounds on 21 March 1988 and losing on a tenth-round knock out against Buster Douglas on 11 February 1990.

CRICKET

Q **Which county has won the County championship most times?**
Yorkshire have had 29 outright wins since the championship was officially constituted in 1890. Surrey won the title five out of its first six years, and set a record seven consecutive victories under the captaincy of Stuart Surridge (1952-6) and then Peter May (1957-8).

Q **What was the full all-round England Test record of Ian Botham?**
Botham played 102 Tests between 1977 and 1992. With the bat, he scored 5,200 runs at an average 33·54, including 14 centuries. With the ball, he took 383 wickets at an average 28·40, and held 120 catches.

Q **Is it correct that England once played a Test match that lasted ten days?**
Correct. This was the famous Timeless Test in South Africa in 1938-9. An aggregate of 1,981 runs were scored over a period of ten days and they could still not get a result. The match ended in a draw, with England having to dash to get the steam ship back home. Set 696 to win, England were 42 runs short of victory and with five wickets standing when the match was abandoned because of rain. There were 43 hours 16 minutes of actual playing time. Bill Edrich was top scorer with 219 in a Test in which there were five other centurions.

Q **What is the highest ever partnership between England batsmen in Test cricket?**
A fourth wicket stand of 411 between Peter May (285 not out) and Colin Cowdrey (154) against West Indies at Edgbaston in 1957. England looked on the brink of defeat when Cowdrey joined captain May at the wicket but they steered them to 583 for four declared. It was the West Indies who were clinging on at the end of a drawn match at 72 for seven. May's score was a record for an England captain, and West Indies spinner Sonny Ramadhin sent down 127 overs and a record 774 balls during the match.

Q **Did Mike Denness score more Test centuries for England than Mike Brearley?**
Mike Denness scored four centuries in his 28 Tests, with a highest score of 188. Mike Brearley scored nine 50s in 39 Tests. His top score was 91.

Q **Was Alec Bedser's twin brother Eric ever capped by England?**
Eric Bedser travelled to Australia with the MCC in 1950-51, but played in only one tour match. He played 443 matches for Surrey between 1939 and 1961, but never represented England in Test cricket. Alec bowled his heart out in 371 matches for Surrey, and took 236 wickets in 51 Tests.

Q **Which batsman holds the record for most 'not outs' in Test cricket?**
It's more a bowler than a batsman. Tailender Bob Willis was not out in 55 Test match innings. He finished his 90-match Test career with an accumulation of 840 runs (av. 11·50), with a top score of 28 – not out, of course.

Q **What was the highest individual score in first-class cricket before Brian Lara's 501?**
Hanif Mohammad's 499 for Karachi against Bahawalpur in 1958-9.

Q **Where were Nasser Hussain and Min Patel born and educated?**
Hussain was born in Madras and was educated at Forest School, Snaresbrook, London and Durham University. Patel was born in Bombay, and was educated at Dartford Grammar School, Erith College of Technology in Kent and Manchester Polytechnic.

Q **Did England football hero Geoff Hurst play County cricket for Essex?**
The Judge got this reply from Geoff Hurst: 'I played regular cricket for Essex seconds, but just once for the County team – against Lancashire at Liverpool in 1962. I went in at number 8, but I'm afraid I did not not trouble the scorer. I went for a duck in the first innings, and I was stranded at nought not out in the second. I then decided to concentrate full-time on football with West Ham. The first time Bobby Moore and I played in the same side was for the Essex schools cricket team!'

Q **True or false: Denis Compton once played cricket at Highbury football stadium?**
True. It was in Compton's benefit year of 1950 and they staged a full-scale all-star cricket match at Highbury for the Arsenal and Middlesex all-rounder. That was the year Denis bowed out of football after playing for Arsenal in the 1950 FA Cup Final and helping them beat Liverpool 1-0.

Q **How many times did the West Indies win under the captaincy of Clive Lloyd?**
Lloyd was the most successful captain in the history of Test cricket. His record as skipper: played 74, won 36, drawn 26, lost 12. His unmatchable team won a record 11 successive Tests in 1984, and went an astonishing 27 successive Test matches without a defeat between 1981 and 1985. Lloyd missed just one of those matches though injury, and Viv Richards took over as skipper.

Q **What was Clive Lloyd's Test batting average before and after taking on the captaincy?**
His run-making average increased from 38·67 in 36 matches before

becoming captain to 51·30 in his 74 matches as captain. His full Test batting record: 110 Tests, 7,515 runs (av. 46·67), 19 centuries.

Q Has first-class cricket ever been played in England under the eight-balls-an-over law?
There was an experiment with 8-ball overs during the 1939 season, but this was abandoned on the resumption of first-class cricket after the war. The Australians switched from eight-ball to six-ball overs in 1979-80.

Q What is the highest number of catches in a County match other than by a wicket-keeper?
Walter Hammond, one of the greatest of all slip fielders, held ten catches for Gloucesterhire against Surrey at Cheltenham on 16-17 August 1928. He clung on to four in the first innings and six in the second.

Q Has any player in a County match taken six wickets with six balls?
Off-spinner Pat Pocock came closest, taking five wickets in six balls, six in nine and seven in eleven balls for Surrey against Sussex at Eastbourne on 15 August 1972.

Q What was Geoffrey Boycott's top score in Test cricket?
Boycott scored an undefeated 246 against India at Headingley in 1967, but the selectors were unimpressed. The fact that it took him 537 minutes to make the runs brought him a shower of criticism and he was dropped for the next Test. Boycott's full Test batting record: 108 Tests, 8,114 runs (av. 47·72), 22 centuries.

Q Who were the players who represented Australia in the 1948 Test series in England?
Considered by many to be the greatest Test team of all time, Don Bradman's all-conquering Aussies were, with Test appearances in brackets: Sidney Barnes (4), Arthur Morris (5), Bradman (5), Lindsay Hassett (5), Keith Miller (5), Sam Loxton (3), Neil Harvey (2), Doug Ring (1), Ian Johnson (4), Don Tallon (4), Ray Lindwall (5), Bill Johnston (5), Ernie Toshack (4), Bill Brown (2), Ron Saggers (1). They beat Norman Yardley's England team by four Tests to nil, with one drawn. While the Aussies had a generally settled side, England's selectors called up no fewer than 21 players during the series in a vain bid to stop the march of the unbeatable tourists.

Q What was Don Bradman's full record as Australia's Test captain?
Bradman captained Australia in 24 Tests, of which 15 were won, six drawn and three lost. The Don skippered the Aussies in five Test series between 1936 and 1948 and did not lose one of

Don Bradman

them. The responsibilities of captaincy rarely seemed to anchor his quite phenomenal Test run-making record: 52 Tests, 6,996 runs (av. 99·94), 29 centuries, 2 wickets (av. 36·00), 32 catches.

Q **Who was the bowler who took Don Bradman's wicket in his final Test?**

Eric Hollies, the Warwickshire off spinner, was playing in his ninth of 13 Test matches, having made his debut back in 1935. For Don Bradman it was the fifty-second and final Test. The Don got a standing ovation as he walked out to the middle at the Oval on the afternoon of 14 August 1948. England captain Norman Yardley shook his hand and then called for three cheers from his players. Bradman was visibly moved by the reception and his concentration was not as finely tuned as usual as he played forward to a googly from Hollies and was clean bowled second ball for a duck. It was one of five wickets Hollies claimed for 131 runs in a marathon stint of 56 overs. Four runs would have taken Bradman's aggregate to 7,000 Test runs and his average to exactly 100. Australia (389)`beat outclassed England (52 and 188) by an innings and 149 runs, so Bradman did not get another chance to bat.

Q **With which team did Basil D'Oliveira play when he first arrived in England?**

D'Oliveira played for Middleton in the Lancashire League when he first came to England in 1960. He joined Worcestershire in 1965, and played for them until his retirement in 1979. This immensely talented all-rounder scored 18,882 runs at an average 39·66 and took 548 wickets at an average 27·38. He amassed 2,848 runs and took 47 wickets in 44 Tests for England.

Q **How did Mike Brearley's England captaincy record compare with those of Len Hutton and Peter May?**

Their records as captains:

Hutton (1952-5): 23 Tests, 11 wins, 4 defeats, 8 drawn.
May (1955-62): 41 Tests, 20 wins, 10 defeats, 11 drawn.
Brearley (1977-81): 31 Tests, 18 wins, 4 defeats, 9 drawn

Q **How many wickets did Michael Holding take against England in the 1976 Oval Test?**

Bowling on a featherbed pitch, Holding took 8 for 92 and 6 for 57 in the second innings for a West Indies match record aggregate of 14 for 149. The match was also memorable for an innings of 291 by Viv Richards that lifted his total runs for the calendar year to a remarkable 1,710.

Q **Which batsman has scored most boundaries in one Test match innings?**

Surrey left hander John Edrich hammered 57 boundaries during his 310 not out for England against New Zealand at Headingley on 8-9 July 1965. His haul included five sixes and 52 fours in an innings lasting 532 minutes.

Q How old was Colin Cowdrey when he played his final Test for England?
Cowdrey was 41 and three years off the Test stage when recalled to emergency duty on the 1974-5 tour of Australia. But he was still junior to Fred Titmus, who was playing his first Test cricket for seven years at the age of 42. Cowdrey took his Test match appearances to a then record 114 as he faced the speed of Lillee and Thomson. He scored 7,624 Test runs (av. 44·06), including 22 centuries. He was also a fine slip fielder and held 120 Test catches. Knighted at the close of his glittering career, Sir Colin captained England 27 times and led them to eight victories and 15 draws.

Q What is the highest number of runs scored in a single day of Test cricket by an England team?
England scored 503 runs on the second day of the 1924 Lord's Test against South Africa. Jack Hobbs (211) and Herbert Sutcliffe (122) laid the foundation with a record opening stand of 268, and then Frank Woolley (134) and Patsy Hendren (50) piled in as England set a stunning scoring rate of 93 runs an hour. Skipper Arthur Gilligan declared the innings closed at 531 for two, and England won by an innings and 18 runs.

Q Did Godfrey Evans or Alan Knott score most runs for England as batting wicket-keepers?
In 91 Tests, Evans scored 2,439 runs (av. 20·49), including two centuries. He held 173 catches and made 46 stumpings. In 95 Tests, Knott scored 4,389 runs (av. 32·75), including five centuries. He held 250 catches and made 19 stumpings.

Q Has Darren Gough ever played overseas cricket apart from with touring sides?
Gough played for East Shirley in Christchurch, New Zealand, during their 1991-2 season. He won his County cap with Yorkshire the following year, and made his England debut against New Zealand in 1994.

Q Who was the first black captain of a touring West Indies Test team?
It was not until 1960 that the West Indies appointed Frank Worrell as the first black overseas tour captain. He was 36 by then and preparing to follow the other two Ws – Walcott and Weekes – into retirement. He stayed on to lead West Indies in 15 Tests. Nine were won, three lost, two drawn and there was the incredible tied Test at Brisbane in December 1960, which was Worrell's first match in charge. Knighted in 1964, this gentleman of cricket amassed 3,860 runs in his 51 Tests at an average 49·48.

Q What were the Test batting averages of Graeme Pollock and Barry Richards?
These two master batsmen had only limited Test experience because of South Africa's isolation from international sport during the apartheid years. Pollock, rated one of the finest left-handed batsmen of all time, played in 23 Tests, scoring 2,256 runs at an exceptional average 60·97. Richards, reckoned by many to be on a par with his namesake Viv Richards, played in only four Tests, plundering 508 runs at an average

72·57. Barry was a have-bat-will-travel professional, and on his retirement in 1983 had built a mountain of 28,358 runs at an average 54·74.

Q Where and when did Graham Gooch make his Test debut?

This is rattling a skeleton in Gooch's cupboard. He started his Test career with a pair against Australia at Edgbaston in 1975. He batted at number five and was caught by Rodney Marsh in both innings, first off the bowling of Max Walker and then against the pace of Jeff Thomson. It was an inauspicious start to what was to become one of the great England batting careers. When he retired from the Test arena in 1995 he had scored 8,655 runs (av. 43·49), including 20 centuries and a career best 333 against India in 1990. He scored 123 in the second innings for a then record match aggregate of 456. It was the first time that any batsman had scored a triple century and a century in the same Test. England won 10, lost 12 and drew 12 Tests under his captaincy.

Q Have any brothers each scored a century in the same Test?

The Chappell brothers, Ian and Greg, set what were relatively unbeatable standards when they became the first brothers to score a century in both innings of the same Test match. They performed their double against New Zealand at Wellington in 1973-74. Ian scored 145 and 121, Greg a career-best 247 not out and 133 – a remarkable family contribution of 646 runs. They shared a first innings partnership of 264. Australia drew a match in which Bev Congdon and Brian Hastings scored centuries for New Zealand.

Q Which three West Indian batsmen were out when Dominic Cork performed his hat-trick?

Cork performed what was the twenty-second hat-trick in Test match history at Old Trafford in the fourth Test on Sunday 29 July 1995. He bowled skipper Richie Richardson, and with his next two balls had first Junior Murray and then Carl Hooper out leg before wicket. Cork became the eighth England bowler to take a Test hat-trick and the first since Peter Loader's triple against the West Indies at Headingley in 1957. It was Cork's second hat-trick. In his first – for Derbyshire against Kent in 1994 – Hooper was also the third man out lbw.

Dominic Cork

Q Which batsman was at the other end when Ian Botham hammered Australia at Headingley in 1981?

Botham smashed a century off just 87 balls as he and Graham Dilley (56) put on 117 in 80 minutes for the seventh wicket in England's second innings when Australia were in sight of victory. Botham (149 not out) then added 67 in partnership with Chris Old (29). Australia wanted 130 runs to win, and were tumbled all out for the 'Nelson's jinx' total of 111. England won by 18 runs to become the first team this century to win a Test match after being forced to follow on.

Q **How many overs did Bob Willis bowl when polishing off Australia in the 'Botham Test' at Headlingley?**
Willis took eight wickets for 43 runs in 15·1 overs as Australia's last nine second innings' wickets tumbled for 55. During a 90-match Test career, Willis took what was then a record 325 wickets (av. 25·20).

Q **Did Rohan Kanhai ever skipper the West Indies in Test cricket?**
Kanhai succeeded Gary Sobers as captain, and led West Indies to just three victories in 13 Test matches.

Q **Did Tom Graveney ever play as wicket-keeper for England in Test cricket?**
The Judge got this answer from England's master batsman: 'I deputized behind the stumps for Godfrey Evans after he had got a knock in the 1955 Old Trafford Test against South Africa. I kept throughout the second innings against the full force of Frank Tyson, Alec Bedser and Trevor Bailey. It was the only time in my career that I wore the gloves, and I'm proud to say that I conceded only two byes throughout the innings. That was the good news. The bad news was that after the match I found I could bend my little finger at all angles like a piece of rubber.'

Q **What is the lowest innings total by a team in a Test match?**
New Zealand, batting against an England team skippered for the last time by the retiring Len Hutton, managed just 26 runs at Auckland's Eden Park on 28 March 1955. Starting their second innings 46 behind England's total of 246, New Zealand were dismissed in 27 overs by Frank Tyson (2 for 10), Brian Statham (3 for 9), Bob Appleyard (4 for 7) and Johnny Wardle (1 for 0). Bert Sutcliffe (11) achieved the only double-figure score of an innings which lasted 106 minutes either side of the tea interval on the third day. Bob Appleyard took three wickets in four balls and was twice on a hat-trick.

Q **What has been the lowest declaration total in a Test match?**
Australian skipper Lindsay Hassett declared at 32 for 7 wickets against England at Brisbane on 4 December 1950. Struggling on a 'sticky' wicket against the bowling of Trevor Bailey and Alec Bedser, Australia declared their innings when only 192 runs ahead. They took six England second innings wickets for 30 before the close, and went on to win by 70 runs despite a stubborn innings by Len Hutton (62 not out). Twenty wickets fell for 102 runs after lunch on the third day.

Q **Has a team ever been dismissed twice on the same day of a Test?**
India were rushed out for 58 and 82 on the third day of the third Test against England at Old Trafford on 19 July 1952. Twenty-two wickets fell in the day as England stormed to victory by an innings and 207 runs. Fred

Trueman (8-31 and 1-9) and Alec Bedser (2-19 and 5-27) did the damage, with Tony Lock marking his Test debut with four for 36 in the second innings.

Q What is the fastest Test 100 on record in terms of balls received?
Master Blaster Viv Richards recorded the fastest 100 in terms of balls received off just 56 balls against England in his native Antigua on 15 April 1986. He scorched to his century in just 81 minutes. He reached 50 off 33 balls in 46 minutes and declared after scoring 110 not out off 58 balls. It was his twentieth Test 100 and included in his 41 scoring strokes were five sixes and seven fours.

Q Has Alec Stewart scored more than one century in a Test for England?
Stewart became the first England batsman to score a century in each innings against West Indies with scores of 118 and 143 in the fourth Test in Barbados in 1994.

Q Which England batsman has scored the fastest century in a Test match?
The record of 75 minutes was set by Gilbert 'The Croucher' Jessop against Australia at the Oval on 13 August 1902. He came to the wicket in the second innings with England reeling at 48 for five and still needing 215 to win. Starting his innings 20 minutes before lunch, he had reached 29 not out at the interval. He completed his 50 in 43 minutes, and he and F. S. Jackson added 109 in 67 minutes with Jessop's share being 83. Eight minutes later Jessop reached his 100 out of 135, having hit an all-run five, 16 fours, two threes, four twos and 17 singles. Jessop was out two minutes later having made 104 out of 139 in 77 minutes. His whirlwind innings set England up for victory by one wicket.

Alec Stewart

Q What is the highest number of runs scored by any batsman before lunch in a Test match?
Leslie Ames, Kent's wicket-keeper batsman, scored 123 runs for England before lunch on the third and last day of the Test against South Africa at the Oval on 20 August 1935. He was 25 not out at the end of play on the second day, and by lunch the next day had rocketed to 148 not out. Ames

and Maurice Leyland put on 151 runs in 100 minutes. England declared at 534 for six and the game finished in a draw.

Q **Which two batsmen have shared the highest stand in Test cricket?**
Don Bradman (244) and Bill Ponsford (266) put on 451 runs in 316 minutes for Australia's second wicket against England at the Oval on 18 August 1934. Playing at Leeds in the previous Test, Ponsford (181) and Bradman (304) had added 388 runs for the fourth innings. In successive Test innings, they had scored 839 runs together at a rate of 76 runs per hour. Mudassar Nazar (231) and Javed Miandad (280) equalled the partnership record at Hyderabad on 14-15 January 1983. The third-wicket pair scored 451 runs in 533 minutes to put Pakistan on the way to a victory over India by an innings and 119 runs.

Q **From which end at Old Trafford did Jim Laker take most of his record 19 Test wickets?**
Amazingly, Jim Laker took all his 19 wickets from the Stretford End although he frequently switched ends with his Surrey spin 'twin' Tony Lock. Laker took 9 for 37 in 16·4 overs in the first innings and 10 for 53 in 51·2 overs in the second. Ten of his victims were caught, including five by the long-armed, 6ft 6in Alan Oakman at short leg who was deputizing for the injured Tom Graveney. Lock took only one wicket for 106 runs.

Q **Has Alec Stewart ever played Sheffield Shield cricket in Australia?**
Alec played Australian grade cricket, not Sheffield Shield. He went to Australia every winter from 1981 to 1989 to play with the Midland-Guildford club in Perth. His first trip down under came soon after he joined the Surrey staff, where his father, Micky, was the manager. It was in Australia that he developed the competitive edge that has made him one of England's most stalwart players, whether with the bat, fielding at slip or crouched behind the stumps. He was always known as 'Micky's son', but has long since gained recognition in his own right.

Q **What have been the most runs conceded by a bowler in one Test match?**
That doubtful privilege belongs to West Indies leg spinner O. C. (Tommy) Scott, who conceded 374 runs in the 'Timeless Test' against England at Kingston in 1930. His figures were five for 266 off 80·2 overs in the first innings and four for 108 off 25 overs in the second. Rain forced the match to be abandoned as a draw after seven days. The match was notable for the last Test appearance of 52-year-old Wilfred Rhodes, the oldest man ever to play Test cricket.

Q **What have been the most runs conceded by a bowler in one Test match innings?**
'Chuck' Fleetwood-Smith was hit for 298 during England's record total of 903 for 7 declared at the Oval in August 1938. The Australian spin bowler sent down 87 overs for just one wicket. Len Hutton stole the headlines with a then world record score of 364.

Q **What is the fastest century scored in a one day international match?**
Shahid Afridi, a virtually unknown 16-year-old, smashed a century from
just 37 balls for Pakistan against Sri Lanka in the Four-Nations tournament in Nairobi in October 1996. Replacing injured fellow leg spinner
Mushtaq Ahmed, he came in at No. 3 in the eleventh over of the innings
with the score at 60 for one. He played tentatively forward to his first ball
from Kumar Dharmasena. The next disappeared into the car park almost
100 yards behind the bowler. He reached his 50 from 18 balls, just one
short of equalling Sanath Jayasuriya's world record. Ironically, Jayasuriya,
the bowler, bore the brunt of the assault with 28 coming from his first over
and 44 from his first two. When the field spread out after 15 overs, Afridi
opened up with all guns blazing. He equalled Jayasuriya's record of 11
sixes in an innings but lowered his record for the quickest century by an
extraordinary 11 balls. Three of his six fours were just feet away from
landing over the ropes as well. A regular tail-ender during his first season
for Karachi Whites in the Quaid-e-Azam Trophy in Pakistan, Afridi
helped Pakistan amass a record total of 371 for nine in 50 overs. Skipper
Saeed Anwar was his partner and helped himself to a relatively pedestrian
115 from 128 balls.

Q **How old was wicket-keeper Jack Russell when he made his County**
debut?
'Jack' Russell, real name Robert Charles, was the youngest ever
Gloucestershire wicket-keeper when he made his bow at the age of 17
years 307 days against Sri Lanka at Bristol in 1981. He held seven catches
and made one stumping, a record haul for a keeper making his first-class
debut.

Q **How many catches did Greg Chappell hold during his Test career?**
Chappell held 122 catches during his 87-match Test career, overtaking the
120 record set by Colin Cowdrey for a non-wicket-keeper. He set the new
record in his final Test, against Pakistan at Sydney in January 1984, when
he held on to catches to dismiss Mudassar Nazar, Mohsin Khan and Salim
Malik. It was an eventful farewell match for Chappell, who in his last
innings scored 182 to break the 7,000-run barrier. Viv Richards equalled
the record, and then Allan Border set new figures of 156 catches in his 156
Test matches.

Q **Did Nick Knight ever score more than 150 runs in a single innings for**
Essex?
Knight scored what was then a career best 157 for Essex against Sussex at
Chelmsford in 1994, the same year that he switched to Warwickshire.

Q **Who was the first player to complete the double double of 2,000 Test**
wickets and 2,000 runs?
That all-round record was first set by Richie Benaud, who completed the
double double with his 2,000th run against South Africa at Brisbane on 6
December 1963. It was his twenty-eighth and last match as Australia's
captain. He retired at the end of the series with a record of 63 Tests, 2,201

runs (av. 24·45), 248 wickets (av. 27·03). His captaincy record: 28 Tests, 12 wins, 4 defeats, 11 draws, one tie.

Q **Is Ian Botham the only player to have scored a century and taken ten or more wickets in the same Test?**

No, but he was the first to achieve the feat. Playing in the Golden Jubilee Test in Bombay in February 1980 Botham took 6 for 58, scored 114 and then wrecked India's second innings by taking 7 for 48. No other batsman scored 50 in the match. England won by ten wickets on the third day. The feat was emulated by Pakistan captain Imran Khan against India in Faisalabad in January 1983. Imran scored 117 and took 11 wickets for 180.

Q **What relationship is David Graveney to the old England master Tom Graveney?**

Tom is David's uncle, and the brother of David's father, Ken Graveney, who was a distinguished Gloucestershire captain.

Q **Which batsman was at the opposite end when Brian Lara became first to score 500 runs in an innings?**

Wicket-keeper Keith Piper batted with Lara through the last 165 runs of his record 501 for Warwickshire against Durham at Edgbaston in June 1994. It was Piper who pointed out to Lara that he was in sight of the record and that time was running out. It brought a sudden acceleration and the record.

Q **How many of Brian Lara's record 501 runs came in boundaries?**

Lara's score of 501 not out took 474 minutes to accumulate and included 62 fours and ten sixes. He reached 400 with an all-run four, and overtook Hanif Mohammad's 35-year-old record of 499 with a four through the covers off the last but one ball of the match. Bowled off a no ball at ten and dropped behind at 18, Lara settled down to play the innings of a lifetime. He scored 390 runs on the final day to break the record in a match that finished in a draw. Warwickshire's total was 810 for four declared.

Q **How did Brian Lara's record 375 Test runs compare with the previous record set by Gary Sobers?**

Lara's score of 375 against England in Antigua in April 1994 took 766 minutes to accumulate and included 45 fours. West Indies declared at 593 for five. Sobers scored his 365 not out in 614 minutes against Pakistan in Jamaica in 1958, and included 38 fours in his blitz. West Indies declared at 790 for three. Neither Lara nor Sobers hit a six during their run riots. Len Hutton's 364-run record set at the Oval against Australia in August 1938 lasted 797 minutes and included 35 fours and no sixes. England declared at a record 903 for seven.

Q **How old was W. G. Grace when he played his first and last Test matches for England?**

The great WG made his debut for England against Australia at the Oval on 6 September 1880 when he was 28, and marked his entry into international cricket with the first Test century (152) by an England batsman. He

opened the innings with his brother Edward
Mills Grace, and his other brother, George
Frederick, was also in the team (he got a
pair!). Grace was 50 years and 320 days
old when he stepped off the Test stage as
England captain after the first drawn Test
against Australia at Trent Bridge in 1899.
It was his twenty-second Test appearance. Only Wilfred Rhodes (52) has
played for England at an older age, and
he made his Test debut in WG's final
match. WG scored 1,098 Test runs at an
average 32·29.

W. G. Grace

Q **Has any batsman scored a double
century and a single century in the
same County match more than twice?**
Zaheer Abbas, the Pakistani batting
master, achieved this feat on four occasions for Gloucestershire and he was not
out in each innings – 216 and 156 v Surrey
at the Oval (1976), 230 and 104 v Kent at
Canterbury (1976), 205 and 108 v Sussex
at Cheltenham (1977), 215 and 150 v
Somerset at Bath (1981).

Q **Where was Kepler Wessels born, and how did he qualify to play for
Australia?**
Kepler Wessels was born in Bloemfontein, South Africa, and moved to
Australia at the age of 21 to play in Kerry Packer's World Series Cricket.
He qualified for the Australian team after four years in Brisbane and made
his Test debut in 1982. He played 24 Tests for Australia before being
dropped for allegedly recruiting players for the rebel tour of South Africa.
Wessels, who had five seasons with Sussex, returned to his home land,
and was at the forefront of the team when South Africa came back into the
Test arena.

Q **What is the highest partnership ever recorded in a County match?**
The opening stand of 555 between Percy Holmes (224 not out) and
Herbert Sutcliffe (313) for Yorkshire against Essex at Leyton in 1932.

Q **How many overs did Devon Malcolm bowl when taking his nine
wickets against South Africa at the Oval?**
Malcolm bowled 99 balls (16·3 overs) on his way to taking nine South
African second innings' wickets for 57. England won by eight wickets.

Q **Which batsman has scored the fastest triple hundred in Test cricket?**
Wally Hammond hurried to a triple hundred in 288 minutes when going in
at No. 3 for England against New Zealand in Christchurch in 1933. He
hammered a then record ten sixes, including three off successive balls, and

finished on 336 not out. His third 100 took just 47 minutes. It was then the world record individual score. Rain forced the match to be abandoned.

Q **Which batsman holds the record for the highest number of sixes scored in a Test match?**
Pakistan captain Wasim Akram hammered 12 sixes in an undefeated 257 as he led his team to a score of 553 against Zimbabwe at Sheikhupura in October 1996. Adding a record 313 for the eighth wicket with Saqlain Mushtak (79), Akram beat the previous record of ten sixes set by Wally Hammond for England against New Zealand on the 1932-3 tour. Akram also hammered 22 fours in his 489 minutes at the crease.

Q **What is the slowest run rate by any batsman in a Test match?**
Phil Tufnell managed just two runs during 81 minutes at the wicket for England against India at Bombay in 1992-3.

Q **What is the longest a Test batsman has gone without getting a run on the scoreboard?**
The usually belligerent Godfrey Evans stone-walled for 97 minutes before recording his first run in the second innings against Australia in Adelaide in 1947. He held up one end while Denis Compton carved out a match-saving unbeaten century. A more familiar Evans scored 98 before lunch against India at Lord's in 1952.

Q **Which England batsman has scored most centuries in Test cricket?**
It is a three-way tie on 22 centuries between Geoff Boycott (193 innings), Colin Cowdrey (188) and Wally Hammond (140). Both Ken Barrington and Graham Gooch scored 20 Test tons, and Len Hutton amassed 19. Sunil Gavaskar is the world record holder with 34 Test centuries in 214 innings, with Don Bradman second on 29 from just 80 innings. Most double centuries have been collected by Bradman (12), Hammond (7) and Pakistan's Javed Miandad (6). Gary Sobers (26) and Viv Richards (24) top the list of West Indian Test match centurions.

Q **Has any batsman carried his bat through an innings in a Test match more than twice?**
West Indian Desmond Haynes has achieved the feat of opening the innings and still being there at the fall of the tenth wicket three times – 88 v Pakistan Karachi (1987-8), 75 v England at the Oval (1991), and 143 v Pakistan at Trinidad (1992-3).

Q **Has a batsman ever scored more than 300 runs in a single day of Test cricket?**
Don Bradman scorched to 309 on the first day of the 1930 England-Australia Test at Headingley. He raced to 105 by lunch, added 115 between lunch and tea, and then another 89 in the final session. The Don, aged only 21, was out for 334 the next morning, then an individual Test record.

Q **Did wicket-keeper Steve Rhodes win a County cap with Yorkshire before moving to Worcestershire?**
Rhodes was the youngest wicket-keeper ever to represent Yorkshire when

he made his debut for them against Sri Lanka at the age of 17 in 1981. He was restless as understudy to David Bairstow at Yorkshire, and moved to Worcestershire where he was awarded his County cap in 1986.

Q **True or false: Keith Miller got a duck when Australia scored more than 700 runs against Essex?**

True. Don Bradman's 1948 tourists accumulated 721 runs on the first day of their match against Essex at Southend in May. The Aussies were all out ten minutes before stumps, and it was the only time they were dismissed in a day on that memorable tour. Bradman led the run rush with 187, and Bill Brown (153), Sam Loxton (120) and Ron Saggers (104) also scored centuries. Bradman and Brown put on 219 runs in just 90 minutes in a blistering second wicket stand. Keith Miller had no appetite for the massacre and deliberately surrendered his wicket to Trevor Bailey without getting a run on the board.

Q **How many times was Sunil Gavaskar unbeaten on his way to his record collection of runs?**

Gavaskar was not out on 16 occasions while accumulating a then record 10,122 runs (av. 51·12) in his 125 Test matches for India. His highest individual score was an undefeated 236 against West Indies in Madras in 1983-4. He accumulated an all-time record 34 centuries. Allan Border overtook his total with 11,174 runs in 156 Tests (av. 50·56) and was not out a record 44 times. He scored 27 centuries, and had a highest score of 205 against New Zealand in Adelaide in 1987-8.

Q **Which English batsman has scored the slowest century in a home Test match?**

Keith Fletcher, former Essex and England captain, set this record against Pakistan at the Oval in the third and final Test against Pakistan in August 1974. He crawled to a century in 458 minutes and off 329 balls. His marathon finished when he was run out on 122 after 513 minutes at the crease during which he faced 377 deliveries. His innings included ten fours. As a contrast, Zaheer Abbas scored 240 for Pakistan in 545 minutes off 410 balls. The match ended in a draw as the Pakistanis protected their unbeaten tour record.

Q **How did Richard Hadlee's Test wickets haul compare with that of Dennis Lillee's and Michael Holding's?**

Their bowling records:

    Hadlee: 86 Tests, 431 wickets, 9,611 runs, av. 22·29

    Lillee: 70 Tests, 355 wickets, 8,493 runs, av 23·92

    Holding: 60 Tests, 249 wickets, 5,898 runs, av 23·68

Richard Hadlee

Q **Which all-rounder won most Test caps: Ian Botham, Richard Hadlee, Imran Khan or Kapil Dev?**

Kapil Dev led the way with 131 caps for India. Botham won 102, Imran 88 and Hadlee 86. Their all-round records: Kapil (5,248 runs, 434 wickets), Botham (5,200 runs, 383 wickets), Hadlee (3,124 runs, 431 wickets), and Imran (3,807 runs, 362 wickets).

Q **How many times did Ray Illingworth skipper England, and what was his record as captain and chairman?**

Illingworth captained England in 31 Tests, winning 12, drawing 14 and losing five. He both regained and retained the Ashes at the start of the 1970s. In all, he played in 61 Tests, scoring 1,836 runs (av. 23·24) and taking 122 wickets (av. 31·20). His highest Test score was 113 against the West Indies at Lord's in 1969, and his best bowling return was six for 29 against India at Lord's in 1967. England won just six of the 28 Test matches during his eventful reign as chairman and chief selector. He played for Yorkshire and captained Leicestershire.

HORSE RACING

Q **Who was the first National Hunt jump jockey to ride 1,000 winners?**
Stan Mellor, who rode 1,035 winners in 20 seasons from 1952 to 1972. He was followed by John Francome, who reached the 1,000 milestone in 15 seasons (1970-85) and Peter Scudamore who achieved the target in just 11 seasons (1979-89). 'Scu' had ridden 1,677 winners by his retirement in 1993.

Q **Was the great Shergar still in training when he disappeared?**
Shergar had retired to the Aga Khan's Ballymany Stud in Co. Kildare when he was kidnapped on 9 February 1983.

Q **Is it true that the 'Australian wonder horse' Phar Lap was, in fact, not Australian?**
Phar Lap was born in the Seadown Stud, Timaru, New Zealand. He won 37 of his 51 races, including 32 of the last 35.

Q **How old was Sonny Somers when he won his last steeplechase?**
Sonny Somers won two steeplechases at the age of 18 in February 1980, and so became the oldest horse to win a steeplechase. A horse called Wild Aster won three hurdles races in six days in March 1919, also aged 18.

Q **Are fillies allowed to run in the Epsom Derby, and can colts compete in the Oaks?**
Three-year-old colts and fillies contest the Derby. Six fillies have won the race: Eleanor (1801), Blink Bonny (1857), Shotover (1882), Signorinetta (1908), Tagalie (1912), Fifinella (1916). The Oaks is for three-year-old fillies only. Eleanor, the first filly to win the Derby, won the Oaks the next day. Blink Bonny, Signorinetta and Fifinella also completed the Oaks-Derby double.

Q **How do the Grand National records of Golden Miller and Red Rum, compare, and which was considered the greater horse?**
Golden Miller was carrying 12 st 2 lb when he won the 1934 Grand National in a record 9 m 20.4 s. Red Rum beat the record by nearly 19 seconds in 1973, carrying 10 st 5 lbs. Red Rum had three wins and two seconds in the National. Golden Miller, a five times Gold Cup winner, failed to finish in four other bids for the National. The Judge's verdict: Red Rum was the Grand National master, Golden Miller the better all-rounder.

Q **In which race did Buzzards Bay land a sensational long-odds victory?**
Buzzards Bay won Ascot's Queen Elizabeth II Stakes at 50-1 in 1982.

Q **What year did a four-year-old horse win the Epsom Derby?**
Running Rein was disqualified after finishing first in the 1844 Derby. He was later proved to be a four-year-old called Maccabeus, which had the same colouring and a distinctive white star on the forehead. The owner, Alexander Wood, had to go to court to prove that he had no knowledge of the switch that had been mastermined by the former owner, Levi Goodman, as part of a betting coup. The ante-post favourite, Ratan, was nobbled in his box overnight, and another horse, Leander (also suspected of being a four-year-old), had to be put down after a collision with Running Rein halfway through the race.

Q **Is it correct that Lester Piggott once rode Grand National legend Red Rum?**
Lester rode Red Rum in a mile handicap at Aintree on Grand National Day 1968 and was beaten by a short head.

Q **How old was Bruce Hobbs when he rode the winner of the Grand National and was it on a 'foreign' horse?**
Bruce Hobbs was just 17 when he won the 1938 Grand National on Battleship which had won the American Grand National four years earlier. Battleship, the first blinkered winner of the National, was owned by American Mrs Marion Scott.

Q **Who was the first woman rider to complete the Aintree course in the Grand National?**
It was Geraldine Rees, riding Cheers in 1982. She picked her way through the many fallers around her to come in eighth and last of the finishers. Charlotte Brew was the first woman to ride in the National. Her mount, Barony Fort, refused four fences from home.

Q **Who rode more winners, Sir Gordon Richards or Lester Piggott?**
Sir Gordon Richards, champion jockey a record 26 times, rode 4,870 winners between 1920 and 1954. Lester Piggott, who rode his first winner at the age of 13 in 1948, clocked up more than 5,300 winners world wide, including over 4,500 in Britain. Sir Gordon, of course, did not have the benefit of fast world-wide travel. He was 21 and weighing just 6 st 11 lbs when he won the first of his record 26 championships with 118 winners in 1925, and he retired in 1954 after 21,834 races. Piggott won the first of his 11 championships in 1960 and the last in 1982 when he was 46.

Sir Gordon Richards

Q **How many winners did John Francome and Peter Scudamore ride the year they tied for the title?**

Both rode 120 winners in the 1981-2 season. Scudamore was injured in a fall in April and Francome sportingly retired for the season when he rode his 120th winner at Uttoxeter on 1 June.

Q **Which horse was first to win the Eclipse Stakes in successive years in post-war racing?**

Mtoto performed the double in 1987 and 1988, each time ridden by South African jockey Michael Roberts. Polyphontes (1924-5) had been the last horse to win the race two years running.

Q **What price was the Queen's horse, Dunfermline, when it won the Oaks?**

Dunfermline was 6-1 when Willie Carson drove her to victory in the 1977 Jubilee Oaks. Carson completed a Classic double by winning the St Leger on Dunfermline.

Q **Which horse was first past the post in the Grand National that never was?**

The 150th Grand National at Aintree on 3 April 1993 was declared void after a fiasco of false starts. Seven horses and riders carried on and completed the course oblivious to the fact that the race had been abandoned. The horses that finished were, in order: Esha Ness, Cahervillahow, Romany King, The Committee, Givus a Buck, On the Other Hand and Laura's Beau.

Q **Was it a photo-finish when Brigadier Gerard beat Mill Reef in the 1971 2,000 Guineas?**

Brigadier Gerard, with Joe Mercer on board, beat Mill Reef by three lengths and going away in the 2,000 Guineas at Newmarket. Mill Reef, ridden by Geoff Lewis, won the Derby a month later.

Q **On which course did Frankie Dettori first break the 200-winner barrier?**

Dettori became only the sixth jockey to ride 200 winners in a season with a 67-1 treble at York on 1 September 1994. He won the jockey's championship that season with 233 winners. In the exclusive '200' club he joined Fred Archer, Tommy Loates, Sir Gordon Richards, Pat Eddery and Michael Roberts.

Q **How many winners did Doug Smith ride, and how many times was he champion jockey?**

Doug Smith rode 3,111 winners between 1931 and 1967, and he was champion jockey nine times following the retirement of Sir Gordon Richards.

Q **What has been the biggest winning margin between first and second in a Classic?**
Mayonaisse, ridden by George Fordham, won the 1,000 Guineas by 20 lengths in 1859. There were four runners in the field.

Q **When was the first English Classic staged during a Sunday meeting?**
The 1,000 Guineas was run at Newmarket on Sunday, 7 May 1995. There was on-course betting and betting shops opened also for the first time on a Sunday. Harayi (5-1) won the race.

Q **How many races did the chaser Sabin du Loir win, and how old was he when he ran his last race?**
Sabin du Loir became desperately ill when turned out to grass in 1992, and he seemed at death's door. But he made a sudden recovery and recorded his twenty-first victory in his forty-first and last race in the John Bull Chase at Wincanton on 14 January 1993. Sabin du Loir was 14 years old at the close of his long-running career.

Q **Which jockey has had the longest winning streak in British racing?**
Sir Gordon Richards won 12 races in succession at the end of the 1933 season: the final race at Nottingham on 3 October, all six at Chepstow on 4 October and the first five races next day at Chepstow.

Q **What was the first Middle East-trained horse to win an English Classic?**
Balanchine, owned by Sheikh Maktoum Al Maktoum and trained by Hilal Ibrahim in the Middle East, won the Oaks in 1994. Ridden by Frankie Dettori, Balanchine won the Irish Derby three weeks later.

Q **How many times has the Triple Crown been won this century?**
Seven horses have won the 2,000 Guineas, Derby and St Leger in the same year: Diamond Jubilee (1900), Rock Sand (1903), Pommern (1915), Gay Crusader (1917), Gainsborough (1981), Bahram (1935), Nijinsky (1970).

Q **When was the Epsom Derby first shown live on television?**
The Derby was first televised in 1932, with pictures beamed back to the Metropole in Victoria. The first live television broadcast was in 1938 when Charlie Elliott brought 20-1 shot Bois Roussel through from the back of the field to win by four lengths.

Q **True or false: A horse called The Bastard was once a winner at Newmarket?**
True. The Bastard, foaled in 1926 and owned by Lord Rosebery, was a shock 100-1 winner at Newmarket before being exported to Australia where he was renamed The Buzzard. He became one of Australia's most successful sires until his retirement in 1950.

Q **How many English Classic winners did Lester Piggott ride?**
Lester set an all-time record of 30 Classic victories, starting with 33-1 outsider Never Say Die in the 1954 Derby when he was 18. It was the first of

nine victories in the Epsom Classic: Crepello (1957), St Paddy (1960), Sir Ivor (1968), Nijinsky (1970), Roberto (1972), Empery (1976), The Minstrel (1977), Teenoso (1983).

He won the St Leger eight times: St Paddy (1960), Aurelius (1961), Ribocco (1967), Ribero (1968), Nijinsky (1970), Athens Wood (1971), Boucher, (1972), Commanche Run (1984).

His six winners in the Oaks: Carrozza (1957), Petite Etoile (1959), Valoris (1966), Juliette Marny (1975), Blue Wind (1981), Circus Plume (1984).

His five winners in the 2,000 Guineas: Crepello (1957), Sir Ivor (1968), Nijinsky (1970), Shadeed (1985), Rodrigo de Triano (1992).

In the 1,000 Guineas, his two winners were Humble Duty (1970) and Fairy Footsteps (1981).

Lester Piggott

The previous record of 27 Classic winners was set by Frank Buckle back in the nineteenth century.

Q **Was Lester Piggott ever thrown by his horse during a Classic race?**

Not during a Classic, but once before the start and once after the finish. Durtal, the favourite, threw him as he cantered down for the start of the 1977 Oaks. She bolted and dragged Piggott along at racing speed with one foot caught in an iron. His foot was finally released when Durtal collided with a rail and was withdrawn from the race. Piggott was also thrown by Gay Time after passing the post in second place in the 1952 Derby when he was just 16. Gay Time bolted and Piggott returned to the unsaddling enclosure minus his saddle and horse, and he was ordered by the stewards to weigh in as he was. Piggott was delayed so long that he was too late to go ahead with a planned protest against the winner, Tulyar, who he claimed had interfered with his run for the line. Lester also suffered bad falls in the 1992 Breeders' Cup Classic in Florida and in a 1994 meeting at Goodwood.

Q **How many Derby and Grand National winners did Vincent O'Brien train?**

Known as the Master of Ballydoyle, O'Brien trained six Epsom Derby winners and three Grand National winners in three successive years. He won a total of 44 European Classics, as well as the Prix de l'Arc de Triomphe three times. Before switching to the flat, he also captured four Gold Cups and three Champion Hurdles. Among the great horses he trained were Nijinksy, Sir Ivor and Cottage Rake.

Q **Who was the first woman to saddle a Grand National winner at Aintree?**
Jenny Pitman is the First Lady of Aintree. She saddled Grand National winner Corbiere at Aintree in 1983, and was leading in the winner again 12 years later when Royal Athlete was first past the post.

Q **Has the great National Hunt trainer Martin Pipe had any winners on the flat?**
Pipe, best known for his phenomenal success with jumpers, had his most productive season on the flat in 1983 with 12 winners. He has won the Ascot Stakes with Right Regent and the Windsor Castle Stakes with Atall Atall.

Q **Who was the first woman to ride a winner at Royal Ascot?**
Gay Kelleway won the Queen Alexandra Stakes on Sprowston Boy at Royal Ascot on 19 June 1987.

Q **What were the horses that Michael Dickinson saddled in the first five places in the Gold Cup?**
The horses trained by Dickinson that finished 1-2-3-4-5 in the 1983 Cheltenham Gold Cup were Bregawn, Captain John, Wayward Lad, Silver Buck and Ashley House.

Q **Who rode Silver Buck to a hat-trick of victories in the King George VI Chase?**
It was Tommy Carmody who achieved the unprecedented feat of winning the King George VI Chase three years in succession, but only the second two were aboard Silver Buck. He started the sequence on another Michael Dickinson trained horse, Gay Spartan.

Q **What was the jumping record that made Arkle a legend in the world of steeplechasing?**
Arkle (1957-70) won three Cheltenham Gold Cups and had at least one success in all of the major steeplechase races apart from the Grand National. He finished first in 26 races over the jumps and won what was then National Hunt record prize money of £74,920.

Q **How old was Steve Cauthen when he won the Kentucky Derby on Affirmed?**
'Wonder Kid' Cauthen was 18 when he won the 1978 Kentucky Derby on Affirmed, which went on to become the eleventh horse to complete the American Triple Crown. Affirmed was the first horse to win more than $2,000,000.

Q **What was Fred Archer's racing record, and how old was he when he died?**
The legendary Fred Archer rode 2,748 winners from 8,048 mounts, including 21 Classic victories (six St Legers, five Derbys, four Oaks, four 2,000 Guineas and two 1,000 Guineas). He was champion jockey 13 times in succession, exceeding 200 winners in five consecutive seasons.

Depressed by the death of his wife and child and weak from weight reducing, Archer committed suicide in 1886 at the age of 29 and while reigning champion.

Q **At which fence was there mayhem in the 1967 Grand National when Foinavon went on to win?**
The monumental pile-up was at the twenty-third fence, one after Becher's. Foinavon picked his way through horses falling all around him and went on to land a stunning 100-1 victory. Only 18 of the 44 starters finished the course, most of them going out at the twenty-third fence.

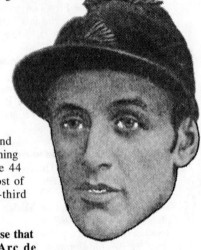

Fred Archer

Q **What was the name of the horse that beat Sir Ivor in the 1968 Arc de Triomphe?**
The race was won by Vaguely Noble, ridden by Willie Williamson. Lester Piggott was second three lengths away on English Derby winner Sir Ivor.

Q **How did the idolized jumper Desert Orchid get his name, and how much prize money did he win?**
Desert Orchid was out of Grey Mirage and Flower Child. His 34 wins from 72 races between 1983 and 1991 netted a record £654,413.

Q **With which horses did Fulke Walwyn triumph in the Grand National?**
Walwyn, who was considered one of the greatest amateur riders of the century, won the Grand National on Reynoldstown in 1936. He fractured his skull in a fall two years later and had to give up riding. The Welshman switched to training, and won the 1964 National with Team Spirit.

Q **Was Lammtarra making his racing debut when he won the Epsom Derby in 1995?**
Lammtarra had raced once before, winning the Washington Singer Stakes over seven furlongs at Newbury 302 days before the Epsom Derby. Walter Swinburn steered Lammtarra to victory, making up six lengths in the last furlong and a half to win his third Derby by a length. His previous triumphs were on Shergar (1981) and Shahrastani (1986).

RUGBY UNION

Q **Who has scored most points during a first-class Rugby Union career?**
England international full-back Dusty Hare, a farmer when he was not playing rugby, amassed 7,337 points in an 18-year career that started in 1989. He was the number one kicker for Nottingham (1,800 pts) and Leicester (4,427 pts). He also scored 240 points in 25 matches for England between 1974 and 1984, another 88 points for the British Lions and 782 in other representative matches.

Q **What has been the fastest try scored in international rugby?**
H. L. (Bart) Price, of Oxford University, Leicester and, later, Harlequins, touched down inside ten seconds of England's match against Wales at Twickenham on 20 January 1923.

Q **Who has played most Test matches for the British Lions?**
Willie John McBride played 17 Tests for the British Lions as well as 63 matches for Ireland. He skippered the Lions team that beat the Springboks 3-0 with one Test drawn in the 1974 tour of South Africa. This was his fifth Lions tour, and he later managed the Lions on their 1983 tour to New Zealand. He has also coached the Irish team following a playing career in which he was one of the most respected forwards in the game.

Q **Did Serge Blanco win all his international caps as a full-back?**
Blanco won 81 of his international caps as a full back, with another 12 appearances coming on the wing. He made his debut on the right wing and scored the first of his 38 tries in the Five Nations match against Scotland in Paris on 17 January 1981.

Q **Is it correct that the great Serge Blanco was not French by birth?**
Blanco was born in Caracas, Venezuela, on 31 August 1958. He grew up in France, and played all his club rugby with Biarritz.

Q **What was the time of Jonah Lomu's first try against England in the 1995 World Cup?**
The phenomenal New Zealand wing scored after just 60 seconds in the semi-final played in Cape Town on 18 June 1995. He gathered a bouncing ball and powered through the tackles of Tony Underwood, Will Carling and Mike Catt for the first of his four tries in the 45-29 crushing of England.

Q How many caps did Gerald Davies win in the centre for Wales?
Davies, one of the most exciting backs of all time, won 35 caps on the wing for Wales and 11 at centre. He scored a record-equalling 20 tries for Wales and another three for the British Lions.

Q Which England wing of the 1950s was known as the Old Dancing Master?
Peter Jackson, who used to side-step defences to death. He played for Old Edwardians and then Coventry, and in 20 matches for England scored six tries. He is best remembered for his spectacular last-gasp try that beat Australia at Twickenham in 1958.

Q Did Andy Irvine play any games on the wing for the British Lions?
Andy Irvine toured three times with the British Lions. He played twice on the wing in South Africa in 1974, and was at full back in four Tests in New Zealand in 1977 and in three matches against South Africa in 1980. He also played four times on the wing in his 51 appearances for Scotland.

Q Was Colin Meads ever sent off while playing for the All Blacks?
Meads, a magnificent lock forward capped 55 times by New Zealand, was sent off against Scotland at Murrayfield in 1967.

Q Where were the Underwood brothers, Rory and Tony, born?
Rory was born in Middlesbrough, Yorkshire, on 19 June 1963. Tony was born in Ipoh, Malaysia, on 17 February 1969.

Q How many times was Gareth Edwards capped by Wales?
Edwards made a record 53 consecutive inter- national appearances from winning his first cap for Wales against France in 1967 when he was 19. He bowed out in 1978 after a final match against France without having missed a single match over a span of 11 years. At 20 years and seven months he was the youngest ever player to captain Wales.

Gareth Edwards

Q What is the highest number of points scored by a club side during a season?
Welsh club Neath scored 345 tries on the way to accumulating 1,917 points in just 47 games in 1988-9 (an average of 40·78 points a match).

Q **Did England fly-half Rob Andrew ever play for an overseas club?**
Andrew spent part of the 1991-2 season with Toulouse in France. In England, he played for Cambridge University, Nottingham and Wasps before taking goals to Newcastle as director of Rugby.

Q **Who has scored the longest international drop-kick goal on record?**
The record was set by South African Gerry Brand against England at Twickenham on 2 January 1932. His successful drop kick from inside his own half was measured at 90 yards (82 metres).

Q **When were the first Middlesex Sevens staged and who were the first winners?**
Harlequins beat St Mary's Hospital 25-3 in the first Middlesex Sevens final in 1926. There were six internationals in the all-star Quins line-up: J. C. Gibbs, R. H. Hamilton-Wickes, V. G. Davies, J. R..B. Worton, J. S.. Chick, W. F. Browne and W. W. (Wavell) Wakefield, who later became a Tory MP and president of the RFU and, in 1963, first Baron Wakefield of Kendal.

Q **With which club was Bill Beaumont playing when he captained England?**
Beaumont joined Fydle from Ellesmere College and played all his 34 matches for England (21 as captain) while with the Lancashire Club. He led England to their first Grand Slam for 23 years (1980), and in the same year captained the British Lions in South Africa.

Q **True or false: The United States have won an Olympic Rugby Union gold medal?**
The United States rugby union team won not one, but two Olympic gold medals. They beat France in both the finals of 1920 and 1924.

Q **What is the greatest number of tries scored by any player in a representative match?**
Russian-born Prince Alexander Obolensky set the record on 31 August 1936 when he scored 17 tries for the touring British team against a Brazilian XV at Niteroi. The final score was 82-0. Earlier in the year 'Obo' had scored his two classic tries against New Zealand at Twickenham.

Q **When was the first international rugby union match televised?**
The first international covered by BBC cameras was on 19 March 1938. The handful of viewers saw Scotland run in five tries on the way to a 21-16 victory over England at Twickenham to clinch the Triple Crown.

Q **In which international match did Pontypool first field five forwards in the Wales pack?**
The famous 'Pontypool Five' were Staff Jones, Jeff Squire, Eddie Butler, John Perkins and Graham Price. They first played together in the same Wales pack in the 23-9 victory over Ireland at Cardiff Arms Park on 5 March 1983.

Q **What was Ollie Campbell's kicking record with Ireland?**
Campbell scored 217 points in 22 matches for Ireland (1976-84), and his 52 points in the 1983 championship season was then a Five Nations record. His dropped goal and six penalties for 21 points against Scotland in 1982 was then an individual Irish record. He was also top scorer on two tours with the British Lions in South Africa (1980) and New Zealand (1983).

Q **What has been the highest official attendance for an international Rugby Union match?**
A crowd of 104,000 gathered to watch Scotland beat Wales 12-10 at Murrayfield on 1 March 1975. It was the only defeat of the season for Wales.

Q **In what positions did Mike Gibson win his international caps?**
Gibson won 69 caps for Ireland (1964-79), 25 at fly-half, four on the wing and 40 at centre. He was capped 12 times by the British Lions.

Q **What was the highest number of points scored in a single international match by Phil Bennett?**
Bennett accumulated 34 points (2 tries, 10 conversions and 2 penalty goals) for Wales against Japan in Tokyo on 24 September 1975. Wales won 82-6.

Q **Which country has scored most points in an official international match?**
New Zealand beat Japan 145-17 in the World Cup in Bloemfontein on 4 June 1995. They ran in 21 tries, 20 of which were converted by Simon Culhane.

Q **What were the highest number of points scored by Rob Andrew in any match for England?**
Andrew compiled a record 27 points for England in the first Test against South Africa in Pretoria on 4 June 1994. He scored five penalties, two conversions, a drop goal and a try in England's 32-15 victory.

Q **How many times did Barry John partner Gareth Edwards in Welsh internationals?**
'King' John partnered Gareth Edwards in all but two of his 25 games for Wales. They also played together five times for the British Lions.

Q **What has been the longest penalty kick landed in a Five Nations match?**
Paul Thorburn scored from 70 yards for Wales against Scotland at Cardiff on 1 February 1986.

RUGBY LEAGUE

Q **What exactly is the Lance Todd Award and who is it named after?**
The Lance Todd Award is decided by a panel of writers and is presented to the man of the match in the Challenge Cup Final. The trophy is named after Lance Todd, a former New Zeland international who played for Wigan and later managed Salford. It was instituted in 1946.

Q **Has the Rugby League Challenge Cup Final ever been staged over two legs?**
For three years during the war the final was held over two legs, with the winner decided on aggregate. The two-leg winners were Dewsbury (16-15 v Leeds, 1943), Bradford Northern (8-3 v Wigan, 1944), Huddersfield (13-9 v Bradford Northern, 1945).

Q **With which League club did Ellery Hanley start his professional career?**
Hanley was signed by Bradford Northern from his Leeds amateur club in 1978 when he was 17. It was three years before he made his Division 1 debut to launch one of the greatest of all careers.

Q **What code of rugby did Shaun Edwards play while he was at school?**
Edwards played both codes, and captained England schoolboys at both Rugby Union and Rugby League. He signed professional on his seventeenth birthday on 17 October 1983, and just 201 days later became the youngest ever player to appear in a Challenge Cup Final when appearing for Wigan against Widnes.

Q **What is the most Rugby League games in succession in which an individual player has scored points?**
David Watkins set the record with Salford when he scored in 82 consecutive games between August 1972 and April 1974.

Q **What was Jim Sullivan's kicking record during his Rugby League career?**
Sullivan was arguably the greatest goal kicker of all time and in any code. In a 25-year career between 1921 and 1946 he kicked 2,867 goals and scored 6,192 points. He joined Wigan from Cardiff rugby union club at the

age of 17 and played a record 921 games for them, mostly at full back. Sullivan's points haul included 160 goals and 329 points in 60 international games, 25 of which were for Great Britain. He kicked 246 during three tours to Australia.

Jim Sullivan

Q **With which Rugby Union club was Martin Offiah playing before making the switch to the League?**
Offiah was was signed by Widnes from Rosslyn Park in 1987, and joined Wigan for a then record £400,000 after being top try scorer with Widnes in his first four seasons of League rugby.

Q **For which clubs did Neil Fox play, and how many points did he score in total?**
Fox amassed 6,220 points (2,575 goals, 358 tries, 4 drop goals) between 1956 and 1978 while playing for Wakefield Trinity, Bradford Northern, Hull Kingston Rovers, York, Bramley and Huddersfield.

Q **Where was Brian Bevan born and for which Rugby League clubs did he play?**
Bevan, who served as a stoker in the Australian Navy during the war, was born in Sydney on 24 June 1924. He started his Rugby League career with Warrington and his jet-paced runs down the wing belied his weak-looking, spindly-legged appearance. Bevan scored a record 796 tries, winding down his career with Blackpool Borough in 1964.

Q **How many times was Andy Gregory on the winning side in the Challenge Cup Final?**
Seven times, twice with Widnes (1981 and 1984) and five times with Wigan Athletic (1988-92). He was only on the losing side once with Widnes – in the 1982 Final.

Q **Did Billy Boston play for any Rugby League club other than Wigan?**
Cardiff-born Boston, discovered while playing rugby in the army as a National Serviceman, played for Blackpool Borough after scoring 482 tries for Wigan. His career total was 560 tries and he was capped 31 times by Great Britain.

Q **Has Joe Lydon ever played Rugby League for an overseas club?**
Lydon, a Challenge Cup winner with both Widnes and Wigan, played for Eastern Suburbs in Sydney for a season in 1987.

Q **What was Alex Murphy's record in the Challenge Cup Final?**
Alex Murphy, one of the quickest scrum-halves ever to play Rugby League, appeared in four winning FA Challenge Cup Finals for three different teams: St Helens (1961 and 1966), Leigh (1971) and Warrington (1974). He was player-coach for three of the finals, and then as a full-time coach steered Warrington (1975), Wigan Athletic (1984) and St Helens (1987 and 1989) to the final.

Q **Which player has scored most tries in a single Rugby League match?**
George West ran in 11 tries for Hull Kingston Rovers against Brookland Rovers in a Challenge Cup tie on 4 March 1905.

Q **What is the biggest win recorded in a British Rugby League match?**
Huddersfield beat Blackpool Gladiators 142-4 in a Regal Trophy first-round tie on 26 November 1994.

Q **How many Welsh Rugby Union caps did Lewis Jones win before becoming a League player?**
Jones had won 10 caps with Wales and two with the British Lions when he signed for Leeds in 1952. He set a record of 496 points in a season in 1956-7 (194 goals and 36 tries).

Q **What is the longest drop kick on record in British Rugby League?**
It was dropped from 61 yards (56 m) by Joe Lydon for Wigan against Warrington in a Challenge Cup semi-final at Maine Road on 25 March 1989.

Q **Which Rugby League footballer has played most games in succession?**
Widnes hooker Keith Elwell set the record when he played 239 consecutive games between May 1977 and September 1982.

Q **What is the biggest attendance for any Rugby League match?**
The Warrington-Halifax Challenge Cup Final replay at Odsal Stadium, Bradford, on 5 May 1954 attracted a crowd of 102, 569.

Q **Who has been the youngest Great Britain Rugby League international?**
Paul Newlove was aged 18 years 72 days when he made his debut for Great Britain against New Zealand at Old Trafford on 21 October 1989.

GOLF

Q **How many major championships has Jack Nicklaus won during his career?**
Since winning the US Amateur title twice (1959-61), Nicklaus has since added these 'major Majors': US Open 1962, 1967, 1972, 1980; US Masters 1963, 1965-6, 1972, 1975, 1986; British Open 1966, 1970, 1978; US PGA 1963, 1971, 1973, 1975, 1980; World Matchplay 1970.

Q **Which golfer has had most victories in the British Open?**
Harry Vardon, the man who gave the game of golf the 'Vardon Grip', won the title six times: 1896, 1898-9, 1903, 1911, 1914.

Q **Has any golfer won the US and British Open titles and US and British amateur titles in the same year?**
The legendary Bobby Jones achieved this unique Grand Slam in 1930. The US media labelled it 'The Impregnable Quadrilateral'.

Q **In which tournament did Brian Barnes once record a 15 for a single hole?**
Barnes put his third shot within four feet of the hole on the short, par-three eighth in the French Open at St Cloud in 1968. He finished with a 15 after a nightmare series of snatched putts plus penalty shots for standing astride the line of a putt.

Q **How many holes did Gary Player pull back when he beat Tony Lema in the World Matchplay final?**
It was not the final, but Player eliminated Lema after trailing by seven holes with seventeen to play at Wentworth in 1965. He squared the match at the thirty-sixth and won it at the thirty-seventh. Player beat Peter Thomson in the final.

Q **Who sank the first hole-in-one screened on 'live' television?**
Tony Jacklin performed the first hole-in-one on television when he aced at the sixteenth at Royal St George's, Sandwich, on his way to a round of 64 and victory in the 1967 Dunlop Masters. Jacklin was bang on target again in the 1978 German Open when his hole-in-one won him a Mercedes sports car.

Q **How old was Gene Sarazen when he achieved a hole-in-one in the British Open?**

Sarazen, a winner of the British Open in 1932, scored a hole-in-one at the age of 71 when competing in the 1973 Open at Royal Troon. He aced with his 5 iron at the 'Postage Stamp' eighth on the first day. At the same hole on the second day he played out of a bunker and holed his second shot. So he had found the hole twice in successive days without need of his putter. This at last wiped out the nightmare memory of his visit to the same course 50 years earlier when he struggled to an 85 and failed to qualify in his first challenge for the Open title.

Q **Who was the first left hander to win the British Open golf championship?**

Bob Charles became the first (and, to date only) left hander to win the British Open when he beat American Phil Rodgers 140-148 in a 36-hole play-off after they had tied on 277 at Royal Lytham and St Anne's in 1963. It was the last play-off decided over 36 holes. Charles was also the first New Zealander to win the Open. He won the title with his putter, averaging just 30 putts a round.

Q **Which golfer used to be nicknamed 'The Walking One Iron?'**

It was a label that was hung on pencil-slim former Ryder Cup player Ken Brown, who is now a course commentator with Sky Sports.

Q **How many times did Sam Snead win the US Open championship?**

It was the one major championship that eluded Slammin' Sam during his distinguished career. He was a runner-up four times. His best chance of winning came in 1939 when he stood on the final tee needing just a six or better to win. Wrong information was fed to Snead, and he was under the impression that he needed a par-five. He went for prodigious recovery shots when he got himself in trouble on the fairway and finished with a disastrous eight.

Q **How old was Nick Faldo when he competed in his first Ryder Cup?**

Faldo was, at 20, the youngest ever Ryder Cup competitor when he was selected for the 1977 team at Royal Lytham when it was the United States v Great Britain and Ireland. He partnered Peter Oosterhuis to beat Ray Floyd and Lou Graham on the first day, and then they caused the shock of the tournament on the second day when they beat the all-star pairing of Jack Nicklaus and Ray Floyd. To cap it all, Faldo had a one-hole victory over Tom Watson on the final day in a match otherwise dominated by the Americans.

Q **Is there a record of the longest drive in an official tournament?**

Californian Mike Austin, aided by a following wind of 35 mph, drove the ball 515 yards (471 metres) in the 1974 US National Seniors Open in Las Vegas. The ball rolled 65 yards (59 metres) past the hole on the par-4 450 yard (59 metres) fifth hole. Austin, 64, drove the ball to within a yard of the green before it started rolling.

Q **What has been the greatest margin of victory in a major golf tournament?**
American Jerry Pate won the Colombian Open by 21 strokes when he shot 262 in the four-round tournament in December 1981.

Q **Is the Royal and Ancient the oldest golf club in the world?**
The oldest club on record is the Gentlemen Golfers, later re-named the Honourable Company of Edinburgh Golfers. It was formed in March 1744, ten years ahead of the Royal and Ancient Club at St Andrews. The first game of golf played over the famous St Andrews links in Fife was on 14 May 1744. It is a contentious issue as to which is the oldest club because the Burgess Golfing Society of Edinburgh claims to have been founded nine years before even the Gentlemen Golfers.

Q **Which golfer has scored most tournament wins in a single year?**
Byron Nelson finished first in 19 of the 30 tournaments that he entered in 1945. He came second in 11 of the other competitions, and averaged 68·33 strokes per round. 'Mr Consistency' was never out of the money in an astonishing run of 111 successive tournaments.

Q **Who has won most professional tournaments during a full careeer?**
In 40 years from 1934, Slammin' Sam Snead registered 164 victories, including a record 84 official USPGA tournament titles. He registered top 10 finishes in the US Open, Masters and PGA while in his mid-50s and, aged 67, he became the first player ever to beat his age in an official PGA event. Born in Hot Springs, Virginia, on 27 May 1912, he recorded 24 holes-in-one.

Sam Snead

Q **Who handed the US Masters jacket to Bernhard Langer when he first won the title?**
Ben Crenshaw was the previous Master who carried out the tradition of handing over the Green Jacket to Langer when he won the US Masters in 1985. He won it for a second time in 1993, with Fred Couples doing the honours.

Q **What is the lowest score for 18 holes in an official tournament?**
Al Geiberger carded a 59 in the second round of the Danny Thomas Classic on the Colonial golf course, Memphis, on 10 June 1977. He started on the tenth tee and reached the turn in 30, coming back in 29. He had six pars, 11 birdies and an eagle. Geiberger, who was 39, sank an eight-foot putt on the final green to break the '60' barrier. Chip Beck repeated the

feat in the third round of the Las Vegas invitational in 1991. Sam Snead (West Virginia1959), Gary Player (Brazilian Open in Rio 1974), David Jagger (Nigerian Open in Lagos 1973) and Miguel Martin (Mar de Plata, Argentine, 1987) are among other players who have recorded a 59 in official tournaments. There have been a handful of 58s recorded, but not in premier tournaments. British golfer Alf Smith scored a 55 in 1936 (29 out, and 26 in) but not in tournament play.

Q **Has any British golfer been under '60' in an official tournament in Britain?**
The nearest has been by Paul Curry, who registered a 60 in the second round of the Bell's Scottish Open at Gleneagles on 9 July 1992. He scored 30 on both the outward and inward halves.

Q **Who partnered Ian Woosnam when Wales won the World Cup?**
David Llwellyn was Woosnam's partner when Wales won the title in 1987. They had an aggregate score of 574, and Woosnam (274) had the lowest individual score.

Q **Where is the longest golf hole in the world, and what is the par score?**
It is reckoned to be the par-seven sixth hole on the Koolan Island golf course in Western Australia which, from tee to flag, stretches 950 yards (868 metres).

Q **Was Severiano Ballesteros the first non-British European to win the Open?**
He was the second (1979) after Frenchman Arnaud Massy, who was the first overseas winner of the British Open in 1907, beating a then record field of 192 rivals at Hoylake where gale-forced winds wrecked the cards of many of the favourites.

Q **How old was Severiano Ballesteros when he won the British Open for the first time?**
Seve was 22 when he won his first Open title at Royal Lytham in 1979. He equalled the course record with a 65 in the second round, and in the final two rounds made a staggering series of recovery shots after continually missing the fairway with his unpredictable drives. Jack Nicklaus and Ben Crenshaw were equal second, three shots behind Seve's total of 282.

Q **Which golfer has had most tournament wins in a season on the European circuit?**
The record of seven wins was set by Australian Norman von Nida in 1947, and equalled by Belgian Flory Van Donck in 1953.

Q **Did any major championship elude the great Arnold Palmer?**
The one major that was always out of his reach was the US PGA championship in which he finished runner-up three times. He won seven majors: US Open (1960), the Open (1961, 1962), US Masters (1958, 1960, 1962, 1964), plus the US Amateur (1954).

Q **Who has won most tournaments on the European circuit?**
Seve Ballesteros clocked up a record 51 victories in the European Order of
Merit tournaments in a career that started in 1974. His first major victory
was the Dutch Open in 1976 when he was 19.

Q **What has been the lowest aggregate score in the US Masters?**
Jack Nicklaus (67, 71, 64, 69 in 1965) and Ray Floyd (65, 66, 70, 70 in
1986) share the record at 271.

Q **Who was the first non-American winner of the Grand Slam?**
Gary Player became the third winner of the Grand Slam (Open, US Open,
Masters and the US PGA) when he won the US Open in 1965. Americans
Ben Hogan and Gene Sarazen were the first two to win all four majors.
Player's honours haul before he started mopping up on the Senior circuit
was three Open titles, the US Masters, the US Open (first overseas player
to win it for 45 years) and the US PGA title twice. He also captured 11
South African Open titles, seven Australian Opens and five World
Matchplay championships.

Q **Which former Ryder Cup golfer was known as 'The Toy Bulldog'?**
Welshman Brian Huggett was fittingly dubbed 'The Toy Bulldog' because
of his determined spirit and great strength of character. He twice battled
into the top three in the British Open (1962 and 1965) and won the
German, Dutch and Portuguese Open titles.

Q **Where and when was Peter Alliss born, and what did he achieve as a
player?**
Alliss, the Voice of Golf, was born in Berlin on 28 February 1931. His
father, Percy, was the club professional in Berlin and one of Europe's
leading players. Percy had a superb swing that Peter inherited, and he was
widely recognized as one of the finest strikers of a golf ball in the world.
He won 20 premier titles in Europe between 1954 and 1969, including the
Italian, Spanish and Portuguese Opens in three successive weeks in 1958.

Q **Who was the first overseas winner of the US Masters tournament?**
South African Gary Player (280) was the first non-USA winner in 1961.

Q **How many times did Henry Cotton win the British Open?**
Three times. Cotton won in 1934 (Sandwich), 1937 (Carnoustie) and
Muirfield (1948). His 1937 victory was exceptional in that the entire US
Ryder Cup team entered.

Q **Was former golfing master Bobby Locke Irish by birth?**
Locke was the son of a Belfastman, but was born in Germiston, Transvaal,
South Africa on 20 November 1917. His achievements included four
British Open titles and 14 victories on the American circuit.

Q **Did Arnold Palmer ever lose a seven shot-lead in a major championship?**
Palmer was leading Billy Casper by seven shots with nine holes to play in

the 1966 US Open. Casper clawed his way back to tie and force a play-off. Palmer was winning by four shots, but Casper – rated one of the greatest putters on the tour – again battled back to take the title.

Q   **What is the lowest 72-hole aggregate in an official tournament?**
Britain's Peter Tupling shot a 29-under-par 255 in the Nigerian Open in Lagos in 1981 (63-66-62-64). Mike Souchak scored 257 in the Texas Open at San Antonio in 1955 (60-68-64-65). The European record was set by Welshman David Llewellyn in the Biarritz Open in 1988, and equalled by his countryman Ian Woosnam at the 1990 Monte Carlo Open (66-67-65-60).

Q   **Who has been the biggest money winner on the world golf tour?**
American Tom Kite was the first golfer to top $9,000,000 in prize money when he scored his nineteenth tournament victory in 1995.

Q   **Who has been the oldest winner of a premier golf championship?**
Not taking into account the recently established seniors tour, the oldest winner was Alex (Sandy) Herd, who captured the British Matchplay championship at the age of 58 in 1923. He had won the Open in 1902.

Q   **True or false: Golfing great Ben Hogan was born in Dublin?**
True, but not Dublin in Ireland. Hogan was born in Dublin, Texas, on 13 August 1912. He gained golfing immortality between 1946 and 1953 by winning the US Open title four times, the US Masters twice, the American PGA twice and the British Open at his first and only attempt in 1953 to complete the unique hat-trick of the Masters and US and British Open titles in the same year. He continued to play on through middle-age, and as late as 1967, at the age of 54, shot a record-equalling 30 on the back nine of the US Masters on his way to a third-round 66.

Q   **Which golfer was nicknamed 'The Wee Ice Mon', and why?**
This was the label hung on Ben Hogan by the admiring spectators at Carnoustie in 1953 when he won the Open by four strokes (73-71-70-68), setting a then course record on the way. What made his achievements all the more remarkable is that he was

Ben Hogan

told he would not walk again, let alone play golf, after receiving horrendous injuries in a car smash in 1949. He was portrayed by Glenn Ford in a film on his life called Follow the Sun. Hogan was voted America's Sportsman of the Decade in 1956, and in 1965 US golf writers elected him the greatest professional golfer of all time.

Q **Who was the first British golfer to hold the British and US Open titles at one and the same time?**
Tony Jacklin was the first non-American to achieve this double. He won the British Open at Royal Lytham in 1969 and the US Open (by seven shots) in 1970. Only four players had done it before: Bobby Jones, Gene Sarazen, Ben Hogan and Jack Nicklaus. He was the first home-grown British Open winner since Max Faulkner in 1951. Defending the Open title at St Andrews in 1970, he reached the turn in the first round in 29 but play was washed out by a storm. He finished fifth.

Q **Who was the first American-born winner of the British Open?**
Walter Hagen became the first American-born winner of the Open at Sandwich in 1922. A year earlier Scots-born Jock Hutchison had become the first American-based winner of the title.

Q **What did Japanese golfer Isao Aoki win for his hole-in-one at the World Matchplay championship?**
Aoki holed-in-one at the second against David Graham in the 1979 championship at Wentworth. His reward was a Bovis home at Gleneagles, then valued at £55,000. It became known as the 'home-in-one' hole.

Q **Who has had most tournament wins on the ladies golf tour?**
Kathy Whitworth, born in Monahans, Texas, in 1939, has set the pace with 88 victories. She was the first woman to break the million-dollar earnings barrier in 1981. She was Player of the Year seven times and leading money winner for a record eight years.

Q **Which golfer was the first to hold both the British and US Ladies Open titles at one and the same time?**
American Patty Sheehan was first to complete this double in 1993. She had won the British Open in 1992, winning it with 207 shots when storms forced the end of the tournament after 54 holes.

Q **Was Laura Davies the first non-American to win the US Ladies Open championship?**
No, Laura was the second overseas player to win when she triumphed in 1987. Catherine Lacoste, daughter of the great French pre-war tennis ace René Lacoste and former golf star Simone Thion de la Chaume, was the first non-American winner in 1969.

Q **What records did Colin Montgomerie set when winning the 1996 European Masters?**
Montgomerie created four European Tour records when winning the title at the Crans-sur-Sierre course in Switzerland in September 1996. His

aggregate of 260 was a record for the tournament and the lowest score on the Tour in 1996. His 124 tally for the last two rounds (61 and 63) was a Tour record, as was his 18 under par return for the final 36 holes. Montgomerie, 24 under par for the championship, beat fellow Scot Sam Torrance by four shots. Torrance, going into the third day of an incredible tournament with a six-stroke lead, shot 68 on each of the final two rounds and still had to surrender the title to Montgomerie. It was the highlight of a year in which he topped the European Order of Merit for a fourth successive year.

Q **Is Tiger Woods called 'Tiger' because he always used the tiger tees as a youngster?**
The name given to him at birth by his Thai-born mother was Eldrick, but he was called Tiger by his father from toddlerhood. This was in tribute to a Vietnamese soldier called Nguyen 'Tiger' Phong. He had saved the life of Tiger's father when they fought together with the Green Berets against the Vietcong.

ATHLETICS

Q **Did Carl Lewis finish first in three successive World Championship finals in the 100 metres?**

No, but he did record a hat-trick of victories! Lewis won in 10·03 s in 1983, finished second to Ben Johnson in 1987 in 9·93 s, and was first in 9·86 s in 1991. Johnson, first across the line in a world record 9·83 s in 1987, was later stripped of the title by the IAAF following his admission of drug taking. Lewis was installed as champion. Johnson also beat Lewis in another new record 9·79 s in the 1988 Seoul Olympics, but was disqualified after his positive drugs test. Lewis, second in 9·92 s, was awarded the gold medal.

Q **On which track did Roger Bannister first break the four-minute mile barrier?**

The Oxford University cinder track at Iffley Road, Oxford (3 m 59·4 s on 6 May 1954). It had been a clockwise running track when Bannister arrived at Oxford, but when he took over as president of the athletics union one of his first priorities was to turn it into an orthodox counter-clockwise track.

Q **When did Sally Gunnell run her first 400 metres hurdles race?**

Sally clocked 59·9 s in her first competitive 400m hurdles race in 1987. She had specialised in the sprint hurdles event until 1988 (after starting off as a long jumper and winning the WAAA junior title in 1980). From beating the one-minute barrier by just a tenth of a secon in 1987 she progressed to a world record 52·74 s in 1993.

Q **True or false: Olympic decathlon champion Dan O'Brien was born in Finland?**

O'Brien was born in Portland, Oregon, on 18 July 1966. His mother was Finnish, his father a black Afro-American. He was adopted at the age of two by an Oregon couple.

Q **Where and when did Sebastian Coe set his long-standing 800 metres world record?**

Coe was Britain's most complete middle-distance runner, and had 12 world records to prove it: nine outdoor and three indoor. His 800 metres record, virtually a solo run, was on the Firenze track in Florence on 10 June 1981. The photo-electric-cell timing device stopped the clock at a remarkable 1m 41·73 s, a time that has withstood hundreds of challenges. The following month in Oslo, on 21 July, he clocked a world record 2 m 12·18 s for 1,000 metres, which has also stood the test of time. Coe, who became an MP in 1992, took his wife to Florence in 1996 to show her where he had set his 800 metres record, only to find the stadium was now a supermarket!

Q **Who has had the fastest mile and 1500 metres times out of Steve Ovett, Sebastian Coe and Steve Cram?**
Steve Cram wins this battle of the clock. His fastest times: mile (3 m 46·32 s), 1500 m (3 m 29·67 s). Coe: mile (3 m 47·33 s), 1500 m (3 m 29·77 s). Ovett: mile (3 m 48·40 s), 1500 m (3 m 31·36 s).

Q **When did the women's pentathlon become the heptathlon?**
The pentathlon was the standard competition until 1980-81. The heptathlon events are: 100 metres hurdles, high jump, shot, 200 metres, long jump, javelin, 800 metres.

Q **When was the first London Marathon staged, and who won it?**
The London Marathon, inspired by 1956 Olympic steeplechase gold medallist Chris Brasher, was first run on 21 March 1981. The result was a dead heat between American Dick Beardsley and Norwegian Inge Simonsen in 2 hr 11 m 48 s. Britain's Joyce Smith won the women's event in 2 h 29 m 43 s. There was a field of 7,055 starters of which 6,418 finished. By the mid-1990s the entry was regularly over 25,000.

Sebastian Coe

Q **Has a British runner ever won the New York Marathon?**
Steve Jones was the men's winner in 1988 (2 h 08 m 20 s), and Priscilla Welch (2 h 30 m 17 s, in 1987) and Liz McColgan (2 h 27 m 32 s, in 1991) have won the women's event.

Q **What have been the greatest number of world records by an athlete in a single day?**
Jesse Owens set six world records in a single day at Ann Arbor, Michigan, on 25 May 1935 in a track meet billed as the Big Ten Championships. In fact, he set them within a single hour during a blitz that triggered six world records in four events. He had considered pulling out of the meeting because of a back pain, but decided to go ahead after massage treatment. His record breaking spree: 100 yards in 9·4 s (3.15 p. m.), long jump of 8·13 m, 26 ft 8·25 in (3.25 p. m.), 220 yards in 22·6 s, also a record at 200 m (3·45 p. m.), 220 yards hurdles in 22·6 s, also a record at 200 m (4.00 p. m). The long jump record was the first time the eight metre barrier had been broken, and it survived in the record books until Ralph Boston's 8·21 m leap in 1960.

Q **Did Ann Packer set a world record when winning the 800 metres Olympic gold medal?**
Ann, a silver medallist in her speciality event of the 400 metres in the 1964 Tokyo Olmpics, won the 800 metres in a then world record 2 m 1·1 s.

Q **How old was Mary Decker when she first competed in international athletics?**
Mary Decker (now Mary Slaney after marriage to British discus thrower Richard Slaney) was at 14 years 224 days, the youngest ever US international, when she ran the indoor mile for the USA against the USSR in 1973. In the same year she won the 800 metres against the Soviets. It was the start of a long running career in which she set 22 US records at distances from 800 metres to 10,000 metres despite a succession of injury problems.

Q **Did Jonathan Edwards compete in the 1991 World Championships?**
No. He is a committed Christian, and missed the championships because the final was on a Sunday. He has since come to terms with competing on the Sabbath. Kenny Harrison won the 1991 World Championship final, and he beat Edwards to the gold medal in the 1996 Olympics in Atlanta.

Q **Who was the first man to throw the javelin more than 90 metres in competition?**
Germany's Klaus Wolfermann threw the javelin 94·08 m on 5 May 1973, and when on 20 July 1984 East German Uwe Hohn reached 104·80 m it was decided that for safety reasons the specifications had to be changed. Steve Backley reached 90·98 m with a new javelin on 20 July 1990 but its roughened surface brought a quick withdrawal and Backley's previous throw of 89·58 m was recognised as the new world record. It was Backley who was first through the 90 m barrier with the newly accepted javelin in New Zealand on 25 January 1992 when he reached a distance of 91·46 m. Czech Jan Zelezny then became the undisputed master with a procession of throws over 95 m.

Q **True or false: Linford Christie was born in St Andrews, Scotland?**
Christie was born in St Andrews – Jamaica not Scotland. He came to England as a boy and began his athletics career with Thames Valley Harriers.

Q **Which long-distance runner had the nickname 'Puff Puff'?**
Gordon Pirie was known as 'Puff Puff' because of the way he used to blow out his cheeks while running. He puffed through more miles than almost any other runner in history, setting 24 British records at distances from 2,000 metres to 10,000 metres. His peak years were between 1953 and 1955 when he set eight world records.

Q **True or false: Entertainer Bobby Davro's father was a champion miler?**
True. His name is Bill Nankeville, and he won the AAA mile title four

time in five years between 1948 and 1952. It was Roger Bannister who interrupted the run of success in 1951. Nankeville competed for the Old Woking Athletic Club in Surrey before switching to Walton. He finished sixth in the 1948 Olympic 1500 metre final. His son, Robert Nankeville, decided that he needed to change his name when going into show business because he wanted it to fit on the theatre bills!

Q **Which four sprinters repre
sented the USA when they
broke the world 4 x 100
metre relay in Barcelona?**
The quartet who scorched
round the track in 37·40 s in
the 1992 Barcelona Olympics:
Mike Marsh, Leroy Burrell,
Floyd Heard and Carl Lewis.

Q **Who was the first British athlete
to clear 27 feet in the long jump?**
Lynn Davies, 1964 Olympic long jump
champion, cleared exactly 27 feet (8·23
m) in Berne, Switzerland, on 30 June
1968 before coming up against Bob Beamon
in the 1968 Mexico Olympics.

Bill Nankeville

Q **Which pole vault champion was known as the 'Vaulting Vicar'?**
This was the Reverend Bob Richards, who won the Olympic gold medal in Helsinki in 1952 and again in Melbourne in 1956. He won 50 successive pole vault competitions between 1950 and 1952, and was unbeaten in outdoor meetings for three years.

Q **How long was the unbeaten sequence of hurdler Ed Moses?**
Moses was unbeaten for a record 122 400 metre hurdle races from the defeat by West German Harald Schmid in Berlin on 26 August 1977 to 4 June 1987, when his fellow American Danny Harris got the better of him in a race in Madrid. Of his victories, 107 were in finals. He won the gold medal in the 1976 Olympics in Montreal, missed the 1980 Games because of the American boycott and was Olympic champion again in Los Angeles in 1984. He lowered the world record four times.

Q **Did Harold Abrahams ever clear 25 foot in the long jump?**
Abrahams, whose 1924 Olympic 100 metres sprint victory in Paris was featured in the film Chariots of Fire, was a long jump specialist. He set four British long jump records, culminating with 24 ft 2½ in (7·38 m) in 1923. It was a record that survived for 33 years. The 25 ft (7·52 m) barrier was in his sights when he broke a leg while long jumping in May 1925. It was an injury that forced his retirement from athletics.

Q **Which athlete beat Bob Beamon's long jump world record?**
Mike Powell, Beamon's fellow American, set a new mark of 8·95 m in the

1991 World Championships in Tokyo when he ended a run of 15 successive defeats by Carl Lewis. Beamon set his phenomenal 8·90 m world record when winning the Olympic gold medal in Mexico City in 1968.

Q **Where and when was pole vaulter Sergey Bubka born, and was he ever second best to his brother?**

Bubka, the 'King of the Airways', was born on 4 December 1963 in what was then Voroshilovgrad (now Lugansk) in the Ukraine. His brother, Vasiliy, is three years older and started pole vaulting at the same time as Sergy in 1975 when he was 15 and Sergy 12. It was 1981 before Sergy regularly vaulted higher than Vasiliy, and by 1983 – the year of his first world championship victory – he had started his 10-year supremacy in the event.

Q **Who was the first man to run 100 metres in under 10 seconds?**

Bob Hayes ran the first automatically timed sub-10 second 100 metres with a clocking of 9·91 s in the 1964 Olympic semi-finals, but a following wind ruled it out as a record. He ran 10 s dead in the final. Hayes had run a hand-timed 9·9 s 18 months earlier, but this too was counted out because it was wind assisted. Jim Hines ran 9·95 s at altitude in the 1968 Mexico Games.

Q **Was Emil Zatopek making his marathon debut when he won the 1952 Olympic gold medal?**

Yes, it was his first competitive run at the distance. He was such a novice that he asked Britain's race favourite Jim Peters whether the pace was fast enough. He won in 2 h 23 m 03·2 s to complete the then unique hat-trick of victories in the 5000 metres, 10000 metres and marathon. His wife, Dana, won the Olympic javelin on the same day that he collected the 5000 metres gold medal. Zatopek, born in Koprivnice, Moravia on 19 September 1922 (the identical day to his wife), set 18 world records during his long running career and at his peak won 69 successive races.

Q **Where and when did Colin Jackson set his world 110 metres hurdles record?**

Jackson clocked his 12·91s world record in the 1993 World Championships in Stuttgart to end a run of three successive victories by Greg Foster.

Q **Did Florence Griffith-Joyner set world records at 100 metres and 200 metres in the 1988 Olympics?**

'Flo-Jo' set the 100 metre world record in the quarter-final of the US Olympic trials in Indianapolis on 16 July 1988 when she clocked an astonishing 10·49 s. Her winning time in the Olympics in Seoul two months later was a wind-assisted 10·54 s. Her two world individual records in the Olympics both came in the 200 metre, with a run of 21·56 s in the semifinal and then 21·34 s in the final. She completed a hat-trick of gold medals in the sprint relay, and added a silver with the anchor leg in the 4 x 400 metre relay final.

Q **Which long-distance runner holds the world record in the marathon?**
There are no recognised world records in the marathon because courses
and conditions differ to such an extent. The fastest time recorded for the
26 miles 385 yards is 2 h 06 m 50 s by Ethiopian Belayneh Dinsamo at
Rotterdam on 17 April 1988. The fastest by a woman is 2 h 21 m 6 s by
Norwegian Ingrid Kristiansen in the 1985 London Marathon.

Q **Was Mary Peters born in Ireland, and did she set a world record
when winning her Olympic title?**
Mary was born in Halewood, Lancashire, on 6 July 1939, and moved to
Northern Ireland with her father, a doctor. She won the Olympic pentathlon gold medal in 1972 with a world record points haul of 4,801
points, pipping German favourite Heide Rosendahl by ten points.

Q **True or false: Decathlete Daley Thompson was born in Nigeria?**
Thompson was born in Notting Hill, London, on 30 July 1958. His mother
was Scottish and his father Nigerian. It was a mix that worked wonders
because he became the world's greatest all-round athlete, winning the
Olympic title in 1980 and 1984 and setting four world records. He was
also world champion in 1983 and supreme in Europe and the
Commonwealth for eight years.

Q **How many Olympic medals did British all-rounder Mary Rand win?**
Mary Rand won a full set of Olympic medals in Tokyo in 1964 – gold in
the long jump (with a then world record 6.76m), silver in the pentathlon
and bronze in the sprint relay.

Q **When did Dick Fosbury first introduce the 'Flop' high jumping
technique?**
Dick, a graduate of Oregon State University in civil engineering, popul-
arized the 'Fosbury Flop' when winning the Olympic gold medal in the
1968 Olympics in Mexico. He had been experimenting with
it from 1963, gradually leaning further and further back
when using the orthodox scissors style of clearance.
The back-to-the-bar take-off technique saw him
improve from a best of 2·08 m to 2·24 m when winning the gold medal.

Q **Whose record did Christopher Chataway
break when winning his memorable duel with
Vladimir Kuts?**
Chataway conquered Kuts by just a stride in an
unfor-gettable 5,000 metre race under the White
City floodlights in a London v Moscow match in
October 1954. Britain's 'Red Fox' of the track beat
the Russian 'Iron Man' by a tenth of a second in 13 m
51·6 s to lower the world record of 13 m 56·6 s set by
Kuts in the European championships in Oslo two months
earlier.

Chris Chataway

Q **Which athlete was known by the nickname of 'White Lightning'?**
This was the nickname given to Cuban Alberto Juantorena during the 1976 Olympics in Montreal. He performed the unique feat of winning gold medals at both 400metres and 800 metres. Juantorena won the 800 metres in a then world record 1 m 43·50 s, and took the 400 metres gold in what was then a fastest ever time at low altitude of 44·26 s.

Q **Who was the first man to run the mile in exactly four minutes?**
Yorkshireman Derek Ibbotson was first to run a mile in exactly four minutes in 1958, four years after Roger Bannister's historic first sub-four minute mile and a year after he set a then world record of 3 m 57·2 s at London's White City Stadium.

Q **Did David Bedford break any world records during his running career?**
Bedford, one of the most popular personalities of the track in the 1970s, won five consecutive AAA 10,000 metres titles from 1970 to 1974, the highlight coming with a world record 27 m 30·8 s on 13 July 1973.

Q **Is sprinter John Regis the brother of footballer Cyrille Regis?**
They are cousins. John was born in Lewisham, London, on 13 October 1966, Cyrille in French Guyana, on 9 February 1958.

Q **Was Herb Elliott at Cambridge University when he won his Olympic gold medal?**
Elliott started studying at Cambridge in 1961, the year after his magnificent victory in the 1500 metres in the Rome Olympics in a world record 3 m 35·6 s. He retired from athletics at the age of 23, unbeaten over the 1500 metres and mile distance.

Q **Is it true that Brendan Foster broke an Olympic record but did not win an Olympic medal?**
Foster clocked an Olympic record 13 m 20·34 s in his heat of the 5,000 metres in the 1976 Olympics. He finished fifth in the final and took a bronze medal in the 10,000 metres, both races won – as in Munich in 1972 – by the Flying Finn Lasse Viren.

TENNIS

Q **How many titles did Jimmy Connors win during his career?**

Connors captured what was a men's record 109 singles titles between 1972 and 1989. The most successful season of his career came in 1974 when he was just 22, and he won the men's Wimbledon singles title (beating Ken Rosewall), the US Open (Ken Rosewall) and the Australian title (Phil Dent). He was prevented from going for the Grand Slam when he was barred from the French Open because he had not joined the Association of Tennis Professionals.

Q **Who were the first left-handed winners of the men's and women's singles titles at Wimbledon?**

Australian Norman Brookes (1907) was the first men's left-handed champion and the first overseas winner at Wimbledon. It was 1969 before Ann Jones became the first left-handed women's champion with a 3-6, 6-3, 6-2 victory over Billie-Jean King.

Q **What is the biggest attendance anywhere in the world for a tennis match?**

A crowd of 25,578 gathered to see Australia play the United States of America on the first day of the Davis Cup Challenge Round in Sydney on 27 December 1954. An unorthodox 'battle-of-the-sexes' between Billie-Jean King and Bobby Riggs drew a crowd of 30,472 to the Houston Astrodome on 20 September 1973.

Q **What was Bjorn Borg's record in the US Open championship?**

The US Open always eluded Borg. He reached four finals and was beaten each time, twice by Jimmy Connors and twice by John McEnroe. Borg was supreme at Wimbledon (five successive victories, 1976-80) and in the French Open (a record six wins, 1974-5,1978-81). His major successes in the United States came in the US Pro championship that he won for three consecutive years from 1974. He was also the Masters champion in 1979 and 1980. There has rarely been a more consistent player, and he was ranked No. 1 in the world for 109 weeks from 1977 until his retirement in 1981 at the age of 26.

Q **Was Fred Perry an American citizen when he won the third of his Wimbledon titles?**

Perry, the son of a Labour MP and born and brought up in Stockport, Cheshire, was still British when he completed his hat-trick of Wimbledon victories in 1936. He then turned professional and became an American citizen while touring in the States with Donald Budge and Ellsworth Vines. He served with the US Forces during the Second World War.

Q **Where was Andre Agassi born, and did he start his tennis career in the Middle East?**
Agassi was born in Las Vegas, Nevada, on 29 April 1970. He started his tennis career in the United States and was coached from the age of 13 by Nick Bolletieri. His link with the Middle East is that his father, Mike Emmanuel Agassian, was an Armenian who emigrated to the United States from Iran in the 1950s. He was an Olympic boxer and fought as a professional before a spell as a tennis coach.

Q **What is the least number of games contested in a championship final going to five sets?**
Henri Cochet beat his fellow French 'Musketeer' Jacques Brugnon 1-6, 6-1, 6-0, 1-6, 6-0 in the 1927 final of the Cannes championship.

Q **Who was the first unseeded player to win the men's singles title at Wimbledon?**
Full seeding was introduced at Wimbledon in 1927, three years after a modified form of rating the players had first been used. Boris Becker (1985) was the first unseeded player to go all the way through for victory.

Q **True or false: Throughout her career, Christine Truman could see out of only one eye?**
True. Christine was ranked No. 2 in the world in 1959 and in Britain's top three for 12 years despite the handicap of playing with a sightless left eye.

Q **Did Christine Truman ever beat the great Australian champion Margaret Court at Wimbledon?**
The Judge went to Christine, now a perceptive member of the BBC Radio 5 Live tennis commentary team, for this answer: 'One of my most memorable moments was beating Margaret in the Wimbledon quarter-finals in 1961 when she was the number one seed. It was before she became Mrs Court and was plain Miss Smith, and she had won the first of her 11 Australian championships. We had a tremendous match. I lost the first set 6-3 and it looked as if Margaret was going to sweep me off the court. But I managed to square the match by winning the second set 6-4, and squeezed to a 9-7 win in the deciding set after saving two match points. I went on to the final where I was beaten by Angela Mortimer, but it was the victory over Margaret that remains brightest in my memory.'

Christine Truman

Q Who have been the youngest winners of the men's and women's titles at Wimbledon?

Boris Becker (17 years 227 days) was the youngest men's champion when he took the title for the first time in 1985. Charlotte 'Lottie' Dodd was the youngest women's champion (15 years 285 days) when winning the first of her five titles in 1887.

Q Is it correct that Britain's Mark Cox once beat the great Pancho Gonzalez?

Mark Cox became the first amateur to beat a professional after tennis went open when he eliminated the legendary Gonzales in the 1968 British hard court championships. The next day he conquered two-times Wimbledon champion Roy Emerson. Cox, a law graduate from Cambridge University and now a respected BBC commentator, turned professional in 1970.

Q Who was the first player to achieve the double Grand Slam?

Rod Laver was the first to complete a second Grand Slam (i.e. holding at one and the same time the four major championship singles titles: Wimbledon, United States, Australian and French). He first won in 1962 (beating Martin Mulligan at Wimbledon and Roy Emerson in the other three finals), and his second Grand Slam came in 1969 (when he conquered John Newcombe at Wimbledon, Tony Roche in the US final, Andres Gimeno in the Australian and Ken Rosewall in the French.

Q Which doubles partners were first to achieve the Grand Slam?

Australian partners Frank Sedgman and Ken McGregor were first to win the Wimbledon, US, French and Australian doubles titles in 1951. Ken Fletcher and Margaret Court completed the mixed doubles Grand Slam in 1962.

Q Who were the quartet known as the 'Four Musketeers' of tennis?

This was the collective nickname for the four French masters – Henri Cochet, Jean Borotra, Jacques Brugnon and René Lacoste. They dominated the world's tennis courts betwen 1927 and 1932. Lacoste's name continues to be famous through the sports manufacturing business that he started. His nickname was 'The Crocodile' and this is why Lacoste sports gear has this as their logo.

Q When did Sweden's Stefan Edberg win his first Grand Slam title?

Edberg won all four Junior Grand Slam titles in 1983, and captured his first senior Grand Slam title when winning the Australian Open in 1985. His first Wimbledon victory was in 1988 when he defeated Boris Becker.

Q Had Pat Cash won any Grand Slam championships before his victory at Wimbledon?

His Wimbledon triumph in 1987 was his first major title. He was Wimbledon and United States Junior champion in 1982. A succession of injuries prevented him from making a greater impact on the world stage.

Q **Who was the eldest of the three Australian tennis masters Lew Hoad, Rod Laver and Ken Rosewall?**
Ken Rosewall (2 November 1934) was 21 days older than Lew Hoad (23 November 1934). Rod Laver (9 August 1938) was the 'baby' of the trio.

Q **Is it correct that tennis master Donald Budge was a Scot by birth?**
Budge, the first winner of the tennis Grand Slam (1938), was born in Oakland, California, on 13 June 1915. His father was a former Scottish professional footballer.

Q **Does Tim Henman have a special sports hero who has inspired him?**
The Judge went to Britain's tennis hero for this reply: 'When I was young my imagination was captured by stories of the exploits of my grandfather Henry Billington, who played Donald Budge at Wimbledon in 1938. As I developed my interest in sport I was inspired by the single-minded attitude and consistency of Nick Faldo. Other sportsmen particularly admired include basketball's Michael Jordan, and that gentleman of the court Stefan Edberg.'

Q **What nationality was Jaroslav Drobny when he became Wimbledon champion?**
Drobny became a political refugee after leaving his native Czechoslovakia in 1949. He held Egyptian nationality when he won the Wimbledon title at his sixteenth attempt in 1954 by beating Ken Rosewall 13-11, 4-6, 6-2, 9-7. Drobny became a British citizen in 1960.

Q **Is is correct that Jaroslav Drobny was an Olympic medallist?**
Yes, but not at tennis. He was a silver medallist with the Czechoslovakian ice hockey team in the 1948 Olympics.

Q **How old was Ken Rosewall when he won his last Grand Slam title?**
Rosewall was 35 when he won the US men's singles title in 1970 – 14 years after his first victory in the tournament. He was runner-up to Jimmy Connors in the Wimbledon and US championships four years later.

Q **How many Wimbledon championships did Billie-Jean King win?**
Billie-Jean won a record 20 Wimbledon titles between 1960 and 1979 – six singles, 10 women's doubles and four mixed doubles.

Billie-Jean King

She reached her first singles final as Miss Moffitt in 1963 when beaten by Margaret Smith in a minor classic. Seven years later – by then Mrs Court and Mrs King – they produced what is considered the greatest women's final of all time, Margaret winning 14-12, 11-9. Billie-Jean won 39 Grand Slam titles, a total beaten only by the 62 championships captured by her great rival Margaret Court.

Q **Where and when was the first Davis Challenge Cup match staged?**
Launched in 1900 as the 'International Lawn Tennis Championship', it began with the United States defending a challenge from the British Isles by three matches to love. The idea was conceived by Harvard undergraduate Dwight Davis, who persuaded his father to donate the 'Davis Cup'.

Q **How many times did Ivan Lendl reach the Wimbledon singles final?**
He was runner-up twice (1986 and 1987), and a losing semi-finalist on five other occasions. The Wimbledon title was the only Grand Slam to elude him during a career in which he won seven major championships.

Q **Was Fred Perry a world table tennis champion before switching to tennis?**
Perry was world table tennis singles champion at the age of 20 in 1929 before switching full-time to lawn tennis. Ann Jones – then Ann Haydon – was runner up in five world table tennis finals (one singles, two doubles and two mixed doubles), and she represented England in 69 internationals.

Q **Who was the first black winner of a Grand Slam tennis title?**
Althea Gibson won the French championship in 1956, and was the first black winner of a Wimbledon title in 1957. Arthur Ashe was the first black men's winner of a Grand Slam title, winning the US Open in 1968. He followed up by winning the Australian championship in 1970 and became the first black men's champion at Wimbledon in 1975.

Q **Who was the taller player, John McEnroe or Jimmy Connors?**
McEnroe stands 5 ft 11 in, Connors 5 ft 10 in.

Q **How old was Tracy Austin when she won her first Grand Slam title?**
Tracy was just 16 years 271 days old when she won the US women's championship in 1979, two years after playing at Wimbledon at the age of 14 years six months. Jennifer Capriati was, in 1990, the youngest ever seed at Wimbledon (14 years 89 days old).

Q **Did Chris Evert capture more singles titles than Martina Navratilova?**
Chris won a then record 157 singles titles, including 18 Grand Slam championships. Martina surpassed her record with more than 160 Grand Slam singles titles and as many again in doubles competitions.

Q **Did Lew Hoad play in the Wimbledon championships as a professional?**
Hoad, Wimbledon champion in 1956 and 1957, turned professional immediately after he had retained his title. His career was hampered by a

recurring back injury, but he came out of semi-retirement in 1968 to play at Wimbledon after it had become an open tournament. He competed in 1968, 1970 and 1972, but made an early exit each time.

Q **What was the longest game contested at Wimbledon before the intro-duction of the tie-break?**

Pancho Gonzales beat his fellow American Charlie Pasarell 22-24,1-6, 16-14, 6-3, 11-9 in a sensational 1969 first round match at Wimbledon that lasted over five hours and 112 games. Gonzales was booed by the centre court crowd for throwing the second set when his appeal against bad light had been turned down. The match was resumed the following morning with him trailing by two sets, and then he started one of the most memo-rable comebacks in the history of Wimbledon. The 41-year-old Gonzales wore down his former pupil to win the marathon 20 years after his first appearance at Wimbledon.

Q **Which tennis star was known by the nickname 'Little Miss Poker Face'?**

This was Helen Wills Moody, who showed little emotion on court during a remarkable run in which she went unbeaten for seven years from 1926. She did not even drop a set in singles from 1927 to 1933 on her way to 31 major championships.

Q **Is it right that Renée Richards competed in both the men's and women's tournament at Wimbledon?**

Not at Wimbledon, but in the US championships. In 1960, then answering to the name of Richard Raskind, he was beaten 6-0, 6-1, 6-1 in the first round by Neale Fraser. Following a sex change and a name change in 1977, Dr Renée Richards was beaten 6-1, 6-4 in the first round by Virginia Wade.

Q **How many years were there between Evonne Goolagong's two Wimbleton title wins?**

Evonne won her first Wimbledon singles championship at the age of 19 in 1971. She was a runner-up in 1972, 1975 and 1976 and was a married mum when she regained the title as Mrs Cawley in 1980.

Q **Where and when was John McEnroe born, and how much younger is he than Jimmy Connors?**

McEnroe was born in Wiesbaden, West Germany on 16 February 1959 while his father was serving with the US Air Force. Connors was born on 2 September 1952 in East St Louis, Illinois.

Q **How old was Maureen Connolly when she played her last major match?**

'Little Mo' was just 19 when a horse-riding injury forced her retirement in 1954. By then she had already become the first woman to win the Grand Slam and had won nine major singles championships.

OLYMPICS

Q **Was Olga Korbut ever the all-round women's Olympic gymnastics champion?**
No. Her Soviet colleague Lyudmila Turischeva was the all-round champion in the 1972 Munich Games where 17-year-old Olga Korbut first captured the public imagination. Olga finished seventh in the all-round competition following a fall on the asymmetric bars. Four years later in the Montreal Games the all-round title went to Romanian Nadia Comaneci, with Nelli Kim and Turischeva second and third. Olga was fifth.

Q **Has Steve Redgrave won any colour of Olympic medal other than his four golds?**
Redgrave was a bronze medallist with Andrew Holmes in the coxed pairs at the 1988 Seoul Olympics. Just 23 hours later they had taken the gold in the coxless pairs.

Q **How many Olympic boxing champions have gone on to win the professional heavyweight title?**
Eight – Floyd Patterson (middleweight gold medallist, 1952), Cassius Clay, later Muhammad Ali (light-heavyweight,1960), Joe Frazier (heavyweight,1964), George Foreman (heavyweight,1968), Michael Spinks (middleweight, 1976), Leon Spinks (light-heavyweight, 1976), Ray Mercer (heavyweight, 1988), Lennox Lewis (super-heavyweight, 1988). Riddick Bowe was runner-up to Lewis in 1988, and Ingemar Johansson received his silver medal 30 years after being disqualified in the 1952 heavyweight final.

Q **Who were the three New Zealand athletes who won gold medals in the Olympic 1500 metres event?**
Jack Lovelock (1936), Peter Snell (1964) and John Walker (1976). Each of them had beaten the world 1500 metres record before striking gold.

Q **Which Olympic champion was known by the nickname 'His Hurdling Lordship'?**
This was Lord David Burghley, Olympic 400 metre hurdles champion for Britain in 1928 and later the 6th Marquess of Exeter. He was also a sprint hurdler and reached the final of both the 110 metre and 400m hurdles in Los Angeles in 1932. The record-breaking race against the chiming bells around the courtyard of Trinity College at Cambridge (attributed to Harold

Abrahams in the film Chariots of Fire) was in fact Lord Burghley's feat. He later became an MP, and an influential athletics administrator respected around the world.

Lord Burghley

Q **Did Harold Abrahams compete in the long jump as well as the sprints in the 1924 Olympics?**
Abrahams was selected for the 100 metre, 200 metre, long jump and relay, but pulled out of the long jump after the Daily Express published an anonymous letter criticizing his inclusion in so many events. Abrahams used this as an excuse to bow out. Only later did he confess that he wrote the letter himself because he wanted to save his energy for the sprints. He won the 100 metres.

Q **Has there ever been a British-born winner of the Olympic marathon?**
Birmingham-born Thomas Hicks, running for the United States, won in St Louis in 1904 after first-across-the-line Fred Lorz had been disqualified for thumbing a lift!

Q **Has golf ever been included in the Olympic programme?**
Golf was included in the Games of 1900 and 1904, with Americans Charlie Sands and Margaret Abbott emerging as the first champions. George Lyon, an eccentric Canadian who sometimes walked around the course on his hands, was the 1904 champion. He arrived in London to defend his title in 1908 but the sport was scrubbed from the Olympic programme following a boycott by the British team after a dispute over entry conditions.

Q **Where and when was Olympic swimming champion David Wilkie born?**
Wilkie was born in Colombo, Sri Lanka (then Ceylon), on 8 March 1954, and his family returned home to Scotland when he was nine. In 1976 he became the first British male swimmer for 68 years to win an Olympic swimming title when he won the 200 metres breaststroke in a then world record 2 m 15·11 s.

Q **Which athlete has won most medals in the history of the modern Olympics?**
Paavo Nurmi, the 'Flying Finn' of the track, won a record 12 Olympic medals at the Games of 1920, 1924 and 1928, nine gold and three silver. He set 22 official world records at distances ranging from 1500 metres to 20 kilometres, and was a master at the steeplechase and cross-country run-

122

ning. Only Ray Ewry, a specialist at the now discontinued standing jumps, won more gold medals. Confined to a wheelchair as a boy, he strengthened his leg muscles with jumping exercises and won 10 Olympic titles between 1900 and 1908.

Q **Who was the first diver to win three successive Olympic highboard titles?**
Klaus Dibiasi, born in Austria in 1947 of Italian parents, completed the first hat-trick off the highboard when he collected his third gold medal in the 1956 Montreal Olympics. He won his first gold in Tokyo at the age of 17.

Q **What was the Olympic medal-winning record of British rower Jack Beresford?**
Beresford was always recognized as the greatest of all British rowers until the emergence of Steve Redgrave. He competed in five consecutive Olympics, and was preparing for a sixth appearance in the 1940 Games when war intervened. He won a total of three gold medals and two silvers.

Q **What did Dhyan Chand achieve on the hockey field that made him an Olympic legend?**
Dhyan Chand was to hockey what Pele was to football and Bradman to cricket. He was centre-forward in the Indian teams that won the Olympic golds in 1928 and 1932 and captained the 1936 champions who clinched the title with victory over host country Germany in Berlin. In their three Olympic triumphs, Chand-inspired India scored 102 goals and conceded just three.

Q **What was the Olympic weight-lifting record of 'The Great Zhabo'?**
Leonid Zhabotinsky, standing 6 ft 6 in and weighing more than 25 stone, dethroned his previously unbeaten Russian countryman Yuri Vlasov in the 1964 Olympics in Tokyo when he produced a world record jerk at his last attempt to clinch the gold medal. A colourful character who captured world-wide interest with his expressive approach to his sport, he retained his Olympic crown at the age of 31 in 1968 with a total lift of 1,262 lb – identical to his record in Tokyo. He set 17 world records during his career, and created the standards later surpassed by Vasili Alexeev, who was Olympic super-heavyweight champion in 1972 and 1976 and was known to eat as many as 30 fried eggs for breakfast. He set a remarkable 80 world records.

Q **How old was Kornelia Ender when she won her first Olympic swimming medal?**
Ender was 13 when she won a silver medal in the 1972 Munich Olympics. Four years later the strapping East German won four golds and a silver.

Q **Who was the gymnast who performed the 'Mexican Hat Dance' in the 1968 Mexico Games?**
It was Vera Caslavska, the Czech queen of gymnastics, who just two months before the Games had been hiding in her home town of Prague fol-

lowing the invasion of Czechoslovakia by Russian troops. Spurred on by the knowledge that victory over the Russian gymnasts would boost morale at home, Vera produced a series of stunning routines to win gold medals for the combined exercises, horse vault and asymmetric bars. She was also joint first in the floor exercises and gained silvers in the beam and team event. She completely won over the Olympic hosts when she selected the 'Mexican Hat Dance' as the background music for her floor exercise. She had a total haul of seven gold and four silver medals, including her successes in the 1964 Games. Vera brought romance to the Games just a few days after her triumphs in the gymnasium in Mexico when she married Czech 1500 metres runner Josef Odlozil, eighth in the Olympic final, at a Roman Catholic church in the centre of Mexico City.

Q Was Chris Brasher ever disqualified while competing in the Olympics?
Brasher won the 3,000 metres steeplechase in the 1956 Melbourne Olympics, but only after judges had over-ruled a disqualification for allegedly obstructing an opponent just before making his sprint for home and victory by a margin of 15 metres. He was carrying an injury and finished eleventh out of 12 in the 1952 steeplechase final. Brasher, the man who inspired the London Marathon and helped pace Roger Bannister to the first sub-four minute mile, went to Melbourne only as a late-choice third string in the steeplechase. He was a mountaineer and Cambridge graduate who went on to a distinguished career in sports journalism.

Q Who has been the oldest medallist in any Olympic competition?
Sweden's Oscar Swahn was 72 years 279 days old when taking a silver medal in the shooting competition at the 1920 Olympics. He had been the oldest Olympic champion in 1912 when winning a shooting gold medal.

Q Has any competitor won gold medals at the summer and winter Olympics?
Eddie Eagan, light-heavyweight boxing gold medallist at the 1920 Antwerp games, won a second gold medal with the USA four-man bobsleigh team at the 1932 Winter Olympics at Lake Placid. Christa Rothenburger won a speed skating gold medal at 500 metres in 1984 and over 1,000 metres in 1988, and also a silver in the 500 metres. In the Summer Games of 1988 in Seoul, Christa – by then married to her coach Ernst Luding – took the silver medal for East Germany in the 1,000 metre sprint cycle final.

Q Has a European sprinter ever won both the 100 metres and 200 metres gold medals at the same Olympics?
Valeri Borzov, the 'Red Rocket' from the Ukraine, completed the sprint double in the 1972 Munich Olympics. There were sneers after his 100 metre victory in 10·14 s that he only won because the top two Americans had been barred after arriving late for a heat. He silenced the cynics by then winning the 200 metres in a European record 20 s. Borzov, who had been prepared for the Games by a team of Russian scientists, became the first Olympic 100 metre champion to collect a second medal in

the event when he finished third in the 1976 Games.
He later married star Soviet gymnast Lyudmilla
Turischeva.

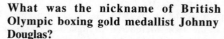

Q **What was the nickname of British
Olympic boxing gold medallist Johnny
Douglas?**
Douglas, middleweight champion in the
1908 London Olympics, was known as
'Johnny Won't Hit Today'. But this was
nothing to do with his boxing style. His ini-
tials were JWT, and he got his nickname
because of his stubborn batting performances
for Essex and England, particularly against the
Australians. He skippered Essex for 14 years from
1911, and scored nearly 25,000 runs during his
career. Douglas also took 1,894 wickets, including the
dismissal of five Yorkshire batsmen in eight balls at
Leyton in 1905. He was an outstanding all-rounder

Valeri Borzov

who also played football for England and the Corinthians, and captained
the team in 15 of his 23 international appearances.

Q **Did the master miler Roger Bannister win an Olympic medal?**
Bannister competed in only one Olympics and finished fourth in the
1,500metres final won by 'unknown' Josef Barthel, of Luxembourg, in
Helsinki in 1952. Two years later the flying doctor became the first man to
break the four-minute mile barrier and won the gold medals in the
Commonwealth and European 1500 metres finals. He then retired to
concentrate on his medical career.

Q **How many gold medals did the 1976 USA Olympic boxing team win,
and who was voted Best Stylist?**
Five: Leo Randolph (flyweight), Howard Davis (lightweight), Ray
Leonard (light-welterweight), Michael Spinks (middleweight), Leon
Spinks (light-heavyweight). Howard Davis won the coveted Val Barker
Best Stylist trophy. Four years later he was outpointed by Scotland's Jim
Watt when challenging for the world professional lightweight title.

Q **At which weight was the Hungarian boxing master Laszlo Papp three
times an Olympic champion?**
Southpaw Papp won at middleweight in 1948 and at light-middle in 1952
and 1956. Papp completed his hat-trick when outpointing Jose Torres in
the Melbourne Games. Torres became world professional light-heavyweight champion in 1965. Papp was the first 'Iron Curtain' boxer officially allowed to turn professional, and he retired as unbeaten European middleweight champion in 1965 after being refused permission by the
Hungarian government to challenge for the world middleweight title. Papp
had 29 professional fights, winning 26 and drawing three. He later became
the trainer of the Hungarian amateur team.

Q **Who was the first swimmer to hold Olympic, Commonwealth and European titles at one and the same time?**
Judy Grinham, of the Hampstead Swimming Club, was first to complete this hat-trick when winning the 100 metres backstroke title in the European championships in Budapest in 1958. Her greatest triumph had come two years earlier in the 1956 Melbourne Olympics when she came from behind to win the 100 metres backstroke gold medal in an Olympic record 1m 12·9 s. Yorkshire's Anita Lonsbrough, gold medallist at 200 metres breaststroke in the 1960 Rome Olympics, also completed the swimming Grand Slam in 1962. She broke the world record when winning her Olympic gold medal.

Q **How many Olympic gold medals did Mark Spitz win in total?**
Nine – two relay golds in the 1968 Games, and his record seven golds in the 1972 Games. The 'Spitz Blitz' was even more remarkable in that a world record was set every time he touched home for gold. He won the 100 metres and 200 metres at freestyle and butterfly, and anchored the USA team to three golds.

Q **Which Olympic champion was known by the nickname of 'Bones'?**
This was Harrison 'Bones' Dillard, the surprising winner of the 100 metres sprint in the 1948 Olympics. He had won 82 successive 110 metres hurdles races, but fell in the Olympic trials. Dillard, who had a slim, rubber-like physique, scraped though in third place in the 100 metres trials and won the gold medal in London with a time of 10·3 s. He then added a second gold medal in the sprint relay. Four years later he won the 110 metres hurdles final in the Helsinki Olympics, and made it four gold medals in the sprint relay.

Q **When was the game of tennis first included as an Olympic sport?**
Lawn tennis was included in the Olympics from the first of the modern Games in 1896 until 1924. It was reinstated in 1988.

SNOOKER

Q **How many world titles did Steve Davis win in the 1980s, and what was his heaviest defeat in that time?**

Davis won six world titles – in 1981, 1983, 1984, 1987, 1988 and 1989. His heaviest defeat came in 1982 when defending his world title for the first time. Tony Knowles beat him 10-1 in the first round of the Embassy World Championships at the Crucible Theatre in Sheffield.

Q **Why is the game of snooker called snooker, and when was it first played?**

In the 1870s, 'snooker' was a slang name given to a raw recruit at the Woolwich Military Academy. Colonel Neville Chamberlain (not he of 'Peace in our time' fame) used the name in a derogatory way to describe his opponent after he had missed a shot during a form of Black Pool in the Devonshire Regiment's officers' mess in Jubbulpore, India, in 1875. It caused such merriment that the officers adopted the name for the pool game to which they gradually added more and more coloured balls. The game of snooker was born. The Billiards Association, formed in 1885, introduced the sport's first set of official rules in 1900.There is also a theory that a form of snooker was being played at the Garrick Club in London in the 1860s.

Q **How old was Stephen Hendry when he won his first world championship?**

Hendry was, at 21 years 106 days, the youngest ever title holder when he beat Jimmy White 18-12 in the 1990 world championship final.

Q **Was Alex Higgins a racehorse jockey before becoming world snooker champion?**

When he was 14, Higgins was an apprentice jockey at the Wantage stables of Eddie Reavey. He was handicapped by increasing weight and gave up his apprenticeship after only one public ride. Higgins won the world snooker title for the first time in 1972 during his debut appearance in the finals.

Q **True or false: Terry Griffiths did not make his first century break until he was in his twenties?**

Griffiths was 24 before he had made his first century break after seven years as a leading Welsh amateur. He turned professional in 1978 and captured the world title a year later, winning snooker's most prestigious prize at his first attempt.

Q **Has any player held the billiards and snooker world titles simul-taneously?**
The great Joe Davis is the only man to have achieved this double, holding both titles for five consecutive years from 1928. He was so superior to all his rivals at the snooker table that he retired from match play in 1946 after winning the title for the fifteenth time. The only player to beat him off a level start through-out his career was his 12-years-younger brother, Fred. In 1955 Joe became the first player to make a maximum 147 break under champi-onship conditions.

Joe Davis

Q **How long had Dennis Taylor been a professional before he won his first major title?**
Taylor had been playing for pay for 13 years when he at last broke his duck by winning the 1984 Rothmans Grand Prix. The following year he hit the jackpot when he beat Steve Davis on the sensational final black of their best of 35 frames world championship final.

Q **Was Cliff Thorburn ever trailing when he beat Alex Higgins to win the world championship?**
Thorburn was 5-9 down and battled back to beat Higgins 18-16 in a mem-orable final at the Crucible Theatre in 1980.

Q **Who was the opponent when Cliff Thorburn made his 147 break in the world championships?**
Terry Griffiths was the player who sat it out as Thorburn became the first player in the history of the world championships to score a maximum 147 in the first round of the 1983 tournament.

Q **Is it true that Ray Reardon was once buried in a mining accident?**
The Judge went to six-times world champion Ray Reardon for the facts: 'I was working a shift at the Florence Colliery in Stoke when I was buried in a roof fall. I was unable to move a muscle until rescued three hours later. I knew I could do myself serious damage if I tried to move, and I kept my concentration going by playing endless frames of imaginary snooker and games of marbles in my mind with my younger brother. It ended my appetite for mining, and soon after I joined the city of Stoke police force before becoming a full-time snooker professional in 1967.'

Q **Which was the first maximum 147 break shown on television?**
Steve Davis scored the first 147 in front of the Granada cameras in the Lada Classic at Oldham in 1982. It featured on ITV's Midweek Sports Special.

Q **Who achieved the first maximum 147 break in an official major tournament?**
John Spencer was the first player to make a 147 break in a major championship in the Holsten Lager International at the Fulcrum Centre, Slough, on 13 January 1979. That was the good news for the three-times world champion. The bad news was that the pockets on the table were oversized and the break did not receive official recognition. There was more bad news for Spencer. The Thames Television camera crew were at a lunch break when he made his clearance, and there were only a handful of spectators in the hall. The first official break was the Steve Davis 147 in 1982.

Q **How old was Ronnie O'Sullivan when he made his first maximum 147 break?**
O'Sullivan was 15 years 98 days old when he made his first competitive 147 in the English Southern Area Amateur Championship at Aldershot on 13 March 1991. It made him the youngest player on record to have made the maximum break. 'Rocket' Ronnie also scored the quickest 147, taking five minutes 20 seconds in his televised first round match against Mick Price in the 1997 World Championships.

Q **What was the first professional title won by Jimmy White?**
White, at 19, became the youngest ever winner of a major professional tournament when he won the 1981 Langs Supreme Scottish Masters title in his first year as a professional. He beat three previous holders of the world crown (Ray Reardon, Steve Davis and Cliff Thorburn) on his way to the title. Aged 18, he had become the youngest ever world amateur champion, and, aged 16, he had been the youngest English amateur champion.

Q **Who was the first winner of the Pot Black tournament on television?**
Ray Reardon was the first winner of the tournament that was introduced on BBC2 in 1969 to coincide with the advent of colour television.

Q **Has anybody ever played tournament snooker with a mini cue, and is it allowed?**
Alec Brown, a professional either side of the Second World War, produced a six-inch mini cue during a tournament at Thurstons in 1938 to play a tight cushion shot. His opponent protested and the referee ruled that he was outside the spirit if not the letter of the law. It was soon after stipulated in the rules that a cue 'must be at least three feet in length and conform to the accepted shape and design'.

Q **Was Stephen Hendry the first Scot to win the world championship?**
No. Hendry was the second Scot after Walter Donaldson, from Coatbridge, who won the title in 1947 and 1950.

Q Was Steve Davis born in Romford, and is he a true Essex man?

The Judge went to Steve Davis for this interesting reply, 'I am an adopted Essex man. I was born and raised in Plumstead in south-east London, and moved across to Essex after I had turned professional with the Matchroom team that have their headquarters in Romford. It was Barry Hearn who turned me into an Essex man, and I have grown to like the county despite all the Essex jokes.'

Q Who did Alex Higgins beat in each round when he won his second world title?

Higgins, an emotional winner of his second world title in 1982, beat Jim Meadowcroft 10-5 in the first round, Doug Mountjoy 13-12 in the second, Willie Thorne 13-10 in the quarter-finals, Jimmy White 16-15 in the semi-finals and Ray Reardon 18-15 in the final.

Steve Davis

Q Which snooker player has won the greatest number of consecutive matches in world-ranking tournaments?

Ronnie O'Sullivan won 70 of his first 72 matches as a professional, including a record run of 38 victories. He was just 16 at the start of his run.

Q What is the fastest frame on record in a world-ranking tournament?

Tony Meo cleaned up the balls in just three minutes against Danny Fowler in a third round frame in the 1988 BCE International tournament.

Q What has been the longest frame in a world-ranking tournament?

Cliff Thorburn ground his way through an 88-minute frame against Paul Gibson in the third round of the 1991 Rothmans Grand Prix.

Q Who was known as the 'Champion with the Lucky White Shoes'?

This was Joe Johnson, who wore what he called his 'dancing shoes' on his way to a surprise world championship triumph at the Crucible in 1986. He started the tournament as a 150-1 outsider, and it was understandable as he had never won a match at the Crucible. He looked on the edge of defeat in the quarter-final against Terry Griffiths when he trailed by three frames with four to play, but he won each of them for a memorable 13-12 victory that launched the legend of the 'lucky white shoes'. Johnson, the Bradford battler, accounted for Tony Knowles in the semi-final, and then played the snooker of his life to conquer hot favourite Steve Davis 18-12 in the final.

Q   **What was the score in the final when John Parrott won the world championship?**
Parrott beat Jimmy White 18-11 after rushing into a 7-0 lead. In the first session he scored 634 points to just 80 by the overwhelmed White.

Q   **When were the world snooker championships first staged at the Crucible in Sheffield?**
The first Embassy World Championships were held at the Crucible in 1977. John Spencer was the winner, beating Cliff Thorburn 25-21 in the final.

MOTOR RACING

Q **Has the British Grand Prix been staged on tracks other than Silverstone and Brands Hatch?**
There have been three other venues for a race first run as the RAC Grand Prix in 1926: Brooklands (1926-7), Donington Park (1935-8) and Aintree (1955, 1957, 1959, 1961-2). There were no races from 1928 to 1934.

Q **Who was the first British winner of the world motor racing championship?**
Mike Hawthorn, driving a Ferrari, beat Stirling Moss to the title by one point in 1958.

Q **For which team did Michael Schumacher have his first Grand Prix drive?**
Schumacher made his debut in the Belgian Grand Prix at Spa-Fracorchamps on 25 August 1991 in a Jordan-191 Ford. The 22-year-old Mercedes-Benz sports car specialist had already made a name for himself by winning the Coupe de Spa sports car world championship race as co-driver to Jochen Mass in Mexico City on 3 June 1990. He was given the Formula 1 drive at the last moment by Eddie Jordan after his Belgian driver Bertrand Gachot had been jailed for spraying CS gas in the face of a London cabbie. Schumacher did not finish the race, but made such an impact in the practice sessions that Benetton controversially signed him before the next race at Monza, in which he finished fifth. His first Grand Prix win came in the 1992 Belgian GP when he beat champion-elect Nigel Mansell into second place.

Q **How many times was Jim Clark world motor racing champion?**
Clark, the son of a Scottish sheep farmer, was Formula 1 world champion in 1963 and 1965. His 25 Grand Prix victories, including seven in 1963, were then records that beat the figures set by Juan Manuel Fangio. He had amassed 274 points from his 72 F1 races when he was killed at Hockenheim on 7 April 1968. His Formula Two Lotus left the track and hit a tree during the first round of the European F2 Championship.

Q **Who was the first man to win the world championship in a car that he had designed himself?**
Jack Brabham, who had won the title in a Cooper-Climax in 1959 and 1960, captured his third championship in 1966 driving his self-designed and constructed Brabham BT 19-Repco. He clinched the title with four

consecutive victories in the French, British, Dutch and German Grand Prix.

Q **When was James Hunt's first Grand Prix victory, and in which car?**
Hunt won his first Grand Prix in a Hesketh at the Dutch GP in Zandvoort on 22 June 1975. He pushed his great rival Niki Lauda into second place, and shook off his early nickname of 'Hunt the Shunt'. James switched to McLaren the following year when Lord Hesketh was forced to pull out of the expensive world of motor racing, and he won the world championship with six victories in 1976. He finished first in 10 of his 92 GP races.

Q **Has Britain's Johnny Herbert ever won the Le Mans 24 hours race?**
Herbert was a winner of Le Mans in 1991 with co-drivers Volker Weidler and Bertrand Gachot in a Mazda 787B.

James Hunt

Q **What has been the closest finish to a Formula 1 Grand Prix race?**
In a blanket finish to the Italian Grand Prix at Monza on 5 September 1971, just 0.61 secs separated Peter Gethin in first place from his BRM team-mate Howden Ganley in fifth place. Ayrton Senna, driving a Lotus, pipped Nigel Mansell in a Williams by 0.014 secs in the Spanish Grand Prix on the new Jerez de la Frontera track on 13 April 1981. There was just half a car length between them as they took the flag.

Q **Where did Nigel Mansell have his first Grand Prix win, and how many GP victories did he have in total?**
Mansell's first Formula 1 win was in the European Grand Prix at Brands Hatch on 6 October 1985. Driving a Williams FW 10-Honda, he beat Ayrton Senna in a Lotus into second place for his first victory in more than 70 Grand Prix starts. Mansell had 31 GP victories from 185 starts, 28 for Williams and three for Ferrari. He placed second 17 times and third in 11 races. He was world champion in 1992, and won the Indycar championship in 1993.

Q **Did Stirling Moss ever win the world motor racing championship?**
Moss won 16 of his Grand Prix races from 1951 to 1961, but was never able to win the championship. He drove in the shadow of Juan Manuel Fangio at the start of his career and was runner-up to The Master each year from 1955 to 1957. In 1958, he lost out to Mike Hawthorn by a single

point. Moss drove a variety of cars including an HWM-Alta, ERA-Bristol, Connaught, Cooper, Maserati, Mercedes-Benz, Vanwall, BRM, Lotus, and Ferguson-Climax. His career was finished by a near-fatal crash at Goodwood in 1962.

Q **Who was the first Formula 1 specialist driver to win the Indianapolis 500?**
Jim Clark won on 31 May 1965 in a Lotus 38-Ford, and Graham Hill won the following year in a Lola T90-Ford.

Q **Was Ayrton Senna leading in the race in which he was tragically killed?**
Senna, the acknowleged king of his generation, was killed at Imola's notorious Tamburello corner while leading in his Williams on lap five of the San Marino Grand Prix on 1 May 1994. The idolized Brazilian won 41 of his 161 GP races, and was world champion in 1988, 1990 and 1991.

Q **What is the Gordon Bennett Trophy and when was it first awarded?**
James Gordon Bennett, who worked in the European office of the New York Herald, put up a trophy for Coupe internationale competition in 1900. It developed into Grand Prix racing in 1906.

Q **Where and when was the first ever motor race staged, and who won?**
It is generally accepted that the first organized motor race was the Paris to Rouen event on 22 June 1894 over a distance of approximately 80 miles. There were 21 starters, and Count Jules de Dion, driving his own designed steam quadricycle, was first to finish in 6 hours 48 minutes and at an average speed of 11·58 mph. The *Petit Journal* newspaper were organizers of the race, but they refused to pay the Count the 5000 francs prize money because he drove without a mechanic accompanying him.

Q **When were turbo-charged engines barred from Formula 1 racing?**
The new 3·5-litre coventionally aspirated engine formula was introduced in 1989. Ayrton Senna, in a McLaren, was the last champion in a turbo-charged car in 1988. Nelson Piquet was the first champion in a turbo-charged car in 1983. Renault, returning to F1 racing after an absence of nearly 70 years, introduced the first turbo-charged car at the British Grand Prix at Silverstone on 16 July 1977. Jean-Pierre Jabouille, driving a Renault RE10, registered the first win in a turbo-charged car when he took the flag in the French GP at Dijon-Prenois on 1 July 1979.

Q **What cars did Niki Lauda drive on the Grand Prix circuit?**
Lauda drove for March (1971-2), BRM (1973), Ferrari (1974-7), Brabham (1978-9) and McLaren (1982-5). He won 25 and finished second in 20 of his 171 GP races, and was world champion in 1975 (Ferrari) and again in 1977 (Ferrari) and 1984 (McLaren) after receiving horrendous burns in an accident at the Nürburgring in the 1976 German Grand Prix.

Q **Who was the first officially recogniszed world motor racing champion?**
Dr Giuseppe (Nino) Farina, a lawyer from Turin, was the first world champion at the age of 44 in 1950. He was driving an Alfa Romeo.

Q **Which drivers have won the world title while driving a Ferrari?**
There have been seven: Alberto Ascari (1952, 1953), Juan Manuel Fangio (1956), Mike Hawthorn (1958), Phil Hill (1961), John Surtees (1964), Niki Lauda (1975, 1977) and Jody Scheckter (1979).

Q **Did Jackie Stewart win his three world titles with the same team?**
Stewart won his first championship in a Matra (1969) and his second two in a Tyrrell (1971, 1973). He set what was then a record 27 Grand Prix victories from 99 races (1965 to 1973). His other GP drives were in a BRM (1965-7) and a March (1970).

Q **When was the British Grand Prix first held at Silverstone and who won it?**
Silverstone, a wartime airfield, staged its first British Grand Prix on 2 October 1948. Maseratis, driven by Luigi Villoresi and Alberto Ascari, were first and second.

Q **Where and when did Alain Prost score his first Grand Prix victory?**
Prost registered his first Grand Prix win in the French GP at Dijon-Prenois on 5 July 1981. It was the first of an all-time record 51 Formula 1 victories. He also had 35 seconds and 20 thirds. The flying Frenchman was world champion in 1985, 1986, 1989 and 1993.

Q **Was Juan Manuel Fangio born in Italy, and how many Grand Prix races did he win?**
Fangio was born in Balcarce, Argentina, on 24 June 1911, and was the son of an Italian house painter who had emigrated to South America. Juan Manuel worked as a garage mechanic before starting his racing career at the age of 17. He won 24 Grand Prix races from 51 starts and was runner-up in another 10 races. Fangio competed in his first Grand Prix in 1950 and was world champion in 1951, 1954, 1955, 1956 and 1957.

Juan Manuel Fangio

Q **Who were the winners of the Birmingham Super Prix, and how many races were there?**
The Birmingham Super Prix round the streets of England's Second City was dropped from the racing calendar after five years. The winners: Luis Perez Sala (1986), Stefano Modena (1987), Roberto Moreno (1988), Jean Alesi (1989) and Eric van de Poele (1990).

Q **Where and when was the European Grand Prix first staged?**
The European Grand Prix was a courtesy title awarded by the FIA until

1983 when it became a race in its own right. Nelson Piquet was the first winner at Brands Hatch on 25 September 1983.

Q **How old was Damon Hill when his father Graham was killed?**
Damon was 15 when his father died in a plane crash on 29 November 1975 at the age of 46. Graham was world motor racing champion in 1962 and 1968. In 1994 Damon won the British Grand Prix, one of the few major races to elude his father in his 14 GP triumphs. His championship triumph in 1996 made him the first son to follow his father as world F1 champion.

Q **Who was the first American driver to win the world Formula 1 motor racing championship?**
Phil Hill, from Miami, Florida, won the title in 1961 at the wheel of a Ferrari. He was better known as a sports car driver.

Q **Was the Indianapolis 500 ever a round in the world championship?**
The Indy 500 was included in the world championship from 1950 to 1960, but only Alberto Ascari of the top European drivers bothered to take part. He failed to finish in the 1952 race.

Q **How old was Emerson Fittipaldi when he won his first world championship?**
Fittipaldi was, at 25 years 273 days, the youngest ever Grand Prix champion when he won the title in 1972. He regained the crown in 1974, and was Indycar champion in 1989.

Q **Where and when did John Surtees win his first Grand Prix as a motor racing driver?**
Surtees, the only man to win world titles on two wheels and four, registered his first F1 victory in the German GP at Nürburgring on 4 August 1963, three years after switching from motor cycles. He won six of his 111 GP races, and was world champion in 1964 when driving for Ferrari.

OTHER SPORTS

Q **How many times was Johnny Leach the world table tennis champion?**
Leach, who perfected the game while serving in the RAF, was champion in 1949 and 1951. He was the last Englishman to win the title before the start of the monopoly by the Chinese with their new-style bats, pen-holder grips and deadly spin.

Q **Is it true that greyhound trainer George Curtis prepared more than 10,000 winners?**
The Judge went to George Curtis, the grand old man of greyhound racing, for this reply: 'I took out a trainer's licence in 1945 and for more than 40 years averaged more than 250 winners a year. I never kept count, but I reckon I have trained more than 10,000 winners.'

Q **Did Jayne Torvill win ice skating titles with any partner other than Christopher Dean?**
Jayne won a British junior and senior title with Michael Hutchison before pairing up with Christopher Dean in 1975. They won the first of a record six successive British titles three years later, and went on to capture four consecutive world titles and the Olympic crown in 1984, when they scored a record nine perfect sixes for their Balero routine. They had an unprecedented total of 12 sixes for their overall performance. Their Olympics comeback in 1994 (when they took the bronze) drew a British record television audience of 23,950,000 viewers.

Q **Why is the game of lacrosse called lacrosse, and where was it first played?**
North American Indians were first to play a primitive form of the game in the early seventeenh century. It was then called 'baggataway'. French settlers in Canada gave the name 'La Crosse' to the stick used by the Indians because of its resemblance to a bishop's crosier. French Canadians took up the game and formed the Montreal Lacrosse Club in 1839. It was first introduced into Britain by a travelling party of Caughnawaga Indians in 1867.

Q **Did cycling master Reg Harris win an Olympic gold medal before turning professional?**
Harris broke an arm shortly before the 1948 Olympics and his preparation was hampered. He had to settle for silver medals in the individual and

tandem sprints. World amateur sprint champion in 1947, he became the king of the professional track. He won the world sprint title three times in succession from 1949 and again in 1954. Harris made a comeback at the age of 54, and won the British sprint title in 1974. He twice set world records for the unpaced kilometre from a standing start (the second of which stood for 21 years), and he also set two indoor world records for the kilometre.

Q Is it true that King Henry VIII invented the sport of Real Tennis?
He helped popularize the sport, but did not invent it. The indoor racket and ball game was first played in the cloisters of French monasteries in the eleventh century. It was originally called Jeu de Paume because the ball was played from the palm of the hand before the invention of rackets. Henry VII was the first English king to master the game, and Henry VIII became one of the

Reg Harris

finest exponents of it and had a court built at Hampton Court Palace in 1530. There were more than 250 Real Tennis courts in Paris by 1600.

Q Is it true that British soldiers were first to play the game of ice hockey?
It is generally accepted that the first 'proper' game of ice hockey was played by members of the Royal Canadian Rifles on a frozen expanse of Kingston harbour, Ontario, in 1860. Most of the soldiers were British born. The game is believed to have derived from a North American ice-pitch sport called bandy. The first official rules for ice hockey were drawn up by W. F. Robertson and R. F. Smith while studying at McGill University, Montreal.

Q How many times did John Lowe and Eric Bristow contest the world darts championship?
They met in three World Darts Organization finals before the formation of the World Darts Council in 1992. Eric Bristow won 5-3 (1981) and 6-2 (1985), with Lowe winning 6-4 in 1987.

Q Did Babe Ruth spend his entire baseball career with New York Yankees?
Babe Ruth began his career as a pitcher with Boston Red Sox in 1914. It was after he was traded to New York Yankees in 1920 that he blossomed into one of baseball's greatest ever hitters. He hit what were then a record

60 home runs in 1927 and 714 career home runs. Babe's career batting average of ·342, including six seasonal marks over ·370 were considered unbeatable. He had made 2,873 hits by the time of his retirement in 1935. Yankee Stadium was erected shortly after he joined the Yankees, and it became known as 'The House that Babe Built'.

Q **On which make of motor cycle was Barry Sheene a world champion?**
Sheene won the 500 cc world titles in 1976 and 1977 on a Suzuki. On his way to retaining his world title in 1977 he set a fastest ever average speed for a world championship race of 135·07 mph (217·37 km/h) in the Belgium GP at Spa-Francorchamps. He won 19 500 cc GP races, the last for Yamaha.

Q **What did O. J. Simpson achieve in American Football that made him such an idol?**
Orenthal James Simpson was simply one of the finest running backs in the history of the sport. He was considered the greatest of all collegiate foot-ballers with USC before he joined the Buffalo Bills in 1969. In 1973 he broke the NFL rushing record with 2,003 yards, and he had a career record – including two seasons with San Francisco 49ers – of 11,236 yards and he scored 61 touchdowns. OJ was also an outstanding sprinter, and in 1967 he helped the USC team set a world sprint relay record.

Q **How many titles did David Bryant win in the world bowls championships?**
Bryant, the master of the greens, had a total of six title victories in the world outdoor championships. He was singles champion in 1966, 1980 and 1988, shared in the triples in 1980 and lifted the Leonard Team Trophy in 1984 and 1988. He was equally dominant indoors, winning the singles title in the first three years of the championships, and the pairs with Tony Allcock six times between 1986 and 1992.

Q **How old was Giacomo Agostini when he started competing on the moter cycle circuit?**
Agostini was 18 when he competed in his first road race in 1961 at the start of a career in which he won an all-time record 15 world motor cycling titles. Seven of his championships were at 350 cc and eight at 500 cc. He had most of his success with MV Augusta before a brief switch to Yamaha.

Q **Which sport is known to its followers as 'the roaring game'?**
This is curling, and is so called because of the sound made by the curling stones as they speed across the ice rink towards the tee. The origins of the sport are believed to belong in Holland in the fifteenth century, but it is in Scotland where the game was developed and organised from the seventeenth century.

Q **Why is the game of badminton so called, and where and when was it first played?**
The name of the game is derived from the seat of the Duke of Beaufort in Gloucestershire, Badminton House, where guests were invited to spend weekends playing shuttlecock in the nineteenth century. There is no

concrete evidence of where and when the game originated. A similar game was played in China over 2,000 years ago, and for centuries children played a form of battledore and shuttlecock. Army officers drew up the first modern rules while playing the game in India in the 1870s. The Badminton Association was founded in England in 1893.

Q **Was Greg Louganis ever beaten in an Olympic diving competition?**
Louganis won a silver medal at highboard in the 1976 Games when aged 16, and he finished sixth at springboard. He missed the 1980 Games because of the US boycott, but came into his own in 1984 when he completed the springboard and higboard double. He repeated the feat in 1988 despite hitting his head on the springboard during the preliminary round. Only Austrian Klaus Dibiasi (three golds and two silvers) has won more Olympic diving medals.

Q **Has any American footballer been voted Most Valuable Player in the Super Bowl more than twice?**
Joe Montana, former San Francisco 49ers quarterback, won the award three times – against Cincinnati Bengals (1982), Miami Dolphins (1985) and Denver Broncos (1990).

Q **When was the Tour de France first staged, and how long a race is it?**
The Tour de France was first held in 1903, with French cyclist Maurice Garin the first winner. The distance of the race was set at 5,000 kilometres in 1911, but since 1930 it has generally been around 4,000 kilometres.

Q **On which horse did David Broome win the world show jumping title?**
Broome was world champion on Beethoven in 1970, and he helped Great Britain win the team trophy in 1978. He also holds the record of six King George V Gold Cup victories on six different horses – Sunsalve (1960), Mister Softee (1966), Sportsman (1972), Philco (1977), Mr Ross (1981) and Lannegan (1991).

Q **How many Grand Prix motorcycle races did Mike Hailwood win?**
Hailwood won 76 Grand Prix races between 1961 and 1967 before swiching to Formula 1 motor racing. His best place on four wheels was second in the 1971 Italian Grand Prix. He returned to his first love and won the Formula 1 world title on two wheels in 1978 to add to his world championships at 500 cc (1962-5), and at both 250 cc and 350 cc (1966-7). Most of his rides were with MV Augusta and Honda. His record of 14 wins in Isle of Man TT races stood until 1993.

Q **Has croquet even been included in the Olympics as an official competition?**
Yes, just once in the 1900 Games in Paris when the 20 competitors were all from France.

Q **What was Sean Kerly's goal scoring record for the Great Britain hockey team?**
Kerly was top scorer for Great Britain with 64 goals in 99 appearances. He also scored 45 goals in 79 matches for England. A quick and decisive centre-forward for Southgate, he played a prominent role in helping Great

Britain win the Olympic gold medal in Seoul in 1988.

Q Which ice hockey player was known as 'The Great One'?
This was the one and only Ontario-born Wayne Gretzky, who broke all NHL scoring records during his career with, first, Edmonton Oilers and then the Los Angeles Kings. Before a back injury that threatened his career in 1992 he amassed a record 811 goals in 1,124 games, and was the driving force behind four Stanley Cup victories by the Oilers (1984-5 and 1987-8).

Q Was Britain's ace marksman Malcolm Cooper born in New Zealand?
Cooper, the winner of two Olympic shooting gold medals (1984 and 1988) and six world championships, was born at Camberley, Surrey, on 20 December 1947. He was first taught to shoot as a schoolboy in New Zealand where his father was stationed as a lieutenant in the Royal Navy.

Mike Hailwood

Q Did Olympic figure skating gold medallist Jeanette Altwegg also win a tennis title at Wimbledon?
Jeanette Altwegg had to choose between ice skating and tennis after finishing as runner-up in the 1947 Wimbledon junior championship. Jeanette chose ice skating, and reached her peak in 1952 when she won the Olympic figure skating gold medal to go with her 1951 world title.

Q Where did Robin Cousins finish in the Olympics in the year that John Curry won the gold medal?
Curry was Olympic ice-skating champion in the 1976 Olympics, with 19-year-old Cousins finishing in tenth place. Four years later Cousins won the gold.

Q Was netball a game invented in England or New Zealand?
Netball grew out of basketball in the USA in 1891. New Zealand set up the first national association in 1924 followed two years later by England.

Q In which year did Hank Aaron overtake Babe Ruth's home run record in Baseball?
It was April 1973 when Hank Aaron overtook Babeís 38-year-old record of 714 home runs, and he retired three years later with an all-time haul of 755 home runs. Aaron, born in Mobile, Alabama, in 1934 – the year before Ruthís retirement – started his career in Milwaukee in 1954 and moved with them when they became the Atlanta Braves in 1966. One of

the pioneer black players, he was traded back to Milwaukee for the last two years of his career for two wind-down seasons with the American League Brewers.

Q **Where was Jack Young born, and with which team was he riding when he was world speedway king?**
Jack Young was born in Adelaide, Australia, on 16 April 1924. In Britain he became the first Second Division rider to win the world title while with Edinburgh in 1951. The following season he moved to West Ham, and he further distinguished himself by becoming the fist rider to win two world titles. He reached a then record seven world championship finals.

Q **How many points do you score for hitting the bullseye in darts?**
You score 50 points for hitting the centre (double) bullseye, and 25 points if you hit the outer-ring bullseye.

Q **What was the original name of legendary basketball player Kareem Andul-Jabbar?**
Literally a giant of his sport, the 7 ft 2 in Kareem began life as Lewis Alcindor in New York in 1947. It was after helping UCLA win three consecutive NCAA basketball titles that he embraced the Muslim religion and changed his name to the one with which he rewrote the record books. While playing for Milwaukee and then Los Angeles Lakers, Kareem amassed an NBA record 38,387 points in 1,560 games at an average 24.6 points between 1970 and his retirement in 1989.

Q **Who was the first player to score 100 points in a single basketball game?**
This incredible milestone was set by the 7 ft 2 in Wilt 'The Stilt' Chamberlain on 2 March 1962 when he rattled up 100 points against New York Nicks. Wilt, who played briefly with the Harlem Globetrotters, was twice an All-American while at the University of Kansas before launching his record-breaking NBA career with Philadelphia Warriors in 1960. He moved with the Warriors to San Francisco in 1963 before a spell back in Philadelphia with the 76ers. His final four years were with the Los Angeles Lakers, when he took his career points total to a then record 31,419 points.

Q **Was Michael Jordan an Olympic gold medallist before playing for the USA 'Dream Team'?**
Yes. Jordan was a member of the USA Olympic gold medal winning basketball team in Los Angeles in 1984 while a student at the University of North Carolina and before becoming a legend in the game with Chicago Bulls. He collected his second Olympic gold meal with the 1992 'Dream Team' in the Barcelona Games.

Q **Did Jahangir Khan ever win a major squash title without his opponent scoring a single point?**
Jahangir, the complete master of squash, achieved this extraordinary feat when beating his Pakistani countryman Maqsood Ahmed 9-0, 9-0, 9-0 in the final of the ISPA Championship in 1982. He won a record six world

titles between 1981 and 1988, and was British Open champion for ten successive years from 1982. He won the first of his three world amateur championships at the age of 15.

Q **Was the former British squash champion Jonah Barrington born in Ireland?**
Barrington was born in Stratton, Cornwall, on 29 April 1941. He was educated at Cheltenham College and Trinity College, Dublin.

Q **What was Sonja Henie's ice skating record before she became a Hollywood star?**
Sonja, born in Oslo in 1912, made her Olympic debut at the age of 11 when she finished last of eight in the figure skating. She was undefeated in any competition from the age of 13, and collected ten world titles, six Europeans and three Olympic gold medals before turning professional in 1936 and becoming one of the worldís richest women through a series of Hollywood spectaculars.

Q **Had any amateur wrestler won three Olympic gold medals prior to the 1996 Games?**
This was achieved three times: Carl Westergren (Sweden, 1920, 1924 and 1932), Ivar Johansson (Sweden, two in 1932 and a third in 1936), and Aleksandr Medved (Ukraine, then USSR, in 1964, 1968 and 1972).

Q **Why is the name Nickalls so revered in the rowing world?**
It is a name closely associated with Henley through the exploits of the Nickalls family. Guy Senior won a record 23 Henley medals, as well as an Olympic gold medal in 1908 as a member of the Leander crew in the eights. Guy Junior won 10 Henley titles, including a record seven in the Grand Challenge Cup. Guy Senior dominated the Silver Goblet pairs with his brother Vivian in the 1890s. Their father donated the Nickalls Challenge Cup for winners of the pair oars at Henley.

Q **Did the great American sculler John Kelly ever compete at Henley?**
No, because he was banned. It has been wrongly reported that this was because he was 'a common bricklayer', but the fact is that any member of his American boat club, Vesper, was barred because Henley officials accused them of infringing amateur rules. Kelly, father of the actress who became Princess Grace of Monaco, was the world's No. 1 sculler from 1910 to 1924.

Q **Who was the ice hockey goalminder of whom it was claimed, 'Only the Lord Saves More'?**
This was Bernie Parent, who was rated the king of goalies during a 14-year career with Boston Bruins, Toronto Maple Leafs and the Philadelphia Blazers. He performed so many shut-outs that his fans carried placards reading, 'Only the Lord Saves More than Bernie Parent, the great father of goalies'.

Q **Who is the British swimmer who set eight world records during his career?**
The only British-born swimmer to have achieved that was Murray Rose, but he was a naturalized Australian by the time of his record blitz. Rose

was born in Birmingham in 1939, but emigrated with his Scottish parents to Australia, where he started his swimming career in Sydney. As well as breaking eight world records, Rose won three gold medals in the 1956 Melbourne Olympics (400 metres freestyle, 1,500 metres freestyle and 4 x 200 metres relay). He won a gold, silver and a bronze in the same events in Rome in 1960.

Q **Has any other cyclist matched Stephen Roche's 'Triple Crown' feat of 1987?**
Dubliner Roche had a golden year in 1987, when he won both the Tour de France and Giro d'Italia, and he also won the coveted Rainbow Jersey as world professional road race champion. This was achieved only one previously, by The Master, Eddy Merckx, in 1974

Q **Which Tour de France cyclist was known to the fans as 'The Cannibal'?**
This was a label hung on probably the greatest cyclist ever, Belgium's Eddy Merckx, because of the way he ate up the road on the way to five Tour de France Victories and a record 36 stage victories.

Q **Which motorcyclist was first to introduce the kneeling passenger to sidecar racing?**
The 'kneeler' was first introduced by Eric Oliver in 1954. He and his kneeling passenger, Les Nutt, astonished fans with their new technique in the Isle of Man TT, but they were so successful that their competitors quickly copies them. Oliver, a crack soloist in the late 1930s, switched to sidecar racing after the war and was the first ever world champion in 1949. He won 18 world titles in all ñ usually in his Norton-Watsonian combination ñ and with a variety of sit-in partners including Dennis Jenkinson, Lorenzo Dobelli and Stanley Dibben. Then he got his passenger to kneel to conquer.

Murray Rose

Q **Who was the first Dane to win the world speedway championship?**
Ole Olsen, born in Haderslev, Denmark, on 16 November 1946, was the first Danish winner of the world speedway individual title in 1971. He won again in 1975 and 1978.

Q **Is is correct that speedway king Ivan Mauger was once turned down by a British team?**
When Mauger first arrived in Britain from his native New Zealand at the age of 18 in 1957 he was unable to command a regular place in the

Wimbledon team. Disillusioned, he returned home to Christchurch at the end of the 1958 season. He decided to try again in 1963 and joined Newcastle in the Provincial League at the start of a revived career that saw him win 15 world titles, including a record six individual championships.

Q **With which teams did Willie Mays spend his baseball career?**
Mays played with the New York and then San Francisco Giants, and returned to New York with the Mets for a wind-down season in 1973. He was considered one of the greatest centrefielders in baseball history, and he hit more than 40 home runs in a season six times.

Q **Who was the first ice skater to achieve a 'double lutz' in competition?**
This was American Dick Button, Olympic champion in 1948 and 1952. He first achieved a double lutz in 1944, and was first to a triple loop in 1952.

Q **Has any Alpine skier won all three gold medals in the Olympics?**
Toni Sailer (Austria, 1956) and Jean-Claude Killy (France, 1968) were first to complete the Olympic treble of giant slalom, slalom and the downhill.

Q **Who is Billy Fiske, to whom a memorial plaque has been erected at St Paul's Cathedral?**
Billy Fiske became, at 16, the youngest ever gold medallist in the Olympic bobsleigh competition. He steered the winning 5-man USA bob at the 1928 Games, and four years later was the driver of the winning 4-man bob. Fearless Fiske was a master of the Cresta Run, and often won there during his term breaks from studying at Cambridge University. Married to the Countess of Warwick, he volunteered for the RAF at the outbreak of the Second World War and was the first American pilot killed in the Battle of Britain in 1940, when he was 29. A Billy Fiske Memorial Trophy is a coveted bobsleigh prize.

Q **Who was the first woman cyclist to beat the four-hour barrier for 100 miles?**
Beryl Burton, Britain's greatest woman cyclist, clocked up 100 miles in 3 h 55 m 5 s in 1968, which would have been a men's record just a dozen years earlier. She won more than 150 major titles during her career.

Q **Who was Jocky Wilson's partner when he won the world darts championship?**
Jocky, world darts champion in 1982 and 1989, won the world pairs title in 1988 in partnership with Ritchie Gardner.

Q **Has a any gymnast ever won medals in all the eight categories in the men's Olympic competition?**
Aleksandr Dityatin, the Leningrad gymnastics master, achieved this feat in the 1990 Moscow Olympics. He won golds on the rings, in the individual overall and team events, and collected four silvers and a bronze. Dityatin was the first male Olympian to score a perfect ten in the horse vault.

Q Who was the first breaststroke swimmer to break one minute over 100 metres in a 25-metre pool?
Yorkshireman Adrian Moorhouse was first to break the 60-seconds barrier in a four-lap 100-metre breaststroke race in 1987 with a clocking of 59·75 s.

Q Which world swimming champion was known as 'Mr Machine'?
This was Mike Burton, who was Olympic champion at 1,500 metre freestyle in the 1968 and 1972 Games and also took the 400 metres gold meal in 1968. In all he set seven world and 16 US records at distances from 400 to 1,500 metres. He was so badly injured when knocked off his bicycle by a truck at the age of 12 that doctors said that he would never walk again.

Q How many Olympic equestrian gold metals were won by Richard Meade?
Meade won one individual gold and two team in the Olympic three-day event competitions in the 1968 and 1972 Olympics. His individual gold was won on Laurieston in Munich in 1972.

Q On which show jumping horse did John Whitaker first win the George V Gold Cup?
Whitaker's first victory was on Ryan's Son in 1986. He captured the premier prize in British showjumping again in 1990 on Milton, the magnificent horse on which he twice won the World Cup.

Q How many Olympic gold medals did speed skater Eric Heiden win, and did he later switch to a new sport?
Heiden made a clean sweep on all five gold metals in the men's speed skating in the 1980 Winter Olympics. He created new Olympic records in all the events, and set new world figures for the 10,000 metres. Heiden later had a brief career as a professional cyclist before studying medicine at Stanford University. His sister, Beth, was an American champion at speed skating, cycling and cross-country skiing.

Q How many British Match Race wins were recorded by speedway master Jack Parker?
Parker, a hero of British speedway tracks for a span of 25 years from 1928, registered a record seven British Match Race wins between 2932 and 1951, when they were considered on a par with the world championship. He and his brother, Norman, were exceptional speedway internationals, with Jack scoring more points in Tests than any other English rider.

Jack Parker

He was a top designer and test rider for BSA, the company he joined in 1927.

Q How many world table tennis championships were won by the Rowe twins?
Rosalind, and her left-handed twin sister Diana, won the world table tennis doubles in 1951 and 1954 and were runners-up in 1952 and 1953.

Q Did yachtsman Rodney Pattison win his Olympic titles single-handed?
Pattison was a specialist in the Flying Dutchman class, and so needed a partner each time. He won gold in 1968 with Iain MacDonald-Smith, gold in 1972 with Chris Davies, and silver in 1976 with Julian Brooke-Houghton. He was also World and European champion from 1968 to 1972.

Q What does the word 'Karate' actually mean, and how long has it been a martial art?
Karate was developed from the ancient Chinese art of Shaolin boxing, and later 'Tang Hand'. It was introduced into Japan in the 1920s by Funakoshi Gichin, who gave it the name 'Karate', meaning 'empty hand'. The style that he perfected became known as Skotokan. Karate spread to the west in the 1950s.

Q What exactly is the modern pentathlon, and what is involved?
The Modern Pentathlon started out as a military sport, and has been included in the Olympics since 1912 (when Joe Patton, later General Patton, took part using his Colt revolver). It involves five disciplines: cross-country horse riding, épée fencing, pistol shooting, swimming (300 metres) and, finally, a cross country run (4,000 metres).

Q Has American Football ever been played with 15 players a side on the pitch?
The game evolved in the late nineteenth century from a mix of the British games of soccer and rugby. Under the original rules drawn up at Harvard University there were 15 players a side, but this was reduced to the present 11-a-side as featured in the game today.

Q Is there a sport called Bandy, and has it ever been included in the Olympics?
Bandy, an early form of ice hockey but played with a ball rather than a puck, was included in the 1952 Olympics as a demonstration sport.

Q How old is the Greyhound Derby and where was it first run?
It was first run at London's White City Stadium in 1927 over 500 yards.

Q Where and when was the hare introduced to greyhound racing?
Greyhound racing began in Hendon, North London, in 1876, but it was not until 1926 at Belle Vue, Manchester, that the mechanical hare was introduced seven years after being invented by Owen Smith in the United States.

Q **Which countries participate in the Pan-American Games, and which sports are included?**
The Pan-American Games are open to competitors from 34 affiliated countries from North, Central and South America, and have been staged every four years since 1951. All summer Olympic sports are included, plus baseball, roller skating and softball.

Q **Who was the first BBC Sports Personality of the Year, and who was the first woman to win the award?**
Chris Chataway was the first winner in 1954, the year he broke the 5,000 metres record by beating Vladimir Kuts and helped pace Roger Bannister to the first sub-four minute mile. Swimmer Anita Lonsbrough was the first woman to win the viewers' vote in 1962.

Q **Where and when was the sport of Orienteering first contested?**
Orienteering (cross-country running with the aid of a compass and map) was created in Sweden in 1918 by Major Ernst Killander.

Q **Is it true that Jimmy Greaves was once a motor rally driver?**
Jimmy competed in the 1970 London to Mexico World Cup rally, finishing a creditable sixth in a Ford Escort. He was co-driver to professional rally master Tony Fall.

Q **Who was the first British rider to win a world motorcycling championship?**
Freddie Frith (350 cc Velocette) and Leslie Garham (500 cc AJS) were both winners in the first year of championship racing in 1949, and Eric Oliver (Norton) won the sidecar event in the same year.

Q **How many world motor cycling titles were won by Geoff Duke?**
Duke won six world titles: 350 cc on a Norton in 1951 and 1952, the 500 cc crown on a Norton in 1951, and he completed a hat-trick of 500 cc title victories from 1953 on a Gilera.

Q **What in ice hockey is the Hart Trophy, and after whom is it named?**
The Hart Trophy is presented to the 'Most Valuable Player' in the NHL, and is awarded by the Professional Hockey Writers' Association. It has been awarded annually since 1924, and is named after Cecil Hart, who was an outstanding manager-coach in Montreal. Wayne Gretzky won the trophy a record nine times in the 1980s while with the Edmonton Oilers.

Q **What exactly is a 'sulky' and in which sport does it feature?**
The sulky is the two-wheeled cart on which the driver sits in harness racing.

Q **True or false: Darts player Eric Bristow has been honoured by the Queen at Buckingham Palace?**
True. The 'Crafty Cockney' was awarded the MBE in the New Year's Honours List in 1989. Senior Tory MPs called the award a 'farce' and crit-

icized his 'big, fat, beer gut'. Bristow, who by then had won the world title a record five times, was unmoved. 'They walk to the bar for a Scotch and then fall asleep in the House,' he said. 'I'm fitter than any of them.'

Q **Was the great greyhound Ballyregan Bob ever beaten, and how many races did he have?**

Ballyregan Bob was beaten six times during his record-breaking career. He finished first in 42 out of 48 starts and broke 16 track records on the way. On 9 May 1985, he won the first of what was to be 32 consecutive victories, beating the previous world recOrd set by American greyhound Joe Dump. After clinching the record in 1986 he became a happy stud in the United States at £600 a time.

Q **Is it true that Johnny Leach learned his table tennis skills in China?**

That is incorrect. Johnny Leach was taught how to play at his Essex home by his father, a good-class club player. He developed his game on the tables of the Grenfell Church boys' club in Romford, Essex, and then with the Romford YMCA team. It was while serving in the RAF that he perfected his classic style that turned him into a role model for thousands of young players. Leach won 152 England caps during a 12 year international career from the end of the Second World War, twice winning the world title.

Johnny Leach

Q **Did British judo champion Neil Adams win a gold medal at the Olympics?**

Adams collected a silver medal in the 1984 Games in Los Angeles. The highlight of his career was a world title victory in 1981 when he beat the Japanese favourite Jiro Kase in the final.

Q **Was Joe DiMaggio still playing baseball when he married Marilyn Monroe?**

Joe DiMaggio, an all-time hero of the New York Yankees, retired in 1951 at the age of 37. He married film goddess Marilyn Monroe in 1954.

Q **Why is the name of Hackenschmidt so revered in the world of amateur wrestling?**

George Hackenschmidt, born in Estonia in 1877, was undefeated in Greco-Roman style contests for 11 years from 1900. He was recognized as world champion in freestyle from 1902 to 1908. He was a philosopher, who expounded his views in one of his many books, Man and Cosmic Antagonism to Mind and Sport. His mind-over-matter theories inspired a procession of sportsmen and coaches. At the time of his death in 1968 at the age of 91 he was still carrying out daily exercises that included jumping over the back of a chair 50 times.

Q **Did Captain Mark Phillips ever win the Burghley and Badminton Horse Trials?**
Mark Phillips was four times the winner at Badminton, in 1971 and 1972 on Great Ovation, in 1974 on Columbus and in 1981 on Lincoln. He was once a winner at the Burghley Trials on Maid Marion in 1973.

Q **Where was British table tennis star Desmond Douglas born?**
Douglas was born in Kingston, Jamaica, in 1955, and came to England with his parents at the age of five. He took up table tennis in Birmingham.

Q **What was the overall record of Belgian cyclist Eddy Merckx?**
As well as his five victories in the Tour de France, Merckx won 525 of the 1,800 races he entered in a 13-year professional career.

Q **How old was British diver Brian Phelps when he competed in the Rome Olympics?**
Phelps was just 16 when he became only the second British man to win a diving medal with a bronze in the highboard competition at the 1960 Games.

Q **Has a British weightlifter ever won an Olympic gold medal?**
Launceston Eliott, competing in the one-handed lift in Athens in 1896, was Britain's only Olympic weightlifting champion. He also came second in the two-handed lift. Louis Martin was a silver medallist at middle-heavyweight in 1964.

Q **In ice hockey, if a goalminder saves a penalty can the player who took the shot score from the rebound?**
No. Once he has taken his shot, the player cannot touch the puck again.

Q **Do competitors provide their own horses in the modern pentathlon?**
No. They are supplied by the competition organizers, and the competitors draw for them by lot.

Q **What was the first competition machine ridden by John Surtees?**
Surtees, a world champion on two and four wheels, made his first competition appearance on a Vincent 'Grey Flash' in 1951 when he was 17.

Q **Who carried the Olympic torch on the final lap in the Stadium at the 1948 Olympics?**
John Mark, an Achilles Club sprinter, lit the flame at Wembley Stadium.

Q **Has a royal competitor ever won an Olympic gold medal in any event?**
Crown Prince Constantine of the Hellenes won a gold medal in the yachting Dragon class in Naples in 1960. The 20-year-old Prince was pushed into the water by his mother, Queen Frederika, for the traditional dunking.

Q **Has a British walker ever won two gold medals at the same Olympics?**
George Larner, a 33-year-old Brighton policeman, came out of retirement to compete in the 3,500 metre and 10-mile walks in the 1908 Olympics, and he won them both.

Q **What is the origin of the often-heard ice skating term 'a Salchow'?**
It is a spectacular jump named after its originator Ulrich Salchow, the Swede who was world men's figure skating champion ten out of the first 11 years of this century. The jump starts from a back inside edge and ends with the skater landing on the back outside edge of the other skate.

Q **Who was the first speedway rider to win the world championship while with a Second Division team?**
Jack Young, who won the title in 1951 while riding for Second Division Edinburgh.

Q **Has the finger spin serve ever been allowed in championship table tennis?**
The controversial finger spin serve – spinning the ball before connecting with the bat – was banned from championship play in 1937.

Q **In which sports event is there a 'Rudolph' and a 'Randolph'?**
These are twisting front somersaults in trampolining.

Q **How many lifts can a weightlifter attempt in a major championship?**
The weightlifter is allowed to have three presses, three snatches and three jerks.

Q **How long must a weightlifter support the barbell over his head before a lift is accepted?**
The judges will accept a lift once the lifter has both feet on the same line, with arms and legs fully extended and he is quite motionless.

Q **How many players form a baseball team, and what are their positions?**
Nine: pitcher, catcher, first, second and third basemen, short-stop, left, centre and right-field.

Q **What is the difference in baseball between a home run and a grand slam home run?**
A home run is a hit that allows the batter time to circle the bases to score without stopping at any base. A grand slam home run is a home run hit with a runner on each of the three bases.

Q **Did ice hockey master Chick Zamick end his playing career with Nottingham Panthers?**
The idol of British ice hockey fans in the 1950s and 1960s ended his career with a wind down season with Wembley Lions before retiring in 1964. Zamick scored most of his 800-plus goals for Nottingham Panthers.

Q **Is it true that Great Britain once won the Olympic gold medal at ice hockey?**

Yes, Great Britain were the shock winners of the Olympic ice hockey title at Garmisch in 1936. They included two Canadian-born players in Alex Archer and goalie James Foster, despite protests from the Americans. Canada's 20-match unbeaten run in the Olympics was ended by Britain in the semi-final, and the British team retained their undefeated record by surviving a 0-0 triple overtime tie with the United States in their final match.

Q **Of what material is the puck used in ice hockey generally made?**

An ice hockey puck is made of vulcanized rubber. Australian Dave Hill, innovative former boss of Sky Sport, has been experimenting in America (where he is in charge of Fox TV sport) with a puck that glows on the ice and is therefore more easily followed by viewers.

Q **How many British walkers have won the Olympic 50 kilometre walk gold medal?**

Three: Tommy Green (Los Angeles 1932), Harold Whitlock (Berlin 1936) and Don Thompson (Rome 1960). Sussex-born Norman Read won for New Zealand in the 1956 Melbourne Olympics.

Chic Zamick

Q **What is the commentator referring to in skiing when he talks of the 'vorlage'?**

This is the internationally accepted German term for the forward lean of the skiier. It is also a style of ski trousers.

Q **Who was the first English cyclist to win a stage in the Tour de France?**

Brian Robinson, who was a stage winner in the 1958 Tour.

Q **Who was the first English cyclist to wear the leader's yellow jersey in the Tour de France?**

Yorkshireman Tommy Simpson wore the yellow jersey in 1962.

Q **During a ski race, is it permissible for the skiier to hold both hands on the same stick?**

No. He or she would be disqualified.

Q **What is the Middleton Cup, and where is the final staged?**

It is the cup awarded to the winners of the English inter-county bowls championship, and the final is traditionally held at Mortlake.

Q **Who was the first British show jumper to officially turn professional?**
It was that great character Harvey Smith who led the way in 1972, and it
was reported to have been a sign of the times!

Q **Which motor cyclist was first to win three successive Senior T. T.
titles in the Isle of Man?**
This was John Surtees, who won in 1958, 1959 and 1960 before switching
to Formula 1 motor racing. He completed the senior and junior double in
1958 and 1959.

Q **Has an Olympic swimming champion ever succeeded in swimming the
English Channel?**
Denmark's Greta Andersen, 100 metres champion in the Olympic pool in
1948, swam the Channel six times.

Q **Who was the first non-European to win the women's European
show jumping championship?**
Kathy Kusner, of the United States, won the title in 1967.

Q **What was the tribute paid to the memory of Tommy Simpson following his death in the Tour de France?**
Simpson died on the thirteenth stage of the 1967 Tour. The following day,
all the riders let Simpson's British team-mate Barry Hoban through to win
the fourteenth stage. Hoban later married Simpson's widow.

Q **Is it right that the Serle brothers beat another pair of brothers when
winning their Olympic gold medal?**
Greg and Jonny Serle, coxed by Garry Herbert, beat Italy's legendary
Abbagnale brothers when they won the coxed pairs in the 1992 Olympic
final in Barcelona. The Italians had been world champions seven times,
but were overwhelmed by a blistering finish from the British brothers.

Q **Which American baseball player was known by the nickname 'The
Georgia Peach'?**
This was Ty Cobb, who was the first player elected to the baseball Hall of
Fame. He had 4,190 hits during a career that stretched from 1905 to 1928.
Cobb, born in Atlanta in 1886, spent most of his playing days with Detroit
Tigers apart from two years winding down with Philadelphia Athletics.

Q **Was Richard Bergmann based in England when he won the first of his
world table tennis titles?**
Bergmann, born in Vienna of a Polish father and Italian mother, was 17
when he won the first of his four men's singles world table tennis titles in
1937. He was then living in Austria, and fled to England a year after
Germany annexed his home country. Bergmann served in the RAF and
took out British nationality. His three other world titles came in 1939,
1948 and 1950. His defensive game was reckoned to have been the sound-
est ever seen.

Q **Who was the Borg of Sweden who became famous in the sports world long before Bjorn Borg was born?**
Arne Borg was one of the greatest swimmers of all time. He set 32 world records between 1921 and 1929 at freestyle distances from 300 yards to one mile. He had a twin brother, Ake, who was nearly in his class.

Q **What were the names of the yachts on which Francis Chichester and Alec Rose sailed around the world?**
Gipsy Moth IV (1967, Chichester) and Lively Lady (1968, Rose).

Q **Did twin brothers win gold medals in the boxing ring for the USA in the 1984 Los Angeles Olympics?**
No, but twins brothers won wrestling gold medals: Ed Banach (light-heavyweight) and Lou Banach (heavyweight) were double trouble for opponents in Los Angeles.

Q **Is it true that the first man to swim the English Channel later drowned trying to repeat the feat?**
Matthew Webb, a captain in the Merchant Navy, was the first man to swim the Channel on 24-5 August 1875. The Dover to Calais swim took 21 hours 45 minutes, and it was 36 years before another swimmer completed the crossing. Webb, born in Shropshire in 1848, drowned eight years after his triumph in the Channel when he was attempting to swim the rapids above Niagara Falls.

Q **Did all-rounder Keith Miller represent Australia in any sport other than cricket?**
Keith was an exceptional exponent of Australian Rules Football, and could play in any position on the field. His specialist positions were at full-back or full-forward, and his kicking was both long and accurate. He played for St Kilda Football Club before becoming a wartime pilot, and after the war represented Victoria and then New South Wales in inter-state football. He reluctantly gave up the game to concentrate full time on cricket after twisting an ankle in a 1947 match.

Q **What did Karen Briggs achieve in judo, and where and when was she born?**
Karen Briggs, arguably Britain's most successful judo player, was born in Hull on 11 April 1963. She won four world titles, five European championships between 1982 and 1987, and also captured the highly prized Japanese Open for four successive years from 1983 and again in 1988.

Keith Miller

Q **Why is Mick the Miller so well remembered in greyhound racing, and where was he bred?**

Mick the Miller was bred in Ireland by Father Martin Brophy. Trained by Mick Horan, he won 15 of 20 races in Ireland before going to England in 1929 where he was bought at auction by London bookmaker Albert Williams for 800 guineas. He won 41 of his 61 races in Britain, including 19 in succession in 1929-30. Mick was bought for a record 2,000 guineas after his first Derby victory in 1929, and his new owner, Mrs Arundel Kempton, sent him to Norfolk to be trained by Sidney Orton. He won the Derby for an unprecedented second time in 1930, and appeared to have completed a hat-trick in 1931 when he crossed the line first. But because backmarker dogs were fighting the race was re-run, and Mick finished fourth. A film of his life, Wild Boy, was made in 1935, and following his death in 1935 a taxidermist prepared his body for display at London's Natural History Museum.

Q **Which world darts champion was known by the nickname 'The Limestone Cowboy'?**

This was Bob Anderson, who won the first of three successive World Masters titles in 1986. A civil servant from Swindon, he became the World Professional champion in 1989.

Q **What is the difference between the biathlon and the triathlon?**

The biathlon, an official competition since 1957, is a combination of cross- country skiing and rifle shooting in which competitors ski over pre-pared courses carrying a small-bore rifle. The triathlon, pioneered by Americans in 1974, combines long-distance swimming, cycling and running. There was also a triathlon in the 1904 Olympics, featuring gymnastics and field events.

Q **Where and when was the sport of water-skiing developed?**

It was pioneered by American Ralph Samuelson on Lake Pepin in Minnesota in 1922. He first of all used snow skis and then pine-board skis.

SPORTS TRIVIA

Q **Did singer Johnny Mathis ever compete as an athlete in the Olympic Games?**
No. Mathis was a leading American college high jumper in the 1950s and was preparing to compete in the US Olympic trials for the 1956 Games in Melbourne when his career as a singer took off. He was also an exceptional hurdler and basketball player, and is a golfer with a single-figure handicap.

Q **How and why did the mighty steeplechaser Arkle get his name?**
Arkle was named after a mountain on the Duchess of Sutherland's estate. He ran in 35 races, three of them on the flat and six over hurdles, and was beaten only four times in 26 steeplechases ñ once by a luckless slip, twice by weight handicaps and one by the injury that ended his career on Boxing Day 1966.

Q **How tall is Lester Piggot, and why is he known as The Longfella?**
Lester Piggot is known as The Longfella because, at just a fraction under 5 ft 8 in tall, most of the jockeys had to look up to him.

Q **Was the American jockey Willie Shoemaker taller than Lester Piggot?**
Willie the Shoe, a winner of a staggering 8,833 races from 1949 to 1990, was one of those who looked up to Lester. He stands just 4 ft 11 in.

Q **Is it true that former world speedway champion Ronnie Moore started as a Wall of Death rider?**
True. Moore, born in Hobart, Tasmania, on 8 March 1933, toured New Zealand at the age of 11 as his fatherís pillion passenger in a Wall of Death act. He was runner-up for the world speedway championship at 17 and he won the first of his two titles in 1954.

Q **Was Henry Cooper a plasterer or a greengrocer when he was not boxing?**
Henry was a plasterer in Bellingham, south-east London, when he turned professional. Towards the end of his career he and his Italian-born wife, Albina, owned a greengrocerís shop in Wembley.

Q **Which Tour de France cyclist was known as 'The Angel of the Mountains'?**

Charley Gaul collected this nickname during the 1955 Tour de France when on the mountain stage he left his rivals 15 minutes in his wake. The iron man from Luxembourg was King of the Mountains on nearly every tour in which he competed, and he was the overall winner in 1958.

Q **Why was the Grand National once known as the National Lottery?**

Lottery won the Grand National in 1839. He was such an exceptional horse that race organizers used to have steeplechasers that were 'open to all horses except Lottery'.

Q **Which West Indian Test cricketer was nicknamed 'Big Bird'?**

This was former Barbados and Somerset fast bowler Joel Garner. He stood just over 6 ft 8 in tall, and, as he ran in to bowl to them, batsmen described the experience as like facing a swooping bird with a huge wing span. His most memorable bowling feat was his five wickets for four runs off 11 balls that sealed victory for the West Indies in the 1979 World Cup final against England at Lord's.

Q **Why was the 1974 Charity Shield at Wembley known as 'The Battle of the Bare Chests'?**

Billy Bremner (Leeds) and Kevin Keegan (Liverpool) were sent off for fighting each other, and as they reached the touchline each of them tore off their shirts and walked bare-chested to the dressing-rooms.

Q **Is it true that Jimmy Greaves at one stage in his career played home matches at Wimbledon?**

The Judge got this answer from Greavsie: 'I know how this started. When my wife Irene and I first got married back in 1958 we lived rent free in a flat at Wimbledon's then football ground at Plough Lane when they were in the Isthmian League. I used to help sweep the terraces and do odd jobs around the ground before we got a place of our own in Essex. I was 18 then and had already established myself in the Chelsea first-team. So the answer is that I never played for Wimbledon, but I was at home there!'

Jimmy Greaves

Q **Why is it that we never see flat-raing jockeys with moustaches or beards?**

The Judge had a string of trainers and jockeys working on this one. Geoff Lewis told The Judge that Australian jockey Peter Cook has a moustache, but he cannot think of anybody else. Trainer Toby Balding said, with tongue in cheek, that they either do not want to carry any extra weight or are concerned about wind resistance. A more serious theory was that trainers set a high standard of discipline, and discourage jockeys from being anything but clean shaven. They dare not show up at gallops with any facial stubble.

Q **Which England Test cricketer was nicknamed Picker, and why?**
This was how fast bowler Graham Dilley was known to his England teammates. Would you believe 'Picca' Dilley?

Q **In which year did the racing tipster Prince Monolulu die and how old was he?**
Prince Ras Monolulu, famous for his 'I gotta horse' tips, died in 1965 at the age of 84. He was the self-styled chief of the Falasha tribe of Abyssinia, and came to England in 1902. It was in the 1920 Derby that he established himself as a tipster when he collected £8,000 backing Spion Kop at 100-6.

Q **Did former British heavyweight champion Joe Erskine play rugby for Wales?**
Joe Erskine played fly-half for Wales. . . as a schoolboy international.

Q **Was American heavyweight boxer Tommy Morrison related to Hollywood legend John Wayne?**
Tommy claims to be a distant relative of John 'The Duke' Wayne, whose real name was Marion Morrison.

Q **Has Arsenal tube station always been so called when there is no such district at Arsenal?**
It became Arsenal tube station in 1932, and was a publicity coup by the then Highbury manager Herbert Chapman. He nagged London Transport into changing the name of the station from Gillespie Road.

Q **Did Arsenal ever wear blue and white socks before switching to the traditional red?**
Herbert Chapman introduced blue and white hopped socks back in the late 1920s because blue was a fast dye and did not run when washed. Red socks were re-introduced at the start of the 1969-70 season.

Q **Has a Hollywood film ever been made about the first of the modern Olympics in Athens?**
Yes, in 1954. It Happened in Athens starred Jayne Mansfield and 1948-52 Olympic decathlon champion Bob Mathias. It did not win any medals.

Q **Why is Frankie Dettori known as Frankie when his initial is L?**
His Christian name is Lanfranco, and he has always been Frankie to his fellow jockeys. He is the son of an exceptional jockey, and his mother was a circus trapeze artist.

Q **Can you name the four footballers with three Os in their surname who played football for England?**
Most football fans manage to name Peter Osgood, Tony Woodcock and Ian Storey-Moore. The one and only Pelham Von Donop is the missing fourth man! He won two England caps against Scotland in 1873 and 1875, and played for the Royal Engineers in two FA Cup finals.

Q **Was there an outstanding American footballer called Johnny Blood?**
This was the 'ghost' name of Johnny McNally, a brilliant running back between the wars with Green Bay Packers, Pittsburgh Pirates and the Steelers. He played under the pseudonym of Johnny Blood in the 1920s to protect his amateur status, and got the idea for his name after watching Rudolph Valentino starring in the silent film classic Blood and Sand.

Q **Did Duncan Goodhew deliberately shave his head bald to get more speed in the swimming pool?**
Duncan lost his hair following a childhood illness.

Q **Is it true that the legendary C. B. Fry was once offered a kingdom?**
Yes. The Great All-rounder was once offered the kingdom of Albania but turned it down. He was England cricket captain in six Tests, set a world long jump record, played for England at football, won an FA Cup medal with Southampton in 1902 and was a top-flight rugby player. He also found time to become a first-class honours graduate in classics at Oxford.

Q **Was a film ever made on the life story of the great decathlete Jim Thorpe?**
Jim Thorpe: All American, starring Burt Lancaster in the title role, was released in 1951. Its British title was *Man of Bronze*. Thorpe, whose original Indian name was Wa-tho-huck (meaning Bright Path), won both the pentathlon and decathlon in the 1912 Olympics in Stockholm. When King Gustav of Sweden presented him with his second medal, he said, 'Sir, you are the greatest athlete in the world.' Thorpe replied, 'Thanks King.' Twelve months later he was stripped of his medals when it was discovered that he had been paid $14 a week 'expenses' to play baseball. It was 1982 and 29 years after his death before he was reinstated as double Olympic champion. Replica medals were presented to his daughter. Thorpe was a master at American Football and baseball, but died in poverty at 62.

Q **Did Rocky Marciano ever box in Wales during the Second World War?**
Rocky never boxed outside the United States. His only fight in Wales, while based there with the US Army in 1945, was during a bar-room brawl in a Swansea pub. He flattened an Australian soldier who

Rocky Marciano

159

unwisely picked on him. Rocky did not start his boxing career until after the war, making his professional debut in 1947 with a third-round knock-out victory over Lee Epperson in Holyoke, Mass, close to his hometown of Brockton. It was the first of 49 successive victories, and he retired as undefeated world heavyweight champion in 1955.

Q **Is it correct that Frank Bruno had dancing lessons during his boxing career?**
Terry Lawless, Frankís manager at the time, arranged for him to attend Roy Castle's school of dancing to help improve his balance. The lessons came in handy when Bruno started appearing in pantomime.

Q **When Miss Erika Roe made her famous streak at Twickenham was she alone?**
Erika was one of two streakers who revealed themselves during the half-time break in the England-Australia match on 2 January 1982. Her friend, Sarah Bennet, came on to the pitch at the same time, but it was Erika who got all of the publicity.

Q **Did Hollywood film star George Raft ever box as a professional?**
Raft had 17 professional fights as a lightweight before switching to dancing and then acting. He was stopped inside the distance seven times, and after his last stoppage decided to hustle for a living around the pool halls. Throughout his Hollywood career he was alleged to have Mafia links.

Q **Is it true that the Duke of Wellington played Test cricket?**
There were no Test matches during the Iron Duke's lifetime. He was a keen cricketer and played for All Ireland when a junior officer.

Q **Did Harlem Globetrotters star Meadowlark Lemon play basketball in the major league?**
Meadowlark – real name Meadow Lemon – joined the Globetrotters immediately on leaving the US Army in 1945 without any major league experience. He was the 'Clown Prince' of the Globetrotters until leaving in 1979 to set up his own road show, 'Meadowlark Lemon's Bucketeers'.

Q **Which was the first League club to install an artificial pitch?**
Queen's Park Rangers were first to lay down a synthetic pitch in 1981. Terry Venables was manager at the time, and ten years earlier he and his co-author Gordon Williams had written a football novel called They Used to Play on Grass.

Q **Why do England and Scotland play their Rugby Union internationals for the Calcutta Cup?**
The Calcutta Rugby Football Club in India was disbanded in 1877, and to keep the name alive the British members decided to put up a trophy to be contested between England and Scotland. They drew hundreds of rupees from the club bank account and had them moulded into a cup that has three snake handles and a silver elephant as the lid piece. The Calcutta Cup inscription reads: presented to the rugby football union by the

Calcutta football club as an international challenge trophy to be played for annually by England and Scotland, 1878.

Q **Where and when was Chelsea manager Ruud Gullit born?**
Gullit was born in Amsterdam on 1 September 1962. His mother was Dutch and his father played international football for Surinam.

Q **Why do older supporters of Charlton Athletic refer to them as 'The Haddicks'?**
It is the local pronunciation of 'Haddocks', which was a nickname given to the club in its early years when their players used a meeting room in East Street that was above a fish shop. The fish shop proprietor was a keen supporter and used to stand on the terraces waving a wooden stick with a haddock nailed to the top. 'Robins' or 'Valiants' became more popular nicknames for the club from the Valley.

Q **Has any footballer scored for England with his first kick in international football?**
Bill Nicholson, Tottenham half-back in the immediate post-war years, scored with his first touch for England inside the first 30 seconds of England's match against Portugal at Goodison Park on 19 May 1951. England won the match 5-2. Nicholson, deputizing for the injured Billy Wright, never won another cap. He became an outstanding Tottenham manager, and there is a Bill Nicholson Stand at White Hart Lane in his honour.

Q **Why did the historic over in which Gary Sobers hit six successive sixes take so long?**
There was a four-minute delay between the fifty and sixth deliveries by bowler Malcolm Nash at Swansea in 1968 while the umpires debated whether Sobers had been caught on the boundary. They finally decided that the fielder had taken the ball over the rope and authorized a fifth successive six. Sobers, batting for Notts against Glamorgan, smashed the final ball out of the ground to become the first man in history to hit six sixes off a six-ball over.

Q **True or false: Johan Cruyff was signed by Ajax on the recommendation of his mother?**
True. His mother was a cleaner at the Ajax stadium, and she persuaded the club coaching staff to give her twelve-year-old son a trial.

Q **Did Joe Louis, the boxer, ever play professional football for Liverpool?**
Joe Louis paid a goodwill visit to Anfield in 1944 while serving with the US Army during the Second World War. He signed forms while at the ground, but it was purely a PR exercise and he returned to the United States soon after to continue his reign as world heavyweight champion.

Q **Why was British boxer Harry Mallin known as 'The Well Chewed Champion'?**
Mallin was adjudged to have been beaten just once in his career of more

than 200 contests, and the result was reversed in extraordinary circumstances. The judges awarded Frenchman Roger Brousse a disputed points decision over Mallin in their 1924 Olympic middleweight quarter-final. A Swedish member of the International Olympic Committee watched the bout from a ringside seat and saw Brousse bite the London policeman on the chest (this was before gumshields were in common use). A medical examination revealed teeth marks on Mallin's chest, and the Frenchman was disqualified. Mallin went on to retain the title that he had won four years earlier in Antwerp.

Q **Was Luciano Pavarotti the first opera singer to take part in the opening ceremony of a top sports event?**
Pavarotti's performance in the build-up to the 1990 World Cup finals in Italy sounded familiar. The great Swedish tenor Jussi Bjorling sang at the opening ceremony to the European athletics championships in Stockholm in 1958.

Q **Why is a £500 bet known as 'a monkey' in betting parlance?**
It is believed to have started with the British soldiers serving in India. The Indian 500-rupee banknote was decorated with an illustration of a monkey.

Q **Is it true that Muhammad Ali collapsed at the weigh-in for his world title fight against Richard Dunn?**
Sort of. Ali had so many of his entourage accompanying him on the stage for his weigh-in at a Munich theatre that it collapsed under their combined weight and it took an hour to release everybody from beneath the shattered floorboards.

Q **Why was Alan Ball the only England player to arrive home from the 1970 World Cup without a medal?**
All the players were presented with a commemorative medal by the organizers of the tournament in Mexico. Ball was so disgusted by England's 3-2 quarter-final defeat by West Germany that he threw his medal out of a hotel window.

Q **Has a postman ever won the Embassy World Snooker championship?**
Terry Griffiths was a former postman. Welshman Griffiths delivered one of the biggest shocks in world snooker championship history when he won the title at his first attempt in 1979.

Q **Who was first to call Nat Lofthouse 'The Lion of Vienna'?**
There are a lot of claims for this one. In the view of The Judge, it was Daily Express sports-writing master Henry Rose. He used the description in his report of England's 3-2 victory over Austria in Vienna in 1952 when Lofthouse raced half the length of the pitch to score a dramatic late winner, getting himself knocked out in the process. Henry, a legendary character in Manchester, was one of the ports journalists who lost his life in the 1958 Munich air crash. His daughter, Ardele, later became a leading *Coronation Street* scriptwriter.

Q **Has a pregnant jockey ever ridden a Grand National winner?**
This trick question has been popping up in quizzes since Mr Frisk won the National in 1990. Trainer Kim Bailey later revealed that his pregnant wife, Tracey, had been riding out on Mr Frisk during the build-up to the race. Pandora Bailey was born three months later, and Kim claimed that she was the youngest ever jockey to ride a National winner!

Q **How much did comedian Freddie Starr pay for the steeplechaser Miinnehoma?**
Freddie bought Miinnehoma at auction for 35,000 guineas, making his bids by sticking out his tongue. He had his tongue in his cheek when collecting his £115,606 prize money (plus cash from a huge wager) after Miinnehoma had won the 1994 Grand National.

Q **Why did it take six hours before Chris Finnegan was confirmed as Olympic boxing champion?**
That was how long it took Chris to produce a urine sample after he had won the middleweight title in the 1968 Olympics. The IOC drug tester had to accompany him to a Mexican nightclub, where Chris downed a dozen bottles of beer before he could produce a sample.

Q **Why was golfer Harry Bradshaw said to have 'bottled' the Open golf championship?**
Bradshaw's drive at the fifth hole in the second round of the 1949 Open at Sandwich lodged against the neck of a broken beer bottle. The Irishman elected to play as it lay. He took a sand iron and smashed through the glass to send the ball 30 yards towards the hole. Bradshaw got down in six on the par-four hole, and at the end of the final round was tied with Bobby Locke, who went on to win the play-off.

Q **Was David Coleman the original presenter of** *A Question of Sport*?
No. David Vine was the first in the chair, with Henry Cooper and Cliff Morgan as the team captains when the programme was first launched in 1970. Since Coleman took over in 1979 – after a stint presenting Come Dancing – the team captains have included Emlyn Hughes, Bill Beaumont, Willie Carson, John Parrott and Ally McCoist. Coleman was a Manchester champion miler and editor of a local newspaper in Cheshire at the age of 23 before switching to a broadcasting career.

David Coleman

Q **Did an Englishman or an Australian batsman face the first ball in Test cricket?**
There has been many an argument over this one. The first batsman to face a ball in Test cricket was Kent-born Charles Bannerman, but he was playing for Australia. He faced the opening ball from Nottinghamshire bowler Alfred Shaw in the first Test at Melbourne Cricket Ground on 15 March 1877. He scored the first of his 165 runs of Shaw's second ball. Bannerman was one of four English-born players in the Australian team, and there was also a Southern Irishman. Australia won by 45 runs, and there was a carbon copy result on the same ground in the Centenary Test of 1977.

Q **Was there ever a Football League title-winning club called Nelson?**
Lancashire club Nelson played in the League for ten years from 1921. They won the Third Division (North) championship in 1922-3 but were relegated the following year. In 1926-7 they scored 104 goals. That was the good news. The bad news is that they conceded 136, a record for the Third Division. In their final season they became the first team to lose all their 21 away matches. Chester took their place in the League in 1931.

Q **Which batsman once got himself lost on the London underground?**
This was Leicestershire wicket-keeper Tom Sidwell, who was one not out overnight against Surrey at the Oval in 1921. Making his way to the ground the next morning he managed to get himself lost on the London underground. He arrived too late to bat, and it went down in the scorebook as 'absent, lost on tube'.

Q **Have Leyton Orient ever played their home matches at Wembley Stadium?**
When known as Clapton Orient in 1930, the Os played two League games at Wembley because their own ground was being reconstructed.

Q **Why is Alan Shepherd named as the man who has hit the most famous of all golf shots?**
Apollo 14 astronaut Shepherd was the first man to hit a golf shot on the moon. He struck a 6-iron while on the 1971 space mission.

Q **Has there been a Hollywood film focusing on the Epsom Derby?**
Not a Hollywood movie, but an English-made film called Derby Day. Made in 1951, it starred Anna Neagle, Michael Wilding and Googie Withers.

Q **Why was a policeman accused of causing an affray during the hockey finals in the 1960 Rome Olympics?**
France got the ball into the net during a match against Belgium while the Belgian players were standing still because the whistle had gone. The umpire awarded a hotly disputed goal, which proved to be the match winner. There were furious protests from the Belgians, who said they had played to the whistle. During the after-match inquest, it was discovered

that the whistle had been blown by a policeman directing traffic just outside the ground.

Q **Which American athlete was known as 'The Stork in Shorts'?**
This was long-legged former world mile record holder Jim Ryun.

Q **Who portrayed Muhammad Ali in the biopic on him called *The Greatest*?**
Ali played himself. The part of his trainer, Angelo Dundee, was played by Ernest Borgnine.

Q **What is meant when the term 'Carpet' is used in the world of betting?**
'Carpet' is a nineteenth-century Cockney rhyming slang for drag (carpet bag). Drag was a hard-labour prison sentence of three months, and carpet in betting parlance means the number three.

Q **Did Kevin Keegan have a top ten hit as a pop singer during his playing career?**
Kevin did not make the top ten, but he made it into the top 40 with his recording of *Head Over Heels*. He recorded it while playing for Hamburg. 'The laugh was on me,' Kevin told The Judge. 'I had so little faith in the record that I took only upfront money and did not bother with royalties. It cost me a small fortune because the record was a big hit in several countries.'

Q **Why is the Lincoln City football club known to its supporters as 'The Red Imps'?**
The Lincoln Imp is the county emblem of Lincolnshire, taken from a carving of an impish creature that features in Lincoln Cathedral.

Q **Which international Rugby Union player was nicknamed 'Mighty Mouse'?**
This was Scottish international forward Ian McLaughlan, whose autobiography was called *Mighty Mouse*.

Q **What was the name of the film in which Bobby Moore and Pele appeared with Sylvester Stallone?**
It was called *Escape to Victory*. Sylvester Stallone, Michael Caine, Bobby Moore and Pele used a football match as a cover for an escape from a German prisoner-of-war camp.

Q **Why did Muhammad Ali have to be presented with a replica gold medal during the 1996 Olympics?**
Ali won an Olympic gold as Cassius Clay in the 1960 Rome Games. On his return to the

Muhammad Ali

United States he threw his medal into the Ohio River as a protest at being refused service in a 'whites only' restaurant. A special presentation was made to him 36 years later during the Atlanta Olympics, with a replica gold medal being hung around his neck by IOC President Juan Samaranch during a moving ceremony before the basketball final.

Q **What did golf master Lee Trevino's father do for a living?**
Lee's father was a gravedigger at a cemetery in Texas.

Q **Which world champion boxer was featured in the film *The Great White Hope*?**
Jack Johnson, the first black world heavyweight champion. The title was based on the search for a 'White Hope' to topple him.

Q **Who was the deaf mute who won a world boxing championship?**
Mario D'Agata, an Italian who took the world bantamweight title from Frenchman Robert Cohen in 1956. They used to flash lights on the corner posts to signal when the bell had gone.

Q **What was so unusual about Len Shackleton's autobiography *Clown Prince of Football*?**
A chapter entitled *What Directors Known About the Game* was left completely blank.

Q **In which film did Robert Redford appear as a baseball player?**
It was *The Natural*, based on the novel by Bernard Malamud.

Q **What did boxing champion Joe Frazier and Liverpool football captain Ron Yeats have in common?**
Both Joe Frazier and Ron Yeats were trained to be slaughtermen.

Q **Is it true that Stanley Matthews was the son of a professional boxer?**
His father was Jack Matthews, a featherweight known as the 'Fighting Barber of Hanley'. It was his father who instilled into him the importance of fitness and training, and for more than 70 years Matthews – the first footballer knighted – has gone through a routine of exercises every morning.

Q **Has former England manager Sir Alf Ramsey had a public house named after him?**
There is a pub in Tunbridge Wells, Kent, called the Alf Ramsey. Sir Alf was guest of honour on opening day and pulled the first pint.

Q **True or False: Johnny Weissmuller won an Olympic medal for water polo?**
True. Weissmuller, considered by many experts to have been the greatest sprint swimmer of all time, somehow found the energy to pick up a bronze medal with the USA polo team after winning golds in the 100 metres, 400 metres and relay in the 1924 Amsterdam Olympics. Four years later he retained his 100-metre title and helped the USA 4 x 22 metres team win

the relay. Weissmuller, who broke 28 world records from 100 yards to 880 yards, later found even greater fame as the screen's first talking Tarzan.

Q **Was Terry Venables ever a tailor before becoming a football manager?**
While at Chelsea in the 1960s, Terry started a tailoring business in partnership with Stamford Bridge colleagues including George Graham, John Hollins, Ron Harris and writer Ken Jones. The suit fittings were done by a professional tailor. Other ventures by the creative Venables while still a player included the invention of a ladiesí wig, singing with the Joe Loss Band and writing in partnership with Gordon Williams. They created the TV private detective Hazell.

Q **Has a batsman ever been twice bowled for a duck with successive balls?**
Glamorgan tailender Peter Judge was the last man out against the Indian tourists in 1946 when he was bowled first ball by leg spinner Chandra Sarwate. India enforced the follow-on and, as time was running out, the Glamorgan skipper signalled to Judge to stay out in the middle to open the next innings. Sarwate was again the bowler, and he clean bowled Judge with the first ball.

Q **True or false: Cuban leader Fidel Castro was once a professional baseball player?**
False, but he was a good enough pitcher to be given a trial by a scout for the New York Giants. Castro then had his baseball ambitions overtaken by revolutionary plans.

Q **Have triplets ever competed in any sport in the Olympic Games?**
Czechoslovakia selected the Svoboda triplets for an international athletics match in 1927, but they did not compete in the Olympics. Alois (high jump), Jiri (javelin) and Joseph (discus) were all top class athletes.

Q **Has there ever been a two-handed javelin competition in the Olympics?**
Yes, in Stockholm in 1912. Finland's Juho Julius Saaristo, runner-up in the conventional javelin event, won with a combined throw of 109·42 metres. He set a then world record of 61 metres with his right hand.

Q **Why do horse racing veterans sometimes refer to Newbury racecourse as 'the prison'?**
Newbury racecourse was converted into a prisoner of war camp in 1915.

Q **Exactly what happened in the 'Great Boxing Brawl of Porthcawl'?**
The 'Great Brawl of Porthcawl' was the title given to the after-fight battle that took place in the ring between boxers Brian London and Dick Richardson and their supporters. London knocked down Richardson's chief second after being stopped with a cut eye by what he claimed was a deliberate butt in the eighth round of their European heavyweight title fight on 29 August 1960. This sparked a ring brawl involving at least a

dozen people. London, whose father and brother (both ex-fighters) joined in, was later fined a record £5,000.

Q **Why could it be claimed that the 'Three Degrees' once played for Chelsea?**
Chelsea signed three medical students from Queen's Park when football re-started after the First World War: David Cameron, Ken McKenzie and John Bell. All three went on to get their doctor's degrees.

Q **What is the connection between 007 James Bond and an Olympic weight-lifting medallist?**
Harold Sakata won a silver medal for the USA in the light-heavyweight weightlifting division in the 1948 London Olympics. He later became a professional wrestler (billed as Tosh Togo) and a Hollywood actor. His most famous role was that of Oddjob in the James Bond film Goldfinger.

Q **Why do Aussies refer to a sportsman called Snowy Baker as being the greatest all-rounder in history?**
Reginald 'Snowy' Baker was a silver medallist in the middleweight boxing division in the 1908 Olympics. He also took part in the springboard diving and freestyle swimming competitions. Snowy was an Australian rugby international, and it was claimed that he was outstanding in 29 different sports. He later moved to Hollywood where he taught Douglas Fairbanks to fence, ride and swim, and starred himself in several silent films. Baker was the man who put the swash into the Fairbanks buckle.

Q **Did Rob Andrew get a cricket as well as a rugby Blue at university?**
Andrew captained Cambridge University at both cricket and rugby in 1985.

Q **Why is a pacemaker in an athletics race often referred to as 'a hare'?**
This goes back to the days of hare-and-hounds races at English public schools, when the 'hares' would leave a paper trail for the 'hounds' to follow.

Q **Why is it that supporters at sporting events are known as fans?**
There are several theories, but the one that appeals most to me is that the aristocrats who used to sponsor bare-knuckle fighters were known as The Fancy, and all those who followed boxing soon came to be known as fight fanciers ... and then fans. It is also said to be an abbreviation of fanatical.

Q **Which footballer was known as 'The Rubber Man', and why?**
This was Brazilian goal master Leonidas da Silva, who was known as 'O Homen Borracha' because his legs seemed like rubber as he bounded past tackles. It is a nickname that would suit Newcastle's Faustino Asprilla.

Q **Why was the kick-off to the 1974 World Cup Final in Munich delayed?**
There had been a superbly organized 90-minute opening ceremony. Then, just as English referee Jack Taylor was about to blow the whistle for the kick-off to the final between West Germany and Holland, he noticed the

little matter that they had forgotten to replace the touchline and corner flags!

Q Did Sir Robert Peel, when Prime Minister, own a horse that won the Derby?
No, but his brother – Colonel Jonathan Peel – did. It was Colonel Peel who lodged a protest against the winner of the 1844 Derby Running Rein, which was later proved to be a four-year-old ringer called Maccabeus. Peel's horses, Orlando and Ionian, finished second and third, and were later installed as winner and runner-up.

Q Which of England's goalkeepers was nicknamed 'The Cat'?
Bert Williams, of Wolves. Chelsea's Peter Bonetti was nicknamed Catty.

Q Has there ever been a midnight horse race meeting in England?
There was a midnight steeplechase staged at Hooton Park, Cheshire, in 1930, with the course lit by blazing torches attached to the rails. The race was a recreation of the 7th Hussars Midnight Steeplechase of 1839. It attracted a crowd of 20,000 people, but all ended in confusion because the horses were completely put off by the shadows, the flames of the torches and the roars of an unruly crowd.

Q Was Jack Charlton the best man at the wedding of his brother Bobby?
No. Bobby chose his then Manchester United team-mate and best pal Maurice Setters to do the honours when he married Norma in 1961. Ironically, Setters was later to become Jack's 'best man', or certainly right hand man. He was number two to Jack when he turned the Republic of Ireland into a team respected throughout the world of football. A Devonian who had been feared for his tackling, Setters was coach at Hillsborough when Jack managed Sheffield Wednesday.

Q Is it true that a competitor in an Olympic 200 metres final took more than a minute to finish?
Haseley Crawford, Trinidadian winner of the 100 metres gold *Bobby Charlton* medal in the 1976 Olympics in Montreal, pulled up with an attack of cramp in the 200 metres final. He fell to the track clutching his leg, and then slowly jogged to the finishing line. His time from gun to tape was 1 m 19·60 s.

Q Why was Irish jump jockey Johnny Lehane known to his fellow jockeys as 'Tumper'?
Because if anybody upset him he would threaten to 'tump' them!

Q **Was Linford Christie the first Olympic champion to be disqualified for false starting in a final?**
Yes, but he would have survived under the old rules. There were, for instance, seven false starts before the runners in the final of the men's 100 metres in the 1912 Olympics finally got away. The race was won by American Ralph Craig, who had been responsible for the first three breaks. Thirty-six years after his Olympic triumph Craig was back in Olympic action with the United States yachting team in the 1948 London Games.

Q **Who was known as the 'Little Mouse' of the athletics world?**
Don Thompson, the tiny, bespectacled London insurance clerk who won the 50 kilometre walk in the 1960 Rome Olympics. He had collapsed with exhaustion in the 1956 Games, and had vowed to make proper preparations for the Rome Olympics. He got himself acclimatized for the sultry heat of Italy by turning the bathroom at his home into a steam room where he used to follow a series of explosive exercises while wearing a tracksuit.

Q **Is it true that entertainer George Formby was a professional jockey?**
George Formby was an apprentice jockey but had to give it up due to increasing weight. He switched to making a living with his little ukelele in his hands.

Q **Has a Sioux Indian ever won a track gold medal in the Olympics?**
Billy Mills, a US Marine born in Pine Ridge, South Dakota, was a shock winner of the 10,000 metres in the 1964 Olympics. Mills, half Sioux, had been educated at a school for Native Americans in Kansas after being orphaned at 12. He was presented with a ring made from Black Hills gold by the Oglala Sioux tribe, given warrior status and an Indian name meaning: Loves His Country.

Q **Have three British brothers ever won Olympic medals in the same event?**
The Wyld brothers, of Derby, Frank, Leonard and Percy, won a bronze medal in the 4,000 metres team pursuit cycle race in the 1928 Olympics.

Q **Is it true that George Best once went through an entire match playing the ball only with his left foot?**
True. It was to win a bet he had struck with a friend. In another match he passed the ball only to team-mate David Sadler, who was playing in the middle of the Manchester United defence. George told The Judge: 'David had moaned at me before the match that I never passed the ball to him. He was sick to death of receiving it by the time the game was over.'

Q **Did a former Wimbledon champion get charged with murder?**
Not a champion, but a runner-up. Baronet's son Vere Thomas St Leger Gould, lawn tennis champion of All Ireland and runner-up at Wimbledon in 1879, was found guilty of murdering a Danish widow while in France in 1907. He was given a life sentence, and died in a cell on Devil's Island.

Q **True or false: An Olympic gymnastics champion had only one leg?**
True. American George Eyser, winner of two gold medals, two silvers and a bronze in the men's gymnastics at the 1904 St Louis Games, had a wooden leg.

Q **What was the trophy that Jack Charlton received from his team-mates during the 1966 World Cup finals?**
Jack's name was drawn out of the hat for the routine drug test so many times at the end of the tournament he was presented with a baby's potty with lettering on it that read, 'The Jimmy Riddle Cup'.

Q **Has a vicar ever scored a goal in an FA Cup final at Wembley?**
Not at Wembley, but the Reverend Kenneth Hunt scored for Wolves in their 3-1 1908 FA Cup Final victory over Newcastle United at Crystal Palace.

Q **Is it true that a jockey had the only win of his career in Australia's top race, the Melbourne Cup?**
Ray Neville got a ride on outsider Rimfire in the 1948 Melbourne Cup after only nine rides as a 16-year-old apprentice. Rimfire won in a photo-finish and Neville was suddenly the most talked-about jockey down under. Amazingly, he never rode another winner and, disillusioned, returned to farm labouring.

Q **True or false: A Wimbledon champion has captained the England football team?**
Max Woosnam, an amateur centre-half with Manchester City, was England football captain in the only international match in which he played in 1922. The previous year he had won the men's doubles at Wimbledon, and the following year he was a runner-up in the mixed doubles. He represented Great Britain in the 1920 and 1924 Olympics.

Q **Has a British sprint champion ever played Rugby Union for England?**
John Young, 1956 AAA 100 yards champion, played for Harlequins and won nine England caps.

Q **It it true that a Bastard has refereed an FA Cup final at Wembley?**
Not at Wembley, to the best of my knowledge, but S. R. (Segal Richard) Bastard refereed the 1878 final at the Oval. Bastard was an international referee who had won an England cap while playing for Upton Park.

INDEX

SPORTS TRIVIA

OTHER BOOKS ON SPORT FROM ANDRE DEUTSCH LTD

CANTONA ON CANTONA

Eric Cantona and Alex Flynn

Eric Cantona has captained both his country and his club. He was one of the main reasons that Manchester United won the Double – the Premiership and the FA Cup - for the second time in three seasons. As a result he was elected the Footballer of the Year in 1996.

With Eric's full involvement, this book examines the man in detail. Eric talks candidly about many subjects, not only football, but matters closer to home – his family and his interests. Eric expresses opinions on subjects as diverse as politics,sponsorship and women.

With a wealth of brand new, striking, black and white photographs from specially commissioned shoots in both Manchester and Marseilles, this book captures all the complex elements of this sporting legend.

0 233 99045 3   *£14.99*

ALEX FERGUSON: TEN GLORIOUS YEARS

Jim Drewett and Alex Leith

For the past ten years Alex Ferguson has been the visionary behind Manchester United's success.What does it take to become one of the greatest football managers of all time? Managing England's most followed team certainly has its pressures and they are revealed in this book.

In this lavishly illustrated account of his time at the club Alex tells of the personalities of which there have been many and the transfers, tantrums and triumphs behind the scenes at Old Trafford.

Ten Glorious Years is a remarkable story. A story of one man's obsession, one man's single determination to succeed. The book finishes with Ferguson's thoughts on his one elusive trophy – the European Cup, the final goal to score.Included in this book, as well as full colour photographs, is a full statistical report for the past ten years.

0 233 99047 X   *£9.99*

RYAN GIGGS: GENIUS AT WORK

Ryan Giggs, Alex Leith and Tim Drewett

Regarded by many as probably the most gifted player of his generation, Ryan Giggs is blessed with a talent that has tormented many opposing defenders. Still in his early twenties, he has already won a fistful of winner medals.

This is a book about football. Ryan expresses his views on his team-mates, Alex Ferguson, the pressures of fame and the expectations, why he plays for Wales and not England and finally what the future holds for him.

Included in this book, as well as full colour photographs, is a full statistical record of Ryan Giggs' career so far.

0 233 99046 1   *£9.99*

Forthcoming titles for autumn 1997

Odd Man Out
A Player's Diary by Brian McClair
0 233 99115 8   £14.99

Living the Dream
by David Beckham
0 233 99148 4   £9.99

Manchester United Diary 1998
0 233 99220 0   £4.99

For children:
Manchester United Annual 1997
0 233 99164 6   £5.50

Current titles available from Chameleon Books

Howzat!
Foreword by Mike Gatting
0 233 99057 7   £7.99

Off the Ball
Foreword by Ray Wilkins
0 233 99056 9   £7.99

The 19th Hole
Foreword by Bernard Gallacher
0 233 99052 6   £7.99

Forthcoming titles for autumn 1997

Sports 'n' All
Hilarious and Bizarre Events From the World of Sport
0 233 99181 6   £7.99

Life's the Pits
Stories and Yarns from the Fast Lane
0 233 99180 8   £7.99

Oh I Say
The Bare-faced Cheek of Life
0 233 99182 4   £7.99

Ruckin' & Maulin'
Stories and Yarns from the Pitches
0 233 99200 6   £7.99

Carling presents **Golden Heroes:**
Celebrating Fifty Seasons of Footballer of the Year
Dennis Signy and Norman Giller
Introduction by Michael Parkinson

Every year, football writers throughout the country vote for their Footballer of the Year. Dennis Signy examines the history of this great footballing occasion.

To celebrate this golden anniversary, every winner describes his winning year and introduces his own dream team. With over 200 photographs including pictures of every winner, and an exclusive introduction by Michael Parkinson, this is a unique celebration of one of the most prestigious events in sport.

0 233 99163 8   *£14.99*

Current titles from André Deutsch
Out of the Rough
Peter Baxter, Jonathan Agnew and David Lloyd

In this inside story of the England tour Peter Baxter and Jonathan Agnew recall dramatic moment of the tour, helped by David Lloyd, the England cricket coach come together to give a blanched view of the teamís controversial performances.

0 233 99158 1   *£15.99*   .

On Top Down Under
Ray Robinson and Gideon Haigh
Foreword by Ian Chappell

This award winning classic has been fully revised and updated to include fall 39 Australian Test captains.

0 233 99122 0   *£9.99*

The Complete Book of Golf

The Ultimate Companion to this maddening, frustrating, addictive and undeniably magnificent game.

0 233 99090 9   *£25.00*

Visions of Football

A Celebration of the world's finest football photography by the Allsport photographic agency.

0 233 99177 8   *£14.99*

From Arlott to Aggers:
Forty Years of Test Match Special

Guaranteed to bring back hundreds of special memories from a tumultuous time in the greatest of all sports.

0 233 99215   *£14.99*

Changing Seasons

A History of Cricket in England, 1945 - 1996
David Lemmon

A remarkable portrait of English Cricket which no enthusiast will want to miss.

0 233 99005 4   *£19.99*

Poms and Cobbers

Rob Steen

The story of the Ashes in the summer of 1997 framed by exclusive contributions from protagonists and supporting players alike. This is a cricket book like no other.

0 233 99210 3   *£19.99*